# GLIMPSES OF HER FATHER'S GLORY

# GLIMPSES OF HER FATHER'S GLORY

*Deification and Divine Light in Longfellow's Evangeline*

TIMOTHY E. G. BARTEL

WIPF & STOCK · Eugene, Oregon

GLIMPSES OF HER FATHER'S GLORY
Deification and Divine Light in Longfellow's Evangeline

Copyright © 2019 Timothy E. G. Bartel. All rights reserved. Except for brief quotations in critical publications or reviews, no part of this book may be reproduced in any manner without prior written permission from the publisher. Write: Permissions, Wipf and Stock Publishers, 199 W. 8th Ave., Suite 3, Eugene, OR 97401.

Wipf & Stock
An Imprint of Wipf and Stock Publishers
199 W. 8th Ave., Suite 3
Eugene, OR 97401

www.wipfandstock.com

PAPERBACK ISBN: 978-1-5326-6012-2
HARDCOVER ISBN: 978-1-5326-6013-9
EBOOK ISBN: 978-1-5326-6014-6

Manufactured in the U.S.A.   APRIL 30, 2019

This book is dedicated to two great lovers of Longfellow:
my grandfather, Willard Bartel, and my father, Richard Bartel.

Who this is we must learn, for man he seems
In all his lineaments, though in his face
The glimpses of his Father's glory shine.

—JOHN MILTON, *PARADISE REGAINED*, LL. 89–91


In narratives where historical veracity has no place, I cannot discover why there should not be exhibited the most perfect idea of virtue; of virtue not angelical, nor above probability, for what we cannot credit, we shall never imitate, but the highest and purest that humanity can reach, which, exercised in such trials as the various revolutions of things shall bring upon it, may, by conquering some calamities, and enduring others, teach us what we may hope, and what we can perform.

—SAMUEL JOHNSON, *THE RAMBLER*, NO. 4

# Contents

*Acknowledgements* • ix

    Introduction • 1
1   The Theological Climate of Longfellow's New England • 14
2   Religious Criticism of Evangeline • 40
3   The Doctrines of Deification and Divine Light in the Church Fathers • 72
4   The Christian Fathers in Longfellow • 103
5   The Religious Elements of Evangeline • 139
6   Deification and Divine Light in Evangeline • 165
    Conclusion • 186

*Bibliography* • 195

# Acknowledgements

MANY THANKS ARE DUE to Gavin Hopps, my PhD advisor at the University of St Andrews, under whose wise direction I conducted the majority of the research and writing of this book. My fellow ITIA postgraduate faculty members Micah Snell, David Baird, Cole Matson, Travis Buchanan, K.J. Swanson, and Simon Vaughan provided valuable feedback on the formulation of my argument. The advice and close readings of Michael O'Neill and Trevor Hart, my PhD examiners, were vital in further strengthening my argumentation concerning *Evangeline* after my doctoral project was complete. The obliging staff of the Houghton Library at Harvard University made it a joy to conduct remote research in their Longfellow manuscript holdings. Finally, I would like to thank my wife, Hope Bartel, whose keen editorial eye has helped to unify the disparate elements and undo the rough edges and slack phrases of this book. Without her, I would not be the writer nor the man I am today.

# Introduction

> Who, in his own skill confiding,
>    Shall with rule and line
> Mark the border-land dividing
>    Human and divine?
> —H.W. LONGFELLOW, "HERMES TRISMEGISTUS"[1]

WHEN HUMANS BECOME LIKE God, they shine with God's light—so the Fathers of the Christian church teach. The nineteenth-century American poet Henry Wadsworth Longfellow, who lived in a nation newly open to visions of the potential divinity and perfectibility of the human, encountered this doctrine in the writings of the Church Fathers, and illustrated it to striking effect in his 1847 poem *Evangeline*. Unfortunately, the critical tradition has not sufficiently recognized the theological heart of Longfellow's poem. We must refamiliarize ourselves with Longfellow's poem and Longfellow's theological sources—both Unitarian and patristic—in order to discern what is at stake in *Evangeline*, which is, I suggest, no less than the question of whether humans can achieve, through ascetic struggle and long-suffering charity, a true state of likeness to God.

## LONGFELLOW AND EVANGELINE

Henry Wadsworth Longfellow was born in 1807, the son of a prominent New England lawyer. He was raised on the literature of the Romantics and the doctrines of the Unitarian preacher William Ellery Channing (Longfellow

---

1. Longfellow, *Complete Poetical Works*, 465.

reports in a letter that he sought to distribute Channing's sermons to his more Puritan peers while an undergraduate at Bowdoin College). In the 1830s and early '40s Longfellow made a name for himself in America and England with memorable lyric poems such as "A Psalm of Life" and "Excelsior." From the outset Longfellow published poems that were deeply ethical and religiously informed. His 1839 collection of lyrics, *Voices of the Night*, for example, ends with the lines "Kyrie eleyson / Christe eleyson!"[2] and his 1841 collection, *Ballads and Other Poems*, includes a short dramatization of the story of Blind Bartimaeus from the Christian New Testament.[3] In 1845, however, Longfellow stepped out beyond didactic lyrics and set his sights on a new project: a long narrative poem based on the British-led deportation of the Acadians—a group of French Catholic colonists—from Nova Scotia in the eighteenth century.

This poem, which became *Evangeline: A Tale of Acadie*, uses the deportation of the Acadians as the backdrop of a tragic romance. The plot is based on a story he heard at a dinner party with Nathaniel Hawthorne and the Reverend H.L. Connolly. Samuel Longfellow, the poet's brother and early biographer, summarizes the poem's origin thus:

> At dinner Connolly said that he had been trying in vain to interest Hawthorne to write a story upon an incident which had been related to him by a parishioner of his . . . It was the story of a young Acadian maiden who at the dispersion of her people by the English troops had been separated from her betrothed lover; they sought each other for years in their exile; and at last they met in a hospital where the lover lay dying. Mr. Longfellow was touched by the story, especially by the constancy of the heroine, and said to his friend, "If you really do not want this incident for a tale, let me have it for a poem;" and Hawthorne consented. Out of this grew *Evangeline*.[4]

Longfellow worked on the poem for two years, from 1845 to early 1847, and the poem was published on November 1, 1847.

*Evangeline* is a poem of 1,399 hexameter lines, divided into two parts of five cantos each.[5] The introductory stanzas of *Evangeline* describe a pastoral

---

2. Longfellow, *Complete Poetical Works*, 6.
3. Longfellow, *Complete Poetical Works*, 17.
4. Longfellow, *Life of Longfellow*, 2:70–71.
5. Notoriously, each line of *Evangeline* is written in hexameter, an approximation in English prosody of the classical hexameter used in Virgil's *Aeneid*. This meter—unorthodox in traditional English language verse—has been controversial since the first reviews: Nathaniel Hawthorne praised it. "Hawthorne's Review of *Evangeline*," 234–35. George Peck bemoaned its "jarring" with the content of the poem. Peck, "Review of

scene of "the forest primeval" beneath which the "hearts" and "home[s] of Acadian farmers"[6] used to dwell. But those homes and people are "forever departed," and now "naught but tradition remains of the beautiful village of Grand-Pré."[7] In the final stanza of the introduction, the narrator calls all who "believe in the beauty and strength of a woman's devotion" to "list to the mournful tradition," "a Tale of Love in Acadie."[8]

Part 1, canto 1, returns in setting to a time when "the little village of Grand-Pré" was still inhabited and happy. Much of the canto describes life in the village and the surrounding farmlands, where the "simple Acadian farmers" "dwelt together in love."[9] We meet Benedict Bellefontaine, "the wealthiest farmer of Grand-Pré," his daughter Evangeline, "the pride of the village,"[10] Father Felician, the "priest and pedagogue" of Grand-Pré, Basil Lajeunesse, a blacksmith, and Basil's son Gabriel, the only young man of the village who Evangeline "welcome[s]" as a suitor.[11]

In canto 2 Basil and Gabriel visit Benedict and Evangeline, and while the young lovers softly woo one another, Basil tells Benedict that

> ". . . the English ships at their anchors
> Ride in the Gaspereu's mouth, with their cannon pointed against us.
> What their design may be is unknown; but all are commanded
> On the morrow to meet in the church, where his majesty's mandate
> Will be proclaimed as law in the land. Alas! In the mean time
> Many surmises of evil alarm the heart of the people."[12]

Though Benedict tries to calm him, Basil is convinced that the English mean harm. Canto 3 begins with the entrance of René Leblanc, the notary public, who contributes to the conversation a parable illustrating the moral that "man is unjust, but God is just, and finally justice / Triumphs."[13] After he tells the parable, Leblanc notarizes the betrothal of Evangeline and Gabriel.

---

Longfellow's *Evangeline*," 7. Matthew Arnold gave the lines qualified compliment: "when they are at their best, they are tenderly elegant; and their fault, when they are at their worst, is to be lumbering." Arnold, *On Translating Homer*, 80. More recent critics have called Longfellow's use of hexameter daring, and even credited it with being a powerful influence on the development of American free verse. See Finch, *The Ghost of Meter*, 36.

6. Longfellow, "Evangeline," ll. 1–9.
7. Longfellow, "Evangeline," ll. 12–15.
8. Longfellow, "Evangeline," ll. 17–19.
9. Longfellow, "Evangeline," ll. 20–58.
10. Longfellow, "Evangeline," ll. 59–61.
11. Longfellow, "Evangeline," ll. 114–21.
12. Longfellow, "Evangeline," ll. 237–42.
13. Longfellow, "Evangeline," ll. 300–301.

Canto 4 describes the events of the next day. In the morning, the village celebrates the betrothal. In the afternoon, while Evangeline waits at home, the men of the village, including her father, Gabriel, and Basil, convene at the church, where they are told by the British soldiers that all their "lands and dwellings and cattle" are now "forfeit . . . to the [British] crown," and that the Acadians will be "transported to other lands."[14] Basil is beaten when he attempts to fight back, and to quell the violence Father Felician preaches an extemporaneous sermon to the men of the village, encouraging them to forgive the English for their actions. The canto ends with Evangeline's worry and eventual consolation, remembering the words of the notary about the inevitable triumph of "the justice of Heaven."[15] In canto 5, the men are let out of the church after a five-day imprisonment, and the Acadians, including Evangeline, Gabriel, and their fathers, are led to the ocean. Though Evangeline assures Gabriel that if they love each other, no harm can come to them, Basil and Gabriel are forced onto a ship while Evangeline is left on the shore with her father and the priest. Benedict Bellefontaine dies of grief as he watches his village burn, and part 1 ends with his burial.

Part 2 of *Evangeline* begins after "many a weary year had passed since the burning of Grand-Pré."[16] Evangeline has remained beside Father Felician, wandering among the exiled communities of Acadians in America, looking for Gabriel. When she is encouraged to settle for someone else, Evangeline responds:

"I cannot.
Whither my heart has gone, there follows my hand,
and not elsewhere."[17]

This response prompts Father Felician to launch into another impromptu sermon—and thematic keynote of the poem—wherein he praises Evangeline and encourages her to "accomplish her work of affection," so that, even if she does not find Gabriel, she will, through her labor, be made "god-like . . . and rendered more worthy of heaven."[18] Evangeline takes Felician's advice and resolves to continue seeking Gabriel. *Evangeline* part 2, canto 1, ends with the narrator's invocation of the muse: "Let me essay, O Muse, to follow the wanderer's footsteps. . . ."[19]

14. Longfellow, "Evangeline," ll. 437–39.
15. Longfellow, "Evangeline," l. 522.
16. Longfellow, "Evangeline," l. 666.
17. Longfellow, "Evangeline," ll. 714–15.
18. Longfellow, "Evangeline," ll. 724–27.
19. Longfellow, "Evangeline," l. 733.

*Evangeline* 2.2 tells the story of Evangeline's journey down the Mississippi and contains some of the poem's most beautiful and famous scenes. Unbeknownst to Evangeline, Gabriel's boat passes hers as she sleeps, and she wakes with a premonition that Gabriel is close. Father Felician tells her that she may indeed be right, for they are near a town of exiled Acadians, where Gabriel might dwell. Canto 2.3 describes the happy reception of Evangeline and Felician by the Acadians of Louisiana. Though Basil is among this community, Gabriel is not, and Basil promises that he will accompany Evangeline in pursuit of Gabriel. *Evangeline* 2.3 closes with another pastoral scene of Evangeline praying in a garden, where she is consoled by a voice from the prairies that whispers, "Patience."[20]

Canto 4 continues the narrative of Evangeline's quest, now with Basil as her guide. They follow Gabriel into the Ozark Mountains, where Evangeline meets and talks with a Shawnee woman, who tells her native legends of lost love. When they arrive at a mission, Evangeline and Basil are told that Gabriel has recently left, but promised to return in autumn. Evangeline waits at the mission for Gabriel at the encouragement of the priest, but Gabriel never returns. The canto ends with a general description of the further wanderings of the aging Evangeline.

In canto 5, Evangeline, who has "not forgotten" Gabriel, nevertheless joins the Catholic order of the Sisters of Mercy in Philadelphia, where she finally feels at home.[21] When a pestilence falls on the city, Evangeline works in the almshouse taking care of the sick and dying, to whom she appears luminous. Evangeline is shocked one day to find Gabriel among the sick; with his last breath, Gabriel strives to say Evangeline's name. She kisses Gabriel as he dies, and whispers, "Father, I thank you."[22] The poem closes with an epilogue, which returns to the "forest primeval" of the introduction, this time describing the lovers as "at rest," having "ceased from their labors" and "completed their journey."[23]

Upon publication, *Evangeline* was lauded in both America and Europe and marked Longfellow's achievement of international fame, a fame that was to last the rest of his life—and to plummet soon afterward, due in part to the ascendancy of twentieth-century modernism. As a result, Longfellow is now almost as famous for falling out of literary favor as he is for achieving it. Only in the last three decades have critics begun seriously to reassess Longfellow's work and influence. *Evangeline* has been of particular interest

---

20. Longfellow, "Evangeline," l. 1057.
21. Longfellow, "Evangeline," ll. 1252–76.
22. Longfellow, "Evangeline," l. 1380.
23. Longfellow, "Evangeline," ll. 1381–89.

in this reassessment, not only because it was Longfellow's—and, indeed, American literature's—first major long narrative poem, but also because it remains one of Longfellow's best poems, most illustrative of his characteristic strengths—metrical dexterity, charming characterization, vivid pastoral scenes, and memorable dramatizations of romantic pathos, often involving marginalized or minority characters.[24]

In his 1993 "Longfellow in the Aftermath of Modernism," which called for a reassessment of Longfellow's oeuvre and influence as a whole, Dana Gioia began a conversation about Longfellow's Unitarianism, calling the poet's famous lyric, "A Psalm of Life," "a masterpiece of Yankee Unitarian agitprop."[25] In his 2009 essay "Evangeline's Mission," Andrew C. Higgins argues that "Christian readers . . . tend to overlook the implications of Longfellow's very sincere Unitarianism."[26] He goes on to show that *Evangeline*'s positive, even heroic portrayal of Catholic characters reveals Longfellow's Unitarian desire for religious tolerance in a time of widespread anti-Catholicism in America. "The most effective vehicle," he writes, "of Harvard Unitarianism was arguably the poetry of Henry Longfellow."[27]

## An Overview of the Argument

It is the argument of this book that when it comes to the spiritual world that Longfellow has created in *Evangeline*, Higgins is half right. Longfellow does indeed present, in a speech by Father Felician in *Evangeline* part 2, canto 1, a doctrine of human godlikeness that is in line with the teachings of William Ellery Channing, Longfellow family friend and foremost figure in American Unitarianism. But in the final scenes of the poem, Longfellow presents a vision of the godlike human that has no parallel in Channing's Unitarian doctrine, a vision that Longfellow found in the writings of the Church Fathers and to which he alludes in his lectures about them, a vision of the deified human shining with divine light.

In order to understand the spiritual world of *Evangeline*, we must familiarize ourselves first with Longfellow's theological sources. Thus this book begins in chapter 1 where Gioia and Higgins suggest we begin—with

24. Recent scholarship reassessing the quality of *Evangeline* and its place in both American literary and Acadian cultural history include Griffiths, "Longfellow's 'Evangeline'"; Seelye, "Attic Shape"; Johnson, "Call of the Archetype"; Willis, "Longfellow, National Literature," and, most importantly for this book, Andrew C. Higgins, "Evangeline's Mission."

25. Gioia, "Longfellow in the Aftermath," 79.

26. Higgins, "Evangeline's Mission," 563.

27. Higgins, "Evangeline's Mission," 564.

the progressive theological climate of Longfellow's New England, taking into account both the Unitarian and Transcendentalist movements and the prominent theological teachings about human godlikeness and divinity in each, an exploration that will pave the way for our later investigation of the theology of human godlikeness in *Evangeline* itself. Further, through Longfellow's own comments on the Unitarianism of Channing and the Transcendentalism of Ralph Waldo Emerson, we will see where Longfellow agreed with and supported these men and their doctrines, but also where he parted ways with them.

In order to situate the present argument within the critical conversation concerning *Evangeline*, the second chapter of this book will provide an overview of the major religious criticism of *Evangeline*, beginning with early reviews by Hawthorne, Whittier, and Brownson. We will then explore the many annotated editions of *Evangeline* from the late nineteenth and early twentieth centuries, which, taken together, highlight two particular passages as thematic keynotes of the poem: Father Felician's "work of affection" speech in *Evangeline* part 2, canto 1 (which, for convenience, we will call the "2.1 keynote"), and the part 2, canto 5, scene wherein Evangeline shines with divine light (which we will call the "2.5 keynote"). We will complete our overview with the two predominant views of *Evangeline*'s religious elements that still hold sway today: the interpretation of Evangeline's piety as primarily domestic, and the interpretation of *Evangeline*'s Catholic elements as primarily motivated by Longfellow's Unitarian commitments, a position represented best by Higgins.

In the third chapter, however, we will part ways with Higgins, and, indeed, all who have gone before, and begin an investigation of the Christian roots of the concept of human godlikeness in its pre-Unitarian form: the doctrine of deification as first articulated by the Church Fathers of the second through fourth centuries. Chief among these Fathers are St Justin Martyr, Tertullian, St Ireneaus of Lyons, Clement of Alexandria, Origen, St Athanasius of Alexandria, St Gregory of Nyssa, and St John Chrysostom. In these Fathers, we will find that the doctrine of deification is intricately connected to two other doctrines: the doctrine of the incarnation, with which Channing strongly disagreed, and the doctrine of the transfiguration of the godlike human with divine light, which, while not antithetical to Channing's theology, plays no part in the Unitarian doctrine of godlikeness that he articulated.

In order to show that Longfellow was indeed familiar with the patristic doctrines of deification and divine light, our fourth chapter will explore the presence of the Church Fathers in the writings of Longfellow. Unfortunately, except for two brief mentions by his biographers, one could read the whole of Longfellow scholarship and remain unaware that Longfellow read, let alone wrote about, the Church Fathers. Those wanting to find the Fathers in Longfellow's published works need to consult the poet's critical notes on *The Golden Legend* and his translations of Dante, or his passing references to the Fathers in his journals and prose works.

There is, however, a much more substantial but less well known resource which reveals Longfellow's familiarity with the Fathers in the years before *Evangeline*—namely, two lectures entitled "The Christian Fathers," written in the early 1830s, which Longfellow presented to his modern languages classes at Bowdoin College. The present argument that the writings and ideas of the Fathers exerted an influence upon Longfellow is based on the previously unpublished manuscripts of these lectures. These "Christian Fathers" lectures are a veritable treasure trove of information about Longfellow's early study of the Fathers, in which the poet reveals his familiarity with the writings of St Justin Martyr, Tertullian, St Cyprian of Carthage, Origen, and St John Chrysostom, among others. It was in these last three Fathers especially that Longfellow found a connection between the doctrine of deification and the doctrine of illumination with divine light—namely, that the goal of the Christian life is to become like God, and that when one becomes like God, one shines with God's light. We will also see a stark contrast between Longfellow's high estimation of the Fathers and Channing's dismissal of the Fathers as unimportant for Christians to read.

In light of this new acquaintance with Longfellow's Unitarian and patristic theological sources, chapters 5 and 6 will focus attention back on *Evangeline*. Chapter 5 presents an overview of the major religious elements of *Evangeline* as a whole. These elements are organized into the categories of theological teachings, spiritual practices and experiences, and religious language. Through our investigation of these religious elements, we will gain a preliminary understanding of the spiritual world of *Evangeline*, including its conceptions of God, man, love, suffering, and redemption.

In chapter 6 we will undertake a line-by-line reading of the keynote passages of *Evangeline*—Father Felician's 2.1 "work of affection" speech and Evangeline's 2.5 transfiguration with divine light—which will be placed side-by-side with those passages in Channing and the Fathers that parallel the theological teachings and spiritual experiences described in the keynote passages. Through this in-depth comparison, we will see that though in the 2.1 keynote Longfellow articulates a doctrine of godlikeness in line with Channing's Unitarian doctrine, in the 2.5 keynote the poet's description of Evangeline's transfiguration with divine light moves beyond Unitarianism into a mystic vision that owes both its imagery and its metaphysics to the Fathers of the church.

## Deification: Terms and Clarifications

Because *deification*—a controversial concept, to say the least—is central to our argument, it will be helpful, at the outset, to clarify the meaning of this term and familiarize ourselves with the current theological conversation concerning deification. Throughout the history of Christian theology, the doctrine of deification has traditionally been seen as a hallmark of the Christian East. Due in part to the emigration of Russian Orthodox scholars to Western Europe in the early twentieth century, deification has recently re-entered the Western theological conversation with new vigor. In France, Jules Gross's 1938 *The Divinization of the Christian according to the Greek Fathers*, and Myrrah Lot-Borodine's 1970 *La Deification De L'Homme Selon la Doctrine des Peres Grecs* presented detailed explorations of the doctrine of deification in the writings of major Greek and Latin Fathers. Since these initial publications, the doctrine of deification has been a continual centerpiece of discussion and debate in Orthodox circles in the West. Over the last decade, non-Orthodox Christian theologians of multiple backgrounds have begun investigations of the possible presence of deification as both a theme and a doctrine in thinkers as varied as Martin Luther, St Thomas Aquinas, and John Wesley.[28]

Arguably the most important work on deification in the last decade has been Norman Russell's 2004 *The Doctrine of Deification in the Greek Patristic Tradition*. In this volume, Russell presents the most helpful taxonomy to date of traditional approaches to deification:

> The early Fathers use deification language in one of three ways, nominally, analogically, or metaphorically. The first two uses are straightforward. The nominal interprets the biblical application of the word "gods" to human beings simply as a title of honor. The analogical "stretches" the nominal: Moses was a god to Pharaoh as a wise man is a god to a fool; or men become sons and gods "by grace" in relation to Christ who is Son and God "by nature". The metaphorical use is more complex. It is characteristic of two distinct approaches, the ethical and the realistic. The ethical approach takes deification to be the attainment of likeness to God through ascetic and philosophical endeavor, believers reproducing some of the divine attributes in their own lives by imitation. Behind this use of the metaphor lies the model of *homoiosis*, or attaining the *likeness* to God. The realistic approach assumes that human beings are in some sense

---

28. For a good overview of this recent boom of ecumenical interest in deification, see Gavrilyuk, "The Retrieval of Deification."

transformed by deification. Behind the latter use lies the model of *methexis*, or *participation*, in God.[29]

Throughout this book, both likeness to God—the ethical approach to deification—and participation in God—the realistic approach to deification—will be considered.

It is important to clarify that the ethical and realistic approaches are not, according to Russell, *competing* approaches to the doctrine of deification, but rather *complementary* approaches that may or may not appear together in the theology of those who hold to a doctrine of deification. "Their meanings," Russell explains, "are distinct, but their spheres of reference overlap."[30] He continues:

> Although [participation] is the stronger term, they both seek to express the relationship between Being and becoming, between that which exists in an absolute sense and that which exists contingently . . . participation occurs when an entity is defined in relation to something else. For example, a holy person is an entity distinct from holiness, but is defined as holy because he or she has a share in holiness. Without holiness, there is no holy person, but the holy person has a separate existence from holiness. To say that the holy person "participates" in holiness conveys a relationship which is (a) substantial, not just a matter of appearance, and (b) asymmetrical, not a relationship between equals. "Likeness" is the name of another "relation" which accounts for the togetherness of elements of diverse ontological type, but in a weaker, non-constitutive way, closer to analogy than to participation. Likeness occurs when two entities share a common property. For example, two holy people resemble each other because they both possess holiness. The boundaries between these distinctions, however, are not rigid.[31]

The patristic and Unitarian texts with which Longfellow was familiar reveal both ethical and realistic approaches to deification, and it will be important in what follows to remember Russell's definitions of ethical and realistic deification and his caveats about the use of the word *deification* as we investigate each text.

It may be helpful to say one final prefatory word about deification. It has been the worry of many Christian theologians, especially those from a Protestant background, that any discussion of the deification of man

---

29. Russell, *Doctrine of Deification*, 1–2.
30. Russell, *Doctrine of Deification*, 2.
31. Russell, *Doctrine of Deification*, 2.

endangers the fundamental ontological distinction between creation and Creator that undergirds the entire Christian conception of the universe. This worry is, indeed, a valid one; after all, it is both difficult and immensely important to be precise with our theological language. It is easy to slip from calling man "godlike" to calling man "God." As we will see in our investigation of Emerson, to call man "God," and to call God "man," creating between them a relationship of complete identity, is to step away from Christian doctrine toward a form of Transcendentalism. This is why the early Fathers from Tertullian onward are careful to clarify that when the Christian attains a likeness to God or participates in God, she does so only by *grace*, and never by *nature*. Some thinkers—including, as we will see, Longfellow himself—only go so far as to call the deified human "godlike." Others, like Vladimir Kharlamov, call the deified human "god," but use a lowercase g to distinguish that human from God the Creator.[32] Russell, as we see above, calls both the ethical and realistic approaches to deification "metaphorical," and clarifies that even in the more robust realistic approach, the notion of participation necessarily implies an "asymmetrical ... relationship" between two ontologically distinct, unequal beings.

## The State of the Study of Nineteenth-Century American Poetry

How will the argument of this book help advance the current critical conversations surrounding the poetry of Longfellow's day? Specifically, why ought we examine the religious elements of *Evangeline* when the most fruitful recent critical work on the text has been in the realms of gender and post-colonial theory? Laurence Buell—whose introduction to Penguin's edition of Longfellow's *Selected Poems* is one of the best recent essays on the poet—argues in his 2003 study *Emerson*:

> Like it or not, there's no getting rid of religion as a force in human affairs. If you think it's nothing more than the opiate of others, you're likely to misunderstand yourself as well as them. Especially if you're trying to come to terms with so religio-centric a culture as the United States was in the early nineteenth-century—and indeed still is.[33]

Following Buell's call to take the religion of nineteenth-century American writers seriously, Martin Kevorkian has recently explored the late writings

---

32. Finlan and Kharlamov, *Theosis*, 6.
33. Buell, *Emerson*, 159–60.

of Emerson, Hawthorne, and Melville, highlighting "these authors' relations to 'organized religion.'"[34] Kevorkian's 2013 *Writing beyond Prophecy* is an elegant model and important step forward in both investigating the lesser studied major texts of American poetry—especially Melville's *Clarel*—and giving serious, sustained attention to the religious and theological elements within them.

If the religious elements in the writings of figures like Melville—whose relationship to organized religion was strained, to say the least—are worthy of close attention, how much more worthy of attention are the religious elements in the poems of a figure like Longfellow? For, though not considered a religious poet in the vein of George Herbert, Longfellow was a deeply religious *man*, as all of his biographers attest, and his poems, from the early "Psalm of Life," "Midnight Mass for the Dying Year," and "Blind Bartimaeus" to the late "My Cathedral," "Hermes Trismegistus," and "The Bells of St Blas," use explicitly religious language and are full of biblical allusions and meditations on the religiously informed ethics of the noble and virtuous life after which the poet himself strove. In the 1881 "Hermes Trismegistus," written in the last year of his life, Longfellow meditates on the difficulties and beauties of divine-human union. He paints a picture of the legendary Hermes, who pondered "the mystic union . . . between gods and men."[35] Longfellow wonders whether such a union is understandable: "Who, in his own skill confiding," he asks, dares to "Mark the border-land dividing human and divine?"[36]

If his religiously informed lyrics were not enough to convince the reader that Longfellow was a poet interested in the Christian theological tradition and its teachings on the human journey toward and union with God, one need look no further than Longfellow's well-known 1865 translation of Dante's *Divine Comedy*. Placed beside the earlier *Evangeline*, Longfellow's *Commedia* shows that all throughout his career, the poet continually returned to stories of those who journey toward God through their search for a human beloved, who are aided in their journeys by the natural, created order, and who experience moments of transfiguration and transformation through encounters with God's heavenly light.

In closely attending to the theological climate of 1840s New England and the theological sources and religious elements of Longfellow's *Evangeline*, I hope to further the critical project of Buell and Kevorkian, and to meditate on those subjects that Longfellow himself time and again places

---

34. Kevorkian, *Writing beyond Prophecy*, x.
35. Longfellow, *Complete Poetical Works*, 465.
36. Longfellow, *Complete Poetical Works*, 465.

at the center of his poems: virtue, self-discipline, and the human journey toward God. The benefits attending our exploration of Longfellow's theological sources, the religious elements of *Evangeline* in general, and the theological vision of *Evangeline*'s keynote passages in particular are twofold. First, our acquaintance with Longfellow's theological sources will deepen our understanding of Longfellow's academic and theological mind. Too often the poet has been painted as a quaint, grandfatherly figure who did no more than quote a few bland platitudes. Yet his own journals, critical notes, and lectures reveal a scholar of immense erudition, able to read and translate a dozen languages, who integrated the literature and legacy of the Old World into the American university more fully and winsomely than anyone before him; a man of genuine religious commitment who explored the fundamental documents and doctrines of his faith, even when preachers of his own tradition called such research and such grounding foolish and unnecessary; and a poet of such felicity and care that he could seamlessly integrate the theology of the early church and his own denomination together into affecting romantic narratives.

Second, our exploration of the religious elements of *Evangeline* will offer to Longfellow studies something it has not seen since the annotated editions of a century ago: a critical reading of the poem as a whole, taking into account new, original research on the unpublished manuscripts of the poet's lectures on the Fathers. It is my hope that such a reading can inspire and offer suggestions for more detailed investigations into Longfellow's structuring of the poem's narrative, use of biblical allusions, and employment of both concrete imagery and semiosis to lend literal texture and allegorical depth to the poem.

# 1

# The Theological Climate of Longfellow's New England

IN THE DECADES BETWEEN Longfellow's birth in 1807 and his publication of *Evangeline* in 1847, New England was dominated by two major, new religious movements: Unitarianism and Transcendentalism. Of the former movement Longfellow was a lifetime member and sometime apologist. Of the latter movement Longfellow was a skeptical, if often lighthearted, critic. Further, Longfellow was friend to major figures in both movements. He knew the champion of American Unitarianism, William Ellery Channing, through his father, and he became acquainted with Ralph Waldo Emerson through the eminent Transcendentalist's regular lectures in Cambridge. The year Channing died, 1842, Longfellow wrote a poem in his honor, and when Longfellow himself died in 1882, the very elderly Emerson spoke at his funeral. It was in the writings of Channing and Emerson that Longfellow encountered the new, dominant theological systems of the American nineteenth century, and it is to the theology of each that we must look if we are to develop a proper contextual framework within which to understand the religious elements of *Evangeline*.

## WILLIAM CHANNING AND UNITARIANISM

William Ellery Channing was born in 1780 in Newport, Rhode Island. A child of revolutionary New England and Calvinist Congregationalism, he nevertheless spent his university years at a Harvard University newly open to the modern political philosophy of Britain and Europe. After Harvard,

Channing moved to Richmond, Virginia, where he worked as a tutor. Gary Dorrien describes Channing's years in Richmond as "a soul-marking spiritual crisis,"[1] wherein Channing "encountered the reality of slavery as an institutionalized social system."[2] Appalled, Channing turned to "radical authors not assigned at Harvard: Voltaire, Rousseau, and William Godwin. Under the spell of Godwin's vision of a egalitarian utopian society, he wrote wild letters to his friends and relatives that called for a communist transformation of America."[3] Stirred to action by his experiences in the South, Channing moved back to New England and began to preach a new, liberal Christianity that called for the abolition of the slave trade and rejected the trinitarianism and determinism of Calvinism.

According to Dorrien, Channing was at first hesitant to use the term *Unitarianism* to describe his theology. This was largely due to the bad light in which English Unitarianism—preached by figures like Joseph Priestley—was viewed in New England. "Priestley-style Unitarianism was hard-edged, politically radical, philosophically materialist, and theologically Socinian, but New England liberal Christianity was mildly rationalist, sentimental, and enfranchised . . . Priestley's attack on the Platonist corruption of early Christianity was too radical for them, since they were spiritualizing neo-Platonists."[4] Further, Channing and other "liberal Christians were appalled by Priestley's materialism and sweeping rejection of traditional Christianity."[5] But this does not mean that there was nothing new about Channing's liberal theology, for his doctrine developed into a non-incarnational, anti-trinitarian system that rejected the traditional, Nicene definition of Christ's divinity, and was closer, Dorrien argues, to the theology of Arius, which was condemned by the early Ecumenical councils.[6] By the second decade of the nineteenth century Channing was upholding and defending what he called "Unitarian Christianity" against its detractors.

## *Channing and the Longfellow Family*

In 1814 Channing was approached by an old Harvard classmate, Stephen Longfellow, who was undergoing a spiritual crisis.[7] Stephen had rejected

1. Dorrien, *American Liberal Theology*, 16.
2. Dorrien, *American Liberal Theology*, 15.
3. Dorrien, *American Liberal Theology*, 16.
4. Dorrien, *American Liberal Theology*, 24.
5. Dorrien, *American Liberal Theology*, 24.
6. Dorrien, *American Liberal Theology*, 24.
7. Thompson, *Young Longfellow*, 13.

Calvinism, but did not know where else to turn. Stephen's wife Zilpah and their two sons, Stephen Jr. and Henry, regularly attended their local Unitarian church, but the skeptical Stephen Sr. did not. To Zilpah's delight, Channing led Stephen back to religious faith, and Stephen joined the Unitarian Church before the year was out. So it was that William Channing came to exert a happy influence upon the family and early life of the future poet Henry Wadsworth Longfellow.

Channing's influence was present both in the church pew and at the hearth during Henry's youth. Edward Wagenknecht stresses the importance of the latter:

> The schools [Henry] attended were of less importance in his training than the earnest but benevolent influence of his home, where the Puritan highmindedness survived, shorn of all its early hardness and fanaticism, and where this world and the next were viewed very much in the spirit of William Ellery Channing, who had been a college classmate of Stephen Longfellow's and an important (possibly even determinative) influence upon Stephen's religious life.[8]

In Henry's letters while at Bowdoin College, the young poet shows signs that he acted the part of an apologist for Channing's theology among his classmates. In an 1824 letter to his friend George Wadsworth Wells, Longfellow writes of the

> little Unitarian society at Bowdoin. I wish something could be done for us; we are as small as a grain of mustard-seed! There are but six members, now, in college, and our library is limited to a hundred or two volumes. I wish you would exert your influence on our behalf. And I want you to purchase twenty-five or thirty copies of a little work called Objections to Unitarian Christianity Considered. I want to distribute one or two of them in this section of the globe.[9]

This "little work" which Longfellow wished to distribute at his school was the 1819 work in which Channing clearly describes the differences between Unitarian doctrine and Puritan doctrine, and argues that Unitarianism is the purer, more rational, and more scriptural of the two.

Longfellow's first mention of Channing in his poetry is in his 1842 poem "To William E. Channing," which he wrote in praise of Channing's abolitionist work and included in his 1842 collection *Poems on Slavery*.

---

8. Wagenknecht, *Longfellow: Full Length Portrait*, 2.
9. Longfellow, *Letters*, 1:94.

Though the poem does not discuss Channing's theology, Longfellow compares Channing to both Luther and St John the Apostle:

> The pages of thy book I read,
>   And as I closed each one,
> My heart, responding, ever said,
>   "Servant of God! well done!"
>
> Well done! Thy words are great and bold;
>   At times they seem to me,
> Like Luther's, in the days of old,
>   Half-battles for the free.
>
> Go on, until this land revokes
>   The old and chartered Lie,
> The feudal curse, whose whips and yokes
>   Insult humanity.
>
> A voice is ever at thy side
>   Speaking in tones of might,
> Like the prophetic voice, that cried
>   To John in Patmos, "Write!"
>
> Write! and tell out this bloody tale;
>   Record this dire eclipse,
> This Day of Wrath, this Endless Wail,
>   This dread Apocalypse![10]

Unbeknownst to Longfellow, who had written the poem en route from Europe back to America, Channing had recently died. But Longfellow did not forget him. In July of 1846, Longfellow, who had written most of part 1 of *Evangeline* but had not begun part 2, returned to Channing. He records in his journal for July 20 a description of his wife, Fanny, reading to the family: "A rainy Sunday. We sat round a wood fire, and F[anny] read Dr. Channing's sermon at the church dedication in Newport; a very interesting discourse, particularly the passage of autobiography and the allusion to the sea-beach at Newport."[11] The sermon on the church dedication at Newport, commonly

---

10. Longfellow, *Complete Poetical Works*, 25.

11. Longfellow, *Life of Longfellow*, 2:51. There is something to be said for Longfellow's interest in descriptions of the sea in his favored theologians. As we will see in chapter 4, Longfellow is quite taken with the seascapes described by third-century writer Marcus Minutius Felix and quotes descriptions of the sea by the fourth-century

called "Christian Worship," was written in 1836, and contains some of the mature Channing's most theologically rich discussions of ontology, soteriology, and worship. In the next section we will explore the Unitarian theology that Channing expounded and defended, and that Longfellow read and praised, in both the mature work "Christian Worship" and the earlier "Objections to Unitarian Christianity Considered."

## *"Objections to Unitarian Christianity Considered"*

In this 1819 essay that Longfellow desired to disseminate at Bowdoin, Channing considers several common objections to New England Unitarianism—namely, that Unitarians do not believe in the divinity of Christ, that Unitarianism takes hope away from Christians, and that Unitarianism leads to unbelief. Throughout, Channing makes clear that Unitarian Christianity is the purest, most rational, and most scriptural form of Christianity.

In the first section, Channing elucidates the Unitarian view of Christ's divinity, which had caused much controversy in the early decades of the nineteenth century. "It is objected to us," Channing writes, "that we deny the Divinity of Jesus Christ."[12] He explains, however, that Unitarians, like most other Christians, do in fact believe in Christ's divinity:

> We believe in the Divinity of Christ's mission and office, that he spoke with Divine authority, and was a bright image of the Divine perfections. We believe that God dwelt in him, manifested Himself through him, taught men by him, and communicated to him his spirit without measure. We believe that Jesus Christ was the most glorious display, expression, and representative of God to mankind, so that in seeing and knowing him, we see and know the invisible Father; so that when Christ came, God visited the world and dwelt with men more conspicuously that at any former period. In Christ's words we hear God speaking; in his miracles we behold God acting; in his character and life we see an unsullied image of God's purity and love. We believe, then, in the Divinity of Christ, as this term is often and properly used.[13]

Though Channing here stresses the intimate connection between God and Christ, he makes plain that Christ and God are separate beings. Christ is the "image" and "representative" of God; in Christ God dwells and through

---

apologist Arnobius in the "Christian Fathers" lectures.

12. Channing, *Selected Discourses*, 71.
13. Channing, *Selected Discourses*, 71.

Christ God acts and speaks. Christ is divine in the sense that he is godly, and God's spokesman, but Christ is certainly not God himself. Channing makes this quite clear: "Whilst we honour Christ as the Son, representative and image of the Supreme God, we do not believe him to be the Supreme God himself. We maintain that Christ and God are distinct beings, two beings, not one and the same being."[14] Channing clearly parts ways with traditional trinitarianism, which teaches that God exists as three persons in one essence, the second person of which is Christ. By distinguishing Christ from "God," Channing is explicitly rejecting the doctrine that Christ is the second person of the Trinity, and therefore God. Channing explains that this trinitarian doctrine "is most unscriptural and unsound. We say that the Son cannot be that same being with his own Father; that he, who was sent into the world to save it, cannot be the living God who sent him."[15] In this passage, Channing does not discuss the distinction between person and essence that is so central to trinitarianism.[16] It is enough for him to point to the scriptures to prove that Christ and God are separate beings:

> If to represent Christ as a being distinct from God, as inferior to Him, be to denigrate him, then let our opponents lay the guilt where it belongs, not on us, but on our Master, whose language we borrow, in whose very words we express our sentiments, whose words we dare not trifle with and force from their plain sense.[17]

It would be a mistake to think that in calling Christ and God two distinct beings Channing was attempting to remove Christ from his central place in Christian doctrine. For Channing, Christ is still the prime spokesperson and example of God to man. He is the intermediary without which man would not have known God's message: "God's forgiving love, declared to mankind by Jesus Christ, and exercised through him, is the foundation of hope to the penitent on which we primarily rest, and a firmer the universe cannot furnish us."[18] Thus Christ's role is twofold—to declare "God's forgiving love" to man, and to exercise that love. The supreme exercise of this

---

14. Channing, *Selected Discourses*, 71.
15. Channing, *Selected Discourses*, 72.
16. Dorrien provides a possible explanation for why Channing does not introduce the person/being distinction: "Channing had no desire to involve 'liberal Christianity' in the well-forgotten early Church debates about the natures of God and Christ." Dorrien, *American Liberal Theology*, 24. Still, the reader familiar with Patristic theology might wish that Channing had provided a clearer engagement with Nicene doctrine.
17. Channing, *Selected Discourses*, 72–73.
18. Channing, *Selected Discourses*, 76.

love was Christ's death on the cross, which "is an important means of our salvation."[19] However, the saving efficacy of Christ's death is not based on a Calvinistic system wherein God is appeased by the sacrifice of a victim, but is based on "the merciful disposition of God toward the human race."[20] Channing thus presents a simpler doctrine than that of the trinitarian Calvinists: Christ, the representative of God, preaches God's forgiving love to sinners and shows this love by dying on the cross, and those who believe Christ's message are forgiven by God. There is no need, Channing argues, for doctrines of incarnation and atonement, for Christ's being and death need not have anything to do with the reconciliation between divine nature and human nature. God the Father reconciles man with himself through simple, forgiving love. And Christ is important because he perfectly preached and perfectly lived this forgiving love.

After his discussion of Christ and God, Channing moves on to a discussion of the Unitarian view of virtue and good works. To those who accuse Unitarians of preaching salvation by works, he explains, "we indeed attach a great importance to Christian works, or Christian obedience, believing that a practice or life conformed to the precepts and example of Jesus is the great end for which faith in him is required, and is the great condition on which everlasting life is bestowed."[21] God forgives and loves all who believe in Christ, but belief is not the final step, for everlasting life is given only to those who follow Christ's example. Far from being an arbitrary requirement, this requirement to live a life of virtue reveals an ontological connection between God and man: "We believe that holiness, or virtue is the very image of God in the human soul, a ray of his brightness, the best gift which He communicates to his creatures, the highest benefit which Christ came to confer, the only important and lasting distinction between man and man." For Channing, then, the *imago dei* is virtue, which God and Christ communicate to man. Further, Channing calls virtue not just the image of God, but also God's light, a "ray of his brightness," which is the most important gift that God can bestow on a human.[22] Here is the sole reference to any sort of concept of divine light in those writings of Channing that Longfellow reports having read. We will see in chapter 4 that this concept, which Channing so briefly mentions, is much more nuanced and pronounced in

---

19. Channing, *Selected Discourses*, 75.
20. Channing, *Selected Discourses*, 75.
21. Channing, *Selected Discourses*, 76.
22. Channing is careful to clarify that "no human virtue, no human obedience can give a legal claim, a right by merit, to the life and immortality brought to light by Christ." Channing, *Selected Discourses*, 76.

the writings of the Church Fathers—especially Origen, St Cyprian, and St John Chrysostom—with whom Longfellow was familiar.

The soteriology of "Objections to Unitarian Christianity Considered" can be summarized thus: God loved man, but man was ignorant of God's forgiving love and of how to live virtuously. Thus God appointed Christ to be the preacher and example of forgiving love and virtue to man. All who believe Christ's message and conform their behavior to his example are not only forgiven by God, but become like him. Finally, God freely bestows immortal life upon all those who believe Christ's message and, through virtue, become godlike. For Channing these doctrines amount to a pure, joyful, scriptural Christianity. While Channing presents these doctrines simply and clearly enough, he does not devote as much to time to the doctrine of human godlikeness as he would in his later sermon "Christian Worship," delivered at the church dedication in Channing's hometown of Newport.

## *"Christian Worship: A Sermon Delivered at the Church Dedication at Newport"*

In this sermon, Channing unfolds a more detailed and mature ontology of the saving relationship between God and man. He does this through considering the implications of calling God "Father," which are fourfold: God creates spirits in his own image, possessing his attributes; God understands the depths and destiny of these spirits; God desires these spirits to be educated in virtue and progress toward perfection; and this progress involves a partaking in the divine nature of God.

First, Channing explains that, just as a human father passes on his natural attributes to his children, so God passes on his attributes to man:

> God is the Father, because he brings into life minds, spirits, partaking of energies kindred to his own attributes. Accordingly the Scripture teaches us, that God made man in his own image, after his own likeness.[23] Here is the ground of his paternal relation to the human race, and hence he is called in an especial sense the Father of those who make it the labor of life to conform themselves more and more to the divine original.[24]

In this passage Channing summarizes his twofold ontology of man—all initially possess "energies kindred to [God's] own attributes." But those who

23. Channing explains in his 1828 sermon "Likeness to God" that the biblical phrase *image of God* is no mere figuration: "God then does not sustain a figurative resemblance to man. It is the resemblance of a parent to a child, the likeness of a kindred nature." Channing, "Likeness to God," 7.

24. Channing, *Works*, 321.

"conform themselves more and more to the divine original" become more complete children of God. Those, on the other hand, who reject God and practice evil distance themselves from the divine likeness.

In order to conform to their divine original, souls must go through a process of education in virtue, which is, Channing argues,

> the great work of a parent . . . There are those who think, that God, if a parent, must make our enjoyment his supreme end. He has a higher end, our intellectual and moral education. Even the good human parent desires the progress, the virtue of his child more than its enjoyment. God never manifests himself more as our Father, than in appointing to us pains, conflicts, trials, by which we may rise to the heroism of virtue, may become strong to do, to dare, to suffer, to sacrifice all things at the call of truth and duty.[25]

Channing's use of the word *virtue* here is significant, for in "Objections to Unitarian Christianity Considered" Channing had argued that virtue was God's image in man and a ray of God's light. In "Christian Worship" virtue is still God's likeness in man, and is particularly that part of God's likeness that enables man to call God his Father "in an especial sense."

It is "pains, conflicts, trials" that lead to virtue, according to Channing. To those who think that such trials obscure God's likeness in man, Channing answers:

> Suffering, trial, exposure, seem to be necessary elements in the education of a moral being. It is fit, that a being whose happiness and dignity are to be found in vigorous action and in forming himself, should be born with undeveloped capacities, and be born into a world of mingled difficulties and aids . . . Were I called upon to prove God's spiritual parental interest in us, I would point to the trials, temptations, evils of life; for to these we owe the character of Christ, we owe the apostle and martyr, we owe the moral force and deep sympathy of private and domestic life, we owe the development of what is divine in human nature.[26]

Sufferings and trials, according to Channing, are precisely what the "undeveloped" soul needs. Suffering is not a hindrance to virtue, but an "aid." Channing gives three examples of suffering as an aid to virtue: Christ, the apostles, and the martyrs. Christ, however, is unique in Channing's

---

25. Channing, *Works*, 323–24.
26. Channing, *Works*, 330–31.

understanding of moral education, for Christ was not merely educated in virtue, but was the one who educated all men about their need for divinity and virtue: "the most celestial worship ever paid on earth was rendered by Christ, when he approached man, and the most sinful man, as a child of God, when he toiled and bled to awaken what was Divine in the human soul, to regenerate the fallen world."[27] Thus Christ fulfills his twofold mission—teacher and example—that Channing described in "Objections to Unitarian Christianity Considered."

Channing makes clear that he is indeed suggesting an overtly optimistic belief in human perfection:

> Human perfection is not a dream. The brightest visions of genius fade before the realities of excellence and happiness to which good men are ordained. In that highest life, the parental character of God will break forth from the clouds which now obscure it. His bright image in his children will proclaim the Infinite Father.
>
> I have thus, my friends, set before you the true object of Christian worship. You are here to worship God as your spiritual parent, as the Father of your spirits, whose great purpose is your spiritual perfection, your participation of a divine nature. I hold this view of God to be the true, deep foundation of Christian worship.[28]

Human perfection is both possible, and the proper end of all, for all were created with undeveloped attributes of divinity. Christ reveals this truth to man, and through suffering man may develop virtue, that likeness to God that is a ray of divine glory. But resemblance to God through sharing God's moral qualities is not the whole of human perfection for Channing.

In the penultimate sentence of the above quotation, Channing refers to 2 Peter, where St Peter says that through God's "very great promises . . . you may become partakers in the divine nature, having escaped from the corruption that was in the world because of sinful desire."[29] Channing could be using this verse in one of two ways: He could be using it to reiterate that the human nature can be called divine because it is made in God's image and through ascesis shares his ethical attributes. Or Channing could mean something more—namely, that the human being can participate in God's own divine nature. It is clear that Channing elsewhere teaches the first principle, but Channing's use of the language of 2 Peter as an explanation

27. Channing, *Works*, 338.
28. Channing, *Works*, 328.
29. 2 Peter 1:4 (ESV).

of God's "great purpose" for man's "spiritual perfection" suggests that his use of the passage refers to a further stage of deification beyond both the initial image of God in man and the man's ethical likeness to God achieved through virtue.

This eventual partaking in the divine nature, which St Peter first described and Channing affirms, is, according to Channing, something that man must believe in and ask for, but that God must ultimately accomplish:

> We must have faith in the human soul as receptive of divinity, as made for greatness, for spiritual elevation, for likeness to God, or God's character as a Father will be to us as an unrevealed mystery. If we think, as so many seem to think, that God has made us only for low pleasures and attainments, that our nature is incapable of godlike virtues, that our prayers for the Divine Spirit are unheard, that celestial influences do not descend into the human soul, that God never breathes on it to lift it above its present weakness, to guide it to a more perfect existence, to unite it more intimately with himself, then we know but faintly the meaning of a Father in Heaven.[30]

Channing describes several extraordinary qualities that the soul gains in its education—namely, godlike virtue, strength, perfection, and unity with God. And Channing directly connects the belief in godlike virtue, strength, perfection, and unity with God with the true understanding of God as Father. According to Channing, if one truly understands that God is his Father, then he will be naturally led to a belief in what, as we saw in the introduction, Norman Russell calls both ethical and realistic deification: that man can be made godlike by sharing God's ethical attributes, and by being united with God in a relationship of intimate participation.[31]

## *Channing and Deification*

Though Channing clearly writes of ethical godlikeness and participation in the divine nature in the two sermons we have examined, there is not a critical consensus that Channing believed in human deification. Gary Dorrien warns that Channing "affirmed that human beings possess the God-given capacity to experience divinity, and he insisted that revelation is knowable only as personal experience, but he pointedly admonished that human beings do not become gods or infallible interpreters of Divinity by virtue of

---

30. Channing, *Works*, 326–27.
31. See Russell, *Doctrine of Deification*, 1–3.

the experience of revelatory feeling."³² Dorrien's main concern here is to discourage too strong a reading of Channing's view of human goodness, for Channing knew all too well the evils of his day, especially those involving human exploitation and slavery. Still, Dorrien does affirm that Channing believed man could "experience divinity." This is a step below saying that Channing believed that man could be united with and participate in divine nature, which Channing explicitly says in "Christian Worship." Further, Dorrien says that Channing does not believe that men become gods. We have seen, however, that Channing does indeed say that man can and should become "godlike."

In Dorrien we encounter the characteristic uneasiness of many modern scholars with doctrines of deification. But if we use Norman Russell's categories of types of deification, it becomes clear that Channing does indeed preach both ethical and realistic deification. As we saw in the Introductions, Russell explains, that "the ethical approach takes deification to be the attainment of likeness to God through ascetic and philosophical endeavor," and that behind realistic deification "lies the model of *methexis*, or *participation*, in God.³³ Though Channing does not discuss philosophical endeavor in the above sermons, in describing the ethical education of the human soul as gradual acquisition of godlike virtue through the ascetic activity of suffering through trials, Channing fulfills Russell's criteria for the ethical approach to deification. And in repeated use of the language of participation in divinity and in God's divine nature, Channing also fits the "model of *methexis*" that under-girds the realistic approach to deification.

The biggest obstacle in the way of simply concluding that Channing preaches a clear doctrine of human deification in those works Longfellow read is that Channing lacks, and even argues against, a primary element in the historical doctrine of deification passed down from the early Church Fathers—namely, the doctrine of the incarnation of Christ. As we will see in chapter 3, the consensus of the Fathers is that the incarnation of the second person of the Trinity, Christ, is the model of the union and participation between human nature and divine nature. According to the Fathers, in Christ's incarnation the human and divine natures, separated because of sin, were reunited, and all who believe in and follow Christ do so with the promise that their human nature will be united to God's divine nature through their belief and obedience. Channing, however, in denying that Christ is God, denies also that Christ united the human and divine natures in his incarnation. Instead, Channing's Christ preaches that all men, merely by virtue of

32. Dorrien, *American Liberal Theology*, 57.
33. Russell, *Doctrine of Deification*, 2.

being created by God, have attributes of divinity in them which have been undeveloped and obscured by human sin. The Unitarian Christ, then, is the model of godlike virtue and the enlightener of man concerning his deified destiny, but this Christ does not unite human and divine nature in any of those new ways that the Fathers describe. This is not to deny that Channing preaches a form of ethical and realistic deification; rather it is to say that Channing presents an account of the ontology behind human deification that differs from that of the Fathers.

## Emerson and Transcendentalism

The American Unitarian movement, under the direction of William Ellery Channing, had rejected the Calvinist doctrine of human depravity in favor of an Arminian view of a morally improvable and even perfectible human nature. Along with this shift came a great trust in human reason to understand both the human self and the created world.[34] Still, Unitarianism continued to hold to the traditional Christian beliefs that the Bible is the unique revelation of God to man and that Christ is the sole savior of the human race. But in the 1830s, the New England Transcendentalist movement would take Channing's doctrines of the reliability of human reason and the godlikeness of man a step further, rejecting Christianity as the unique and uniquely authoritative way to God and moral improvement.

One of the leading figures in the Transcendentalist movement was Ralph Waldo Emerson. Born in 1803 and raised in a Unitarian-leaning Congregationalist household, Emerson attended Harvard Divinity School and traveled in Europe before beginning his ministry as a Unitarian preacher in the early 1830s. Emerson admired and imitated the inspiring eloquence that flowed from Channing's pulpit, but soon became uneasy with the restrictions of even Unitarian doctrine. Lawrence Buell explains that "the point of no return was Emerson's refusal to administer the Lord's Supper—the ritual of communion. He asked his congregation to choose between him and this ceremony in which he no longer believed. More to his relief than his disappointment, they chose the ceremony."[35] Emerson began to employ his talents as a preacher in public lectures in Boston and around New England. When he gave the commencement address to the graduates of Harvard Divinity School in 1838, his words scandalized the region; not only

---

34. Lawrence Buell writes that "the main impetus behind the Unitarian departure from orthodoxy" was "the shift from a Calvinist view of human nature as depraved to an Arminian view of man as improvable." Buell, *Literary Transcendentalism*, 26.

35. Buell, *Emerson*, 15.

did he deny that Christ was God, but also that Christ intended to pass on any authoritative rules or practices. Instead, Emerson called the graduates to look inward, to their consciences, where they would find all the truth and moral guidance they needed. In his first book, *Essays*, published in 1841, he further explained his views on the self in "Self-Reliance" and on God in "The Over-Soul."

Though many were scandalized, others—among them Amos Bronson Alcott, Orestes Brownson, Margaret Fuller, and Henry David Thoreau—were quite taken with Emerson's message, and partnered with him in disseminating Transcendentalist doctrines across the country. Though the name "Transcendentalism" was first given to this group as a title of derision, Emerson and others came to accept and use it.[36] Throughout the 1830s and '40s Transcendentalism spread, both through journals like the *Dial*, which Emerson edited, and through attempts at new styles of living, including the socialist communes of Brook Farm and Fruitlands, as well as Thoreau's famous residence at Walden Pond.

## Emerson and Longfellow

While he was happy to edit the *Dial*, Emerson did not reside in any commune or rustic cabin. He was a member of Boston society, and it was through his activities there that he met Henry Wadsworth Longfellow. Longfellow had moved from Maine down to Cambridge in 1837, when Harvard University snatched him from the relative obscurity of Bowdoin College and appointed him the Smith professor of Modern Languages. Eager to take advantage of all that the Cambridge region had to offer, Longfellow attended the public lectures that Emerson gave in 1838. He reports having heard four lectures in all that year: "Affections," "Being and Seeming," "Holiness," and, most importantly, the controversial "Divinity School Address."

Overall, Longfellow was impressed by Emerson's talents as a speaker, if somewhat confused about Emerson's actual doctrines. After hearing Emerson lecture on March 8, 1838, Longfellow writes,

> This evening Emerson lectured on the Affections: a good lecture. He mistakes his power somewhat, and at times speaks in oracles, darkly. He is vastly more of a poet than a philosopher. He has a brilliant mind, and develops and expands an idea very beautifully, and with abundant similitudes and illustrations.[37]

36. Buell, *Emerson*, 31–32.

37. Longfellow, *Life of Longfellow*, 1:277. After this description, Longfellow includes a joke: "Jeremiah Moses said a sharp thing, the other day, when asked whether he could

Longfellow's description of Emerson's next lecture, on March 28, foreshadows the controversy that would erupt over the "Divinity School Address" one month later: "Hear Emerson's lecture on Holiness, which he defines to be 'the soul of the world.' This lecture is a great bugbear to many pious, feeble souls. Not exactly comprehending it (and who does?) they seem to be sitting in the shadow of some awful atheism or other."[38] Here Longfellow does not explicitly state which side of the argument he is on, though he implies it by calling those who were offended by the lecture "feeble."

Of all that Longfellow wrote about Emerson, it is his remarks on the "Divinity School Address" that have gained the most critical attention, perhaps because it was in this address that Emerson presented his "most forceful statement" of Transcendentalist theology.[39] In a letter dated July 28, 1838, Longfellow writes:

> Emerson continues to make a stir. Not long ago he preached a most extraordinary sermon here; concerning which the Reverend Dean Palfrey said 'what in it was not folly was impiety!' Oh! After all, it was only a stout *humanitarian* discourse; in which Christ and Göthe [sic] were mentioned together as great Philosophers.[40]

In contrast to Lawrance Thompson, who says that Emerson's lecture only "touched [Longfellow] as a bundle of vague and harmless effusions,"[41] Buell takes Longfellow's words about the "Divinity School Address" to be an indication that "the Unitarian community was much readier for Emersonian notions of arts and religion than the acerbity of the miracles controversy would lead us to expect."[42] But though Buell says that Longfellow "obviously considers Emerson's ideas self evident," it is not clear that this is where Longfellow's exasperation with Reverend Palfrey lies. Longfellow's tone indicates at least that he thinks Palfrey should not have been scandalized by Emerson's humanitarianism. It is unclear whether Longfellow thinks that this is because Palfrey should have expected such doctrines from Emerson, because Emerson's doctrines are self-evidently true, or both.

In 1841, Longfellow read Emerson's *Essays*, including "The Over-Soul," which incorporated sections of the lecture "Holiness" that Longfellow

---

understand Mr. Emerson. His answer was 'No, I can't, but my daughters can'" (277–78).
38. Longfellow, *Life of Longfellow*, 1:282.
39. Buell, *Literary Transcendentalism*, 30.
40. Longfellow, *Letters*, 2:87.
41. Thomson, *Young Longfellow*, 260.
42. Buell, *Literary Transcendentalism*, 32–33.

had heard three years before.[43] In 1845–1846, the poet again attended a lecture series by Emerson, this time on "Great Men," including Plato, Goethe, and Napoleon. This time around, Longfellow writes, "Many striking and brilliant passages, but not so much as usual of that 'sweet rhetorick' which usually flows from his lips; and many things to shock the sensitive ear and heart."[44] Despite this mixed review, a month later, Longfellow writes of Emerson, "There is a great charm about him,—the Chrysostom and Sir Thomas Brown of the day."[45] A few days later, Longfellow dined with Emerson, and describes him thus: "rather shy in his manner, but pleasant and friendly . . . We like Emerson,—his beautiful voice, deep thought, and mild melody of language."[46] When Emerson's first volume of verse, *Poems*, appeared later that year, Longfellow praised them:

> [*Poems*] gave us the keenest pleasure; though many of the pieces present themselves Sphinx-like . . . throughout the volume, through the golden mist and sublimation of fancy gleam bright veins of purest poetry, like rivers running through meadows. Truly a rare volume; with many exquisite poems in it . . . containing much of the quintessence of poetry.[47]

It is unsurprising that Longfellow, who continually called Emerson a poet after hearing his lectures, should be most pleased by Emerson's poetry.

In all, Emerson's friendly demeanor and aesthetically pleasing speeches endeared him to Longfellow. But Longfellow appears continually reserved when it comes to Emerson's *ideas*; "oracles," "dark," "shadow," "shock," "mist"—these are the words that Longfellow uses to describe Emerson's work, in addition to the word "beautiful." Longfellow appears to have been unable to apprehend Emerson's ideas clearly. While comfortable with such opacity in Emerson's poems, he seems a little bit frustrated by it in Emerson's lectures.

## *"Holiness"*

The first of encounter that Longfellow had with Emerson's theological teachings was in the lecture "Holiness." Emerson begins this lecture by characterizing two extreme positions: "superstition" and "atheism." Superstition is the

43. Longfellow, *Life of Longfellow*, 1:375.
44. Longfellow, *Life of Longfellow*, 2:27.
45. Longfellow, *Life of Longfellow*, 2:30.
46. Longfellow, *Life of Longfellow*, 2:32.
47. Longfellow, *Life of Longfellow*, 2:69.

adherence to an "imported faith" external to the human soul: "venerate, says Tradition, this book, this saint, this law. Do not vaingloriously stand on your own sense and think forsooth that you must be consulted and reconciled to these doctrines before they can pass current. Here is positive instruction out of heaven. Take this."[48] Such superstition, which is a "quitting of the substance for the shadow" is "impossible," Emerson says. But equally impossible is atheism, the rejecting of everything spiritual and heavenly, which results in

> the solitude of the soul which is without God in the world . . . To him, it is no creation . . . To him heaven and earth have lost their beauty . . . The words Great, Venerable, have lost their meaning; every thought loses all its depth and has become mere surface.[49]

Though Longfellow describes Emerson's detractors as afraid of his "awful atheism," in "Holiness" Emerson makes clear that actual atheism is as undesirable as superstition.

The middle way between a self-denying superstition and miserable atheism is *holiness*. One of the reasons that man is unsatisfied with both superstition and atheism is that both ignore the most important faculty of his human soul, the moral sentiment. "Moral sentiment is the basis of nature. Good and Bad are its first distinction . . . The sentiment is the ultimate fact, and cannot be defined. It is alive, and maketh alive."[50] This passage is indicative of the opacity about which Longfellow complained. The moral sentiment is both the most important thing in man and "cannot be defined." However, Emerson does give us some of its central characteristics: it is in the soul; it is ethical, distinguishing between good and bad; and it is a living thing. Finally, the moral sentiment is the key to holiness—that quality which saves man from both superstition and atheism. Holiness, Emerson explains, is "self surrender to this moral sentiment, the acceptance of its dominion throughout our constitution as the beatitude of man."[51] Through surrendering to the moral sentiment, man progresses to an understanding of the unity of all men: "the advancing soul inhaling the immortal breath of Virtue, recognizes, at once, the identical nature of all men; and feels instantly the omnipotence of this principle shining out of one part of heaven even to the other part of heaven, and how vain is all opposition to it."[52] Once

---

48. Emerson, "Holiness," 341.
49. Emerson, "Holiness," 341–42.
50. Emerson, "Holiness," 344–45.
51. Emerson, "Holiness," 346.
52. Emerson, "Holiness," 346–47.

we begin to listen to and obey the ethical guidance of the moral sentiment, we will see that all have an identical nature; we all have, and can be directed by, the moral sentiment.

Thus the problem with both superstition and atheism is that both reject the moral sentiment, the first by placing authoritative ethical guidance outside of one's soul, and the other by denying the soul entirely. Though in "Holiness" Emerson does not explicitly say that the Christian has no unique revelation or authority above other moral-sentiment–followers, it is implied. And Emerson's descriptions of superstition sound quite similar to traditional Puritan teachings about the depravity of man and the authority of scripture.

## *"The Divinity School Address"*

As mentioned earlier, it was not until the "Divinity School Address" that Emerson publicly revealed his wholly post-Christian teachings. Longfellow called Emerson's ideas "humanitarian," and they do indeed center on man, not God nor the exclusive revelation of Christianity. Emerson opens the address with a description of natural, physical beauty, but soon turns to the beauties that the moral sentiment (now called the "sentiment of virtue") reveals to man:

> A more secret, sweet, and overpowering beauty appears to man when his heart and mind open to the sentiment of virtue. Then instantly he is instructed in what is above him . . . When in innocency, or when by intellectual perception, he attains to say,—"I love the Right; Truth is beautiful within and without, forevermore. Virtue, I am thine: save me: use me: thee will I serve, day and night, in great, in small, that I may be not virtuous, but virtue;"—then is the end of the creation answered, and God is well pleased.[53]

The moral sentiment in man reveals two things, truth and virtue. This is not only a beautiful experience, but is "the end" of man itself, his *telos*. And it pleases God. But that is not all that the sentiment of virtue accomplishes: "If a man is at heart just, then in so far is he God; the safety of God, the immortality of God, the majesty of God do enter into that man with justice."[54] Thus instruction in and love of virtue not only pleases God, but imbues man with God's attributes.

---

53. Emerson, "Divinity School Address," 292.
54. Emerson, "Divinity School Address," 232.

"These facts," Emerson explains next, "have always suggested to man the sublime creed."[55] This creed is not the Christian creed, though on first glance it is compatible with Christian doctrine. This creed states "that the world is not the product of manifold power, but of one will, of one mind; and that one mind is everywhere."[56] Emerson says not just that each man's spirit and mind resemble those of his fellow men, but that all men, in fact, have one mind, one spirit, one animating power. This single mind, when used properly, gives rise to religious sentiment, "our highest happiness."[57] Emerson reiterates that "this sentiment is divine and deifying. It is the beatitude of man."[58] This deifying sentiment "is an intuition . . . It cannot be received second hand. Truly speaking, it is not instruction, but provocation, that I can receive from another soul. What he announces, I must find true in me, or wholly reject."[59] It is this sort of first-hand intuition leading to divinity, bestowed by the religious sentiment, that Jesus possessed, along with all true seers and prophets throughout history:

> Jesus Christ belonged to the true race of prophets. He saw with open eye the mystery of the soul. Drawn by its severe harmony, ravished with its beauty, he lived in it, and has his being there. Alone in all history, he estimated the greatness of man. One man was true to what is in you and me . . . He said, in this jubilee of sublime emotion, "I am divine. Through me, God acts; through me, he speaks. Would you see God, see me; or, see thee, when thou also thinkest as I now think."[60]

Here Emerson makes two important moves: he both restricts true human living and religion to a particular state of spiritual perception, and he opens up the possibility of this true human living to all men regardless of culture or religion. Buell calls this intellectual move "a two edged sword":

> infinitely expansive, ferociously reductive. It would be used to discredit all forms of religion other than the peak experiences of the inspired individual. Institution, civilizations, epochs could be dismissed in a wave. But universal mind theory could be used to grant non-western mythologies the same standing as Judeo Christianity.[61]

55. Emerson, "Divinity School Address," 233.
56. Emerson, "Divinity School Address," 233.
57. Emerson, "Divinity School Address," 233.
58. Emerson, "Divinity School Address," 234.
59. Emerson, "Divinity School Address," 234.
60. Emerson, "Divinity School Address," 235.
61. Buell, *Emerson*, 170.

It is true that Emerson still places Christ in a very high position. Christ "alone" was truly a man. But all can attain true humanity, and thus divinity, in the same way that Christ did. This attainment has little to do with Christianity, for the Christian religion has fallen prey to that dead "second-hand" instruction which Emerson contrasts with the immediate "intuition" of true religious sentiment. "Men have come to speak," Emerson explains, "of the revelation as somewhat long ago given and done, as if God were dead. The injury to faith throttles the preacher; and the goodliest of institutions becomes an uncertain and inarticulate voice."[62] Contextually, these words are harsh and pointed, for he was speaking to new preachers at an institution, Harvard Divinity School, that taught them to be the premier spiritual authorities in the largest institutions of New England Christianity.

The solution to the problem of throttled preachers and inarticulate institutions according to Emerson is, simply, the return of the preacher to the practice and the doctrine of *Self-Reliance*. The preacher must attune his soul (which he shares with all men) to virtue, and obey the soul's moral utterances. Further, the preacher must provoke his congregation to the same Self-Reliance. From such a shift in doctrine and practice, Emerson foresees the possibility of new prophecy, and even new scripture. "I look," Emerson says, "for the new Teacher,"[63] which any man could be, if he would become "a newborn bard of the Holy Spirit ... and acquaint man first hand with the Deity."[64]

## *"The Over-Soul"*

Though the "Divinity School Address" clearly presents a post-Christian view of man and Christ, it still sounds theistic. God and man, though united in those moments when man attains virtue through the moral sentiment, seem to be separate beings in Emerson's theology, just as they are, emphatically, in Channing's. But in the 1841 essay "The Over-soul" Emerson clarifies that "all spiritual being is in man."[65] This spiritual being is what Emerson calls "common nature," that mind/spirit/will that fills and animates all things and unites all men. This "common nature" is not some personal, indwelling Father: "common nature is not social; it is impersonal; is God."[66] If all spiritual being is in man, and this spiritual being is man's common nature, and that

62. Emerson, "Divinity School Address," 237.
63. Emerson, "Divinity School Address," 245.
64. Emerson, "Divinity School Address," 243.
65. Emerson, "The Over-soul," 387.
66. Emerson, "The Over-soul," 390.

common nature is God, then God is nothing more or less than a quality of the human spirit. Buell explains that "Emerson's god is an immanent god, an indwelling property of human personhood and physical nature, not located in some otherworldly realm."[67]

Emerson's God, then, is located in man and in nature, not heaven, which is for him an illusion of superstitious traditionalists who have lost touch with the religious sentiment. Further, Emerson's God is a property of human personhood, but not *every* property, and certainly not the physical appetites or changing whims of the passions. Indeed, in "Holiness" and the "Divinity School Address," Emerson makes it clear that most men are wholly inattentive to their moral sentiment, and even great men see truth and virtue in passing flashes. Perhaps only Christ, Socrates, and the Buddha lived in continual perception of and obedience to their moral sentiments. Thus the word "God," for the Emersonian Transcendentalist, should be applied to that deep, hard to reach, animating property of human nature from which flow all truth, morality, religion, and art.

## *Ego-theism versus Likeness to God*

If Emerson is right that God is the truth-revealing, spiritual property that all men share, then becoming divine is not a participation in some separate being, but an awareness of and obedience to the revelations of that inner property. This "divinity of self," Buell argues, is the "cornerstone of transcendentalism."[68] All men have the divine within, but many do not know this, or have forgotten. Spiritual reconciliation and renewal is a reordering of human properties such that the moral sentiment is given total rule over all human action. There is no personal God to be reconciled to, because he does not exist. He was the result of man misunderstanding his own spirit.

Though William Channing had indeed preached that it is through the soul that humans learn about God's attributes, he could not follow Emerson into the identification of God with a property of the soul. Dorrien explains that Channing "criticized certain Emersonians for having fallen 'into a kind of *ego-theism*' that blurred the distinction between the self as a partaker of divinity and divinity itself."[69] As we have already seen, Channing thinks that the divine attributes of God—the "likeness of God"—come to be in the human soul in two ways: initially, God placed his attributes in man when he created man; after salvation, man imitates God and develops the

---

67. Buell, *Emerson*, 162.
68. Buell, *Emerson*, 16.
69. Dorrien, *American Liberal Theology*, 48.

nascent divine attributes in his soul. This ethical deification of sharing the property of virtue with God then leads to a realistic deification wherein man participates in the divine nature, as articulated in 2 Peter 1:4. Emerson's ego-theistic view dispenses with all but the divine attributes in man. The development of these attributes through obedience to the moral sentiment is all the experience of God that man can have, for God is tantamount to the moral sentiment. This is not to say that such experience is unsatisfying for Emerson, for Emerson describes it throughout his career as the height of human ecstasy.

In Channing's Unitarianism and Emerson's Transcendentalism, then, Longfellow encountered two theological systems that championed the deification of man as their goal. The first preached a non-trinitarian, non-incarnational doctrine of attaining godlikeness through virtue and participation in God the Father's divine nature. The second preached a non-Christian doctrine of the identity of God with the central property of human nature, and the attainment of divinity through obedience to this property. It should now be clear that the attainment of godlikeness was a spiritual concept in which the theological innovators of Longfellow's age were keenly interested. And we will soon see that this concept was also on Longfellow's mind as he composed the second part of *Evangeline*.

## The Critics on Longfellow's Creed

While Buell sees in Longfellow a sympathy with Emerson's "Divinity School Address," no critic has been inclined to say that Longfellow was in any important way a Transcendentalist. Instead, as we will see in some detail in the next chapter, critics over the last century and a half have most often characterized Longfellow as a Unitarian. Still, the poet always comes out looking like a strange sort of Unitarian.

Articulating what had been clear from the beginning of Longfellow's career, George MacCrie in 1875 wrote that Longfellow "cannot be considered as an Evangelical, in the sense of a Calvinistic poet."[70] Four decades later, Augustus Hopkins Strong added to this perspective, describing Longfellow's spiritual maturation as a left-ward journey. Though Strong's language clearly shines a negative light on Longfellow's beliefs, he does describe American Unitarian doctrine rather accurately. During Longfellow's college years at Bowdoin, Strong explains,

---

70. MacCrie, *Religion of our Literature*, 221. "A Calvinist poet," MacCrie goes on to write, "is the great desideratum of our age."

> A sort of religious indifference took possession of him. His attendance at religious services became somewhat perfunctory. He longed for a more mild and ethical preaching; and when a Unitarian church was organized at Brunswick, he gave it whatever support lay within his power. There is little doubt that his enthusiastic willingness to accept a Harvard professorship was to some extent influenced by his desire to emerge into a freer theological, as well as a freer intellectual field. From this time, Longfellow was an avowed Unitarian.[71]

This Unitarianism was characterized, Strong explains, by a "Pelagian" attitude toward man and God which felt no "deep conviction of sin, [nor] felt the need of an atoning Saviour, [and] never shrank from the holiness of God."[72] This led to an "insufficient estimation of Christ . . . Sin to him is a misfortune and a disease, but never guilt and ruin . . . Little sin means a belittled Christ; and of this belittled Christ Longfellow is the apostle."[73] In speaking of a "belittled Christ" and a "Pelagian" attitude Strong refers to those doctrines that Channing called, respectively, the divinity of Christ properly understood, and the perfectibility of man. If Longfellow did indeed ascribe to those doctrines he found in "Objections to Unitarian Christianity Considered" and "Christian Worship," then he would be guilty of Strong's accusations. Further, Strong claims that Longfellow did not believe in the need for an atoning Savior. If Longfellow agreed with Channing that Christ's death was a loving example, not an act of substitutionary atonement, then Strong is right again.

For all this, Strong does not think that Longfellow was wholly devoid of Christian faith, especially in comparison with Emerson. Strong acknowledges that "Longfellow could not sympathize with Emerson's transcendentalism, or with the disjointedness of his thinking."[74] Strong also clarifies that Longfellow did firmly hold to important, minor Christian doctrines. "Longfellow's faith," he writes, "was simply a faith in the historic value of Christ's human example. This is a minor point in Christian doctrine, yet it is an essential point."[75] To summarize, then, Strong sees in Longfellow's works Channing's doctrines of human perfectibility, of Christ's non-equality with God, and of Christ's death as an ultimate example of love rather than a substitutionary atonement. Sadly, Strong does not explore the details of

---

71. Strong, *American Poets and Theology*, 222.
72. Strong, *American Poets and Theology*, 223.
73. Strong, *American Poets and Theology*, 237.
74. Strong, *American Poets and Theology*, 250.
75. Strong, *American Poets and Theology*, 243.

Longfellow's "Pelagian" belief in human perfectibility through the attainment of godlikeness. One is tempted to think that if he had explored this doctrine in Longfellow or Channing, he would have been displeased with what he found.

Though Strong describes Longfellow as an eager and firmly entrenched Unitarian of Channing's school, two subsequent biographers, Lawrance Thompson and Edgar James Bailey, challenge this view of Longfellow. In 1922, Bailey pushed back against Strong's ascriptions of hardline Unitarianism to Longfellow. Longfellow, Bailey writes, "took his unquestioning stand upon the three fundamental doctrines, the goodness of God, the divinity of Christ, and the immortality of the soul."[76] Though the first and last of these doctrines are also tenets of Channing's Unitarianism, the second is not. What, we might ask, does Bailey mean by the "divinity of Christ"? Whatever he means, a few pages later he suggests that Longfellow had at least minor trinitarian leanings:

> The theological concept of the trinity seems not to have greatly interested Longfellow . . . That he accepted the doctrine as truth may perhaps be assumed from the couplet which stands as the fifth of his several experiments in Elegiac Verse, "How can the Three be one? You ask me: I answer by asking, / Hail and snow and rain, are they not three and yet one?" However much or little these lines may be assumed to prove, it is but just to admit that of the several persons in the Trinity, Longfellow in his poems only occasionally mentioned the Holy Spirit and in no place greatly developed his thought of the Father and Son.[77]

Here we encounter one of the great problems in discussing the faith of a poet—namely, the ambiguity of the speaker in any poem. If we can assume that Longfellow himself is speaking in the couplet on the Trinity, then we can conclude that Longfellow not only believed in the doctrine of the Trinity, but also had arguments and analogies for its veracity ready to hand. But we cannot know for certain that Longfellow is the speaker. Bailey does show, however, that Longfellow was capable of presenting a defense for the Trinity and was willing to publish it, two things that cannot be said of Channing.

Lawrance Thompson, writing in 1938, discusses the cost that Longfellow's membership in the Unitarian Church had upon his social standing at Bowdoin College:

> His own Unitarian beliefs had not made him popular among the orthodox members of the faculty. Since his return to Brunswick

---

76. Bailey, *Religious Thought*, 115–16.
77. Bailey, *Religious Thought*, 119–20.

he had affiliated himself with the small, Unitarian group which met regularly, and had assisted by singing in the choir and conducting a Bible class. Such deliberate and flagrant disagreement with the conventional religious belief at Bowdoin did not strengthen his position.[78]

Nevertheless, according to Thompson, Longfellow's attitude toward Unitarianism was quite different from Channing's:

> [Longfellow's] own religious beliefs had been inherited, along with his mildly federalist views on politics, in diluted form from his mother and father. Perhaps if Longfellow had been able to digest and assimilate the meaty Unitarian preaching which Ichabod Nichols had preached in Portland, he might have made out of it something more than a pleasant belief in the fundamental goodness of man and the certainty that all would be saved in an after life. But in religion, as well as in politics, Longfellow was content to fumble with a few ideas and never bothered to get below the surface of them. That Unitarianism was a dynamic, liberating creed to Channing, is certain; that it was a convenience, acquired secondhand by Longfellow is obvious.[79]

Thompson characterizes Longfellow's Unitarianism as a second-hand "convenience" that boiled down to two doctrines: human goodness and universal salvation. Interestingly enough, Channing preaches no universalism in the texts we know Longfellow read. Dorrien, for one, makes a point of stressing Channing's belief in the damning power of human evil. It is strange that Thompson ascribes universalism to the Unitarianism that Longfellow inherited.

In the early twentieth century, then, we find three major Longfellow critics with three different interpretations of Longfellow's Unitarianism. Strong sees Longfellow as Channing's man, fully Unitarian in anthropology, Christology, and soteriology. Bailey toys with the not-baseless idea that Longfellow was a trinitarian; and Thompson returns our attention to Longfellow's Unitarianism, but finds it a lax, vague creed somewhat contrary to Channing's teachings. More recent critics have taken either Thompson's or Strong's view. In 1963, Newton Arvin wrote that "Longfellow's work is pervaded by the fragrance of nineteenth century religious liberalism—undogmatic, eclectic, latitudinarian, and rather vague,"[80] and, as we will see in the next chapter, Jenny Franchot and Andrew C. Higgins have recently

78. Thompson, *Young Longfellow*, 179–80.
79. Thompson, *Young Longfellow*, 263.
80. Arvin, *Longfellow*, 10.

found the republicanism and ecumenism of Unitarian politics in the pages of *Evangeline*.

We will never, most likely, satisfactorily understand what Longfellow did and did not believe about anthropology, Christology, and soteriology in his heart of hearts. Be that as it may, this does not mean that we cannot explore and come to understand those anthropological, christological, and soteriological concepts that drive and shape his written works. The history of *Evangeline* criticism contains much serious, fruitful critical engagement with the religious elements of Longfellow's famous poem. And though it took more than a century to articulate, there is now a dominant interpretation of *Evangeline* wherein Unitarian doctrine drives the political and ecclesial content and themes in the poem. This interpretation will be explored and ultimately challenged over the course of the present book, in favor of a reading wherein Longfellow begins with Unitarian doctrine in *Evangeline* 2.1, but ultimately describes the deification of his protagonist in 2.5 in characteristically patristic terms. We will now turn to the history of the religious criticism of *Evangeline*, wherein we will find, especially in the work of Nathaniel Hawthorne and Arthur Demarest, a brief yet bright foundation upon which to build the argument of this book—that *Evangeline* is, at its theological heart, concerned with the deification and transfiguration of its protagonist, and, by extension, all humans.

# 2

# Religious Criticism of *Evangeline*

Now THAT WE HAVE examined the religious climate of Longfellow's New England, we are in a position to consider the history of religious criticism of *Evangeline*, a poem that was conceived, written, published, and read in a New England abuzz with the theologies of Channing and Emerson. Given that it is a poem full of prayers, chapels, priests, and nuns, *Evangeline* has often invited comments from critics about its religious elements. These comments have sometimes been brief—unelaborated mentions of a biblical reference here or there before moving on to the main, secularly interpreted love-plot—while others have characterized the religious elements as more central, forming a grand theme about human destiny in God.

During Longfellow's lifetime, religious criticism focused on the spiritual example of the heroine, the relationship between the poem's erotic and religious themes, and the poet's portrayal of Roman Catholic characters and traditions. After Longfellow's death, editors and annotators identified "keynote" passages that most clearly articulated *Evangeline*'s moral and spiritual themes. In the early to mid twentieth century, religiously minded critics turned their attention toward the puzzle of Longfellow's own personal theological beliefs, treating *Evangeline* as sometimes evidence for, sometimes irrelevant to, the poet's creed. In the late twentieth century and early twenty-first century, two main strains of *Evangeline* criticism have emerged: first, a reading of the poem as a typical nineteenth-century celebration of domestic piety, of a piece with Longfellow's home-and-hearth–focused lyrics; second, a renewed interest in closely reading the poem in an attempt to discern theological influences, focusing especially on the influence of the Bible and American Unitarian doctrine.

Though critical approaches have varied over time, most critics have agreed on a few points. Many critics have recognized in the poem a potentially controversial Catholic flavor—a strange subject, perhaps, for the Unitarian Longfellow. Further, there has been no doubt about Longfellow's intent for Evangeline to be a moral example for all readers—though some critics have doubted whether the poem's protagonist is, in fact, morally exemplary. One approach critics have avoided on the whole is an allegorical reading of the poem; the possibilities of such a reading have always been pushed aside in pursuit of the more interesting questions and possibilities—to modern and postmodern minds—concerning the poem's historicity. Indeed, religious and theological concerns have always played second fiddle to critical interest in the historicity of the poem and in its subsequent impact on Acadian history. Nevertheless, if we are to undertake an interpretation of the religious elements of the poem, it is necessary first of all to familiarize ourselves with the critical conversation concerning *Evangeline*'s religious elements from the initial reviews up through contemporary voices.

## LONGFELLOW'S CONTEMPORARIES

The plot of *Evangeline* was first given a moral interpretation before Longfellow even wrote it, and the interpretation was given by Longfellow himself. After he was told the story of an Acadian maiden who, when separated from her fiancé by exile, searched for him her whole life, only to find him on his death bed, the poet allegedly proclaimed: "It is the best illustration of faithfulness and the constancy of woman that I have ever heard of or read."[1] Though he did not cast it in explicitly religious terms, this statement provides a direction and focus for most subsequent criticism of *Evangeline*: the moral example of the heroine. Evangeline, Longfellow proclaimed, before he even had named her or written a line of her famous story, was an "illustration of faithfulness and . . . constancy." But Evangeline the character and *Evangeline* the poem would become more than that in the writing of the work, and all subsequent criticism of the poem could be read as a struggle to see how much more than an illustration of simple moral goodness Evangeline is.

### *Hawthorne's Review*

Nathaniel Hawthorne, who was present on the night of Longfellow's above proclamation, was one of the first to review the poem, and though he did so

1. Arvin, *Longfellow*, 100.

anonymously, Hawthorne's review cannot help betraying the novelist's moral perceptiveness. "The impression of the poem," Hawthorne explains, "is nowhere dismal or despondent, and glows with the purest sunshine where we might the least expect it, on the pauper's death-bed."[2] Hawthorne here highlights the surprising abundance of *light* in the poem, which is present, he points out, in surprising places, including "the pauper's death-bed." What is interesting about this particular note is that most critics and readers see—properly, perhaps—the climax of the poem as Evangeline's discovery of Gabriel on his death-bed. But in the stanza before this discovery, we find a light-filled scene wherein Evangeline ministers to the dying poor. And it is this scene in part 2, canto 5, just prior to the climax of the plot of the poem, to which Hawthorne gives his highest praise: "We remember no such triumph as the author has here achieved, transfiguring Evangeline, now old and gray, before our eyes, and making us willingly acquiesce in all the sorrow that has befallen her, for the sake of the joy which is prophesied and realized within her."[3] The scene to which Hawthorne refers is this:

> Thither, by night and by day, came the Sister of Mercy. The dying
> Looked up into her face, and thought, indeed, to behold there
> Gleams of celestial light encircle her forehead with splendor,
> Such as the artist paints o'er the brows of saints and apostles,
> Or such as hangs by night o'er a city seen at a distance.
> Unto their eyes it seemed the lamps of the city celestial,
> Into whose shining gates erelong their spirits would enter.[4]

Hawthorne says that in this scene Evangeline is "transfigured," and the passage does indeed include characteristics of the Transfiguration scenes in the New Testament gospels, wherein Christ, on mount Tabor, shines with brilliant light in the presence of his disciples. According to the Gospel of St Matthew, in the Transfiguration Christ's "face shone like the sun, and His clothes became white as light."[5] Though Evangeline's clothes are not mentioned, the description of "light encircl[ing] her forehead with splendor" does resemble St Matthew's description of Christ's "face [shining] like the

2. Hawthorne, "Hawthorne's Review of Evangeline," 234.
3. Hawthorne, "Hawthorne's Review of Evangeline," 234.
4. Longfellow, "Evangeline," 120. While one could make a case that Hawthorne is referring to the conventionally-conceived climax of the poem, and that by "pauper's death-bed" he actually means Gabriel's death bed, such a case falls apart when we consider that the primary focus of Hawthorne's high praise is the transfiguration of Evangeline. Though Gabriel's death-bed scene does involve morning light on Gabriel's face, it does not describe Evangeline in any way that could be construed as transfiguration.
5. Matthew 17:2 (ESV).

sun." Hawthorne sees Evangeline's transfiguration as the realization of "the joy which [was] prophesied," which makes the reader "willingly acquiesce in all the sorrow" that Evangeline experiences throughout the second half of the poem.

It is worth pausing a moment longer to consider the religious implications of what Hawthorne is saying. There are three elements of Evangeline's story that Hawthorne describes: the prophecy of joy, the sorrow that befalls her, and the realization of the prophesied joy. We have already seen that the prophesied joy is realized in the transfiguration of Evangeline in 2.5. The sorrows of the heroine are many, and are clearly laid out in *Evangeline* 1.5–2.5. They involve first the separation from Gabriel, the death of Evangeline's father, and Evangeline's continual disappointment in her search for Gabriel. What, however, is the prophesied joy? Most likely Hawthorne refers to the words of Father Felician in book 2, canto 1, where the priest explains to Evangeline the future rewards of her search for Gabriel, which he calls her "work of affection":

> "Patience; accomplish thy labor; accomplish thy work of affection!
> Sorrow and silence are strong, and patient endurance is godlike.
> Therefore accomplish thy labor of love, till the heart is made godlike,
> Purified, strengthened, perfected, and rendered more worthy of heaven!"
> Cheered by the good man's words, Evangeline labored and waited.[6]

The joy that Felician promises Evangeline is that of being "made godlike, / Purified, strengthened, perfected, and rendered more worthy of heaven." Unfortunately Hawthorne's brief review does not explore these lines and their theological significance.

Hawthorne's contribution is nonetheless vital, and the critical community has yet to appreciate how valuable a reading of *Evangeline* it truly is. For in the same year that the poem was published, he proposed a reading of the poem wherein joy is prophesied, sorrow is endured, and joy is then realized in a light-filled scene of transfiguration. Such a reading highlights Evangeline's individual, spiritual journey over and above both her quest for her lost lover and her role as an illustration of moral virtue. In doing so, Hawthorne places the true "triumph" of the poem not in the rediscovery of Gabriel, but in the Christ-like transfiguration of the heroine.

---

6. Longfellow, *"Evangeline,"* 105.

## Whittier's Review

The second of Longfellow's literary friends to offer early criticism of the poem, John Greenleaf Whittier famously devoted most of his 1848 review of *Evangeline* to a consideration of whether the poem contained sufficient indignation at the mistreatment and oppression of the Acadians by the British government. But Whittier also provides several early summaries of the religious themes in the poem and the moral example of Evangeline. To Whittier, "the beautiful Evangeline" is "loving and faithful unto death," and is "a heroine worthy of any poet of the present century."[7] The poem itself is

> a simple story of quiet pastoral happiness, of great sorrow and painful bereavement, and of the endurance of a love which, hoping and seeking always, wanders evermore up and down the wilderness of the world, baffled at every turn, yet still retaining faith in God and in the object of its lifelong quest.[8]

Whittier sees dual purposes in Evangeline's quest, dual objects of her faithfulness; first, there is the heroine's "faith in God"; second, there is her faithfulness to "the object of her quest," Gabriel. Though he does not describe the exact connection between the two objects of Evangeline's faithfulness, he does see the poem as Christian in its tone and flavor overall: "It is a psalm of love and forgiveness: the gentleness and peace of Christian meekness and forbearance breathe through it."[9]

Just as we might wish that Hawthorne's review had included more detail about what exactly that joy is which was prophesied and realized in *Evangeline*, we might also wish that Whittier had spent a little less time excoriating the British, and a little more time exploring the connections between the two objects of Evangeline's love and faithfulness, God and Gabriel. Is love and faithfulness to the one a prerequisite of love and faithfulness to the other, or are Evangeline's religious affection and constancy and her erotic affection and constancy incidental to one another? Whatever the case, in Longfellow and his two friends, Hawthorne and Whittier, we find the foundations of most religious criticism of *Evangeline*. To all three *Evangeline* is a poem with Christian themes of love and faithfulness; to Longfellow and Whittier, the moral example of Evangeline is a highlight of the story, and to Hawthorne the imagery of light and transfiguration are the poem's true triumph. Further, a tension emerges in these early reviews between the religious and the erotic. Is Evangeline's quest, full of sorrow and hardship as

---

7. Whittier, *Works of Whittier*, 366.
8. Whittier, *Works of Whittier*, 368.
9. Whittier, *Works of Whittier*, 368.

it is, primarily for the sake of finding her lover, Gabriel, or primarily for the sake of imitating her Savior, Jesus Christ? There is, of course, a possibility of synthesis: as we learn from Longfellow's predecessor, Dante, the human beloved and the divine beloved need not always be in conflict.

## Brownson's Review

Orestes Brownson was a contemporary of Longfellow, but never met the man. Despite his ignorance of Longfellow's person and religious background, he was the first, in his 1849 review of the poem, to attempt a reading that reconciles the dual objects of Evangeline's faithfulness and love. He writes:

> The symbolical meaning of *Evangeline* seems to be a vain pursuit of earthly happiness, never attained until the soul is consecrated to God,—whilst, reactively, with Gabriel it represents man ever losing the happiness that pursues him, by his own impatience and want of resignation. Mr. Longfellow is German enough to conceive these double allegories.[10]

Brownson's reading makes some sense of the events of part 2 of the poem. After all, Evangeline only finds Gabriel after she has become a nun, effectively renouncing the possibility of a future marriage to Gabriel or anyone else. Brownson interprets this taking of orders as a symbol of consecrating the soul to God, and it is only through such consecration, he says, that one can attain the "earthly happiness" of the human beloved.

Such a reading, however, is not without problems. It implies that before Evangeline becomes a nun, she is somehow *not* consecrated to God. But a cursory reading of the poem shows that from the first canto onward Evangeline is a pious, church-going, sacrament-partaking, priest-obeying Catholic. Though Brownson attributes Gabriel's disappointed endeavors to "impatience and want of resignation," he does not explain how exactly Evangeline is unconsecrated prior to her taking of orders as a Sister of Mercy. Is Evangeline herself guilty of the same impatience and want of resignation as Gabriel?

Whatever our final estimate of Brownson's reading, it is possible to discern in it an element similar to Hawthorne's reading, namely that there is some spiritual quality that Evangeline must attain in part 2 in addition to

---

10. Brownson, "Longfellow's *Evangeline*," 84. Brownson is alone in his use of the term *allegory* in the history of Evangeline criticism, and it is debatable whether his interpretation of the poem's "symbolical meaning" should be considered a true allegorical interpretation.

finding Gabriel. For Hawthorne this quality is the joy realized in transfiguration. For Brownson it is the consecration to God found in joining a monastic order, which reveals, perhaps, the final resignation of earthly desires and is, ironically, the only path to attainment of that earthly desire.

In addition to his spiritual, symbolic reading of *Evangeline*, Brownson contributes a meditation on Longfellow's denominational affiliations. A Catholic himself, Brownson praises the "Catholic purity and elevation"[11] found in sections of *Evangeline*, and concludes that

> Evangeline, as a Sister of Charity, is as pure a conception as Protestantism permits. Indeed, her whole character is vastly more Catholic than that of most of our own theologico-romantic heroines, so innocently invented, now-a-days, for the edification of youths, by too zealous converts, who write before they have well tasted the first sweet waters of Catholic purity.[12]

Though Brownson thinks Longfellow is limited by his Protestantism, he recognizes in *Evangeline* Longfellow's acquaintance with Catholicism. However, he warns that "an acquaintance with the interior loveliness of Catholic life may remove the bigotry of Protestants, but reason, prayer, and the grace of God can alone convert them to Catholicity."[13] Late-nineteenth-century Catholic critics eager to claim Longfellow as one of their own would have done well to attend to Brownson's words here.

## Voices from Overseas

In 1849, the French critic Philaréte Chasles published an essay on *Evangeline*, arguing that "in this Anglo-American poet two tendencies are visible; the one, religious, towards the Catholic creed, towards vaster and more liberal Christian ideas: the second, literary, towards the Scandinavian Teutonism."[14] As Brownson before him, Chasles sees the Catholic elements in Longfellow's work as a liberal tendency. Whilst this might strike the contemporary reader as an odd association, we will see in the recent research of Andrew C. Higgins that in the rampantly anti-Catholic atmosphere of Puritan New England, the Catholic sympathies of *Evangeline* would indeed have seemed quite broadminded and progressive on Longfellow's part.

In *Evangeline* Chasles finds

11. Brownson, "Longfellow's *Evangeline*," 60.
12. Brownson, "Longfellow's Evangeline," 69.
13. Brownson, "Longfellow's *Evangeline*," 86.
14. Chasles, *Anglo-American Literature*, 208.

that worship of native land, that impassioned love for the heaven and earth of America, that moral energy and that spirit of indomitable enterprise which characterize the republican of the States. The sentiment of morality, of purity, love of duty, sanctity of the affections and of home, profoundly imprinted on this poem, form its deep soul and its secret inspiration.[15]

To the themes of faithfulness and constancy, affection and love that the American reviewers had already highlighted, Chasles adds several new themes: enterprise, duty, and the sanctity of home. The first of these new themes, that of indomitable enterprise, is indeed clear in the text; Evangeline finds her way through a wilderness that defeats many others, as Charles Calhoun has recently explored in more depth. But the next two themes, the love of duty and the sanctity of the home, are more fraught with complexities. Is it, after all, Evangeline's *duty* to seek after Gabriel? They are engaged, not married, and the Acadian community even encourages her to take another man for a husband, an indication that there was no expectation within Evangeline's culture for a fiancée to behave as Evangeline does. Further, though there are many beautiful scenes of home life in both parts of the poem, the heroine more and more distances herself from domestic scenes and desires, to the point of becoming a nun, effectively rejecting forever both wifehood and motherhood. Thus, if love of duty and the sanctity of home are two themes in *Evangeline*, they are not themes that are explicitly illustrated by Evangeline herself, for she supersedes duty through her supererogatory search and ultimately rejects the domestic life.

While others have found exclusively Christian images and allusions in *Evangeline*, Chasles highlights the poem's pagan elements. He chides Longfellow for including "too many druids, muses, and bacchantes; the looseness of old Europe, and the mythologic dress flout clumsily about the fresh beauties of the child of the forest."[16] Chasles seems to have expected Evangeline, being "the child of the [New World] forest" to have lost all the old mythologies of the Old World. He points to a possible contrariety in the spiritual logic of the poem; how, after all, can a Canadian Catholic girl fit into a world where muses inspire bards and druids chant in primeval forests? How, we may ask—inspired by Chasles—does the spiritual world of *Evangeline* work? What beings populate its heaven and its earth; what magic or miracle perfects its spirits? It is to these questions we will return in our discussion of the spiritual world of *Evangeline* in chapter 5.

15. Chasles, *Anglo-American Literature*, 196.
16. Chasles, *Anglo-American Literature*, 196.

In 1875, George McCrie added a British voice to the conversation about the religious elements of *Evangeline*. McCrie makes clear that he sees *Evangeline* as "a triumph of genius" which may even outstrip the works of Browning and Tennyson.[17] McCrie describes God's place in *Evangeline* as that of both a guide and a providential overseer. Part 2 of the poem, he says, is the story of Evangeline "refusing to part with life's earliest dream, and still believing that God will direct her steps through those labyrinths of nature to the object of her love."[18] Here God is a guide; he is not a second object of Evangeline's love, as he is in Whittier, but the means to her single, erotic end. As McCrie continues to explore the poem, however, his conception of God's role in the story expands. The Edenic Grand-Pré is "the nest as God made it," but is doomed to tragedy, to be "ravished and violated by ruthless hands."[19] Finally, McCrie describes the whole story of *Evangeline*, from the engagement of the lovers to the final scene on Gabriel's death-bed, as "the mere foundation stone and cope stone of a building which God had made frustrate."[20] God is now, in McCrie's conception, a sovereign disappointer of human designs. He is both Evangeline's daily helper and her cosmic hinderer. If this begins to sound Calvinistic, it is because such is McCrie's outlook. He shows his hand in the conclusion of his essay on Longfellow, writing: "A Calvinistic poet! Some may sneer at the term. But we hold this to be the great desideratum of the age."[21] Though he is openly looking for a particular doctrine of God in Longfellow's work which the poet himself would have rejected as incorrect,[22] McCrie does lead us to a new theological question about *Evangeline*: what is God up to in the poem? Is he a benign guide who helps humans find what they love, a stern sovereign who toys with human dreams, or both? In these questions we may find a connection between Chasles and McCrie, for both are interested in the spiritual world of *Evangeline*—how it works, whether it is consistent, and how the human and the divine relate within it.

---

17. McCrie, *Religion of Our Literature*, 209.
18. McCrie, *Religion of Our Literature*, 209.
19. McCrie, *Religion of Our Literature*, 210.
20. McCrie, *Religion of Our Literature*, 212.
21. McCrie, *Religion of Our Literature*, 221.
22. Longfellow's aversion to Calvinism, especially in its American, Puritan form, deserves more detailed treatment than I can give here. Critics agree that if there was one creed that Longfellow was most outspoken against, it was Calvinism. "There can be no doubt," Edward Wagenknecht writes, "that Longfellow did identify Calvinism with intolerance and regard it with sharp impatience." Wagenknecht, *Longfellow: Full Length Portrait*, 294.

## The Age of Annotations

In the three decades following Longfellow's death, his poems were continually collected, selected, and annotated in edition after leather-bound edition. In the numerous annotated editions of *Evangeline* we begin to see certain lines and sections of the poem become highlighted as expressing the main spiritual themes of the poem. Two passages in particular recur as favorites in these annotations, both of them in the second part of the poem. The first is the 2.1.717–727 passage quoted earlier, wherein Father Felician encourages Evangeline to continue her search for Gabriel, a passage that describes those promised joys that Evangeline will receive if she accomplishes her "work of affection," including being made "godlike, / Purified, strengthened, perfected, and rendered more worthy of heaven." The second important section is 2.5.1313–1319, wherein Evangeline ministers to the sick and shines with "gleams of celestial light," the passage that Hawthorne calls Evangeline's "transfiguration" and Longfellow's "true triumph."

### *"Talk not of wasted affection . . ."*

In an 1893 edition of *Evangeline*, the editor[23] calls 2.1.719

> [a] key-note of the poem. It is the lesson Evangeline has to learn, and it is only when she again meets Gabriel, at the close of her life, that the lesson is fully learnt. Through their long separation they have never ceased to love each other, and this love was like a talisman to Evangeline, keeping unworthy thoughts from her, and finding its expression in care for all around her.[24]

Thus Evangeline's love and affection for Gabriel, according to the 1893 editor, do not just "return again to the fountain," but flow over and bless many others. Echoing Hawthorne, the 1893 editor writes that "Evangeline's later life was exactly in accordance with the advice here given by the priest."[25]

The word *keynote* is again used to describe Father Felician's sermon in 2.1 in a 1909 edition of *Evangeline*, edited by Maud Kingsley and Franck Palmer. "These words," write Kingsley and Palmer, "are the keynote of the poem. Evangeline's life was not wasted even though her quest was unsuccessful. The perfect love which she had for Gabriel made her a blessing to

---

23. Sadly, I have not been able to track down the editor's name, which, strangely, does not appear anywhere in the 1893 volume. I shall hitherto refer to him as the "1893 editor."
24. *Evangeline: With Explanatory Notes*, 56.
25. *Evangeline: With Explanatory Notes*, 67.

all with whom she came in contact during her long journey."²⁶ There is an almost uncanny resemblance between the 1893 and 1909 notes; perhaps Kingsley and Palmer used the 1893 notes as a source. Kingsley and Palmer do differ from the 1893 editor slightly, though, for they call Evangeline's quest "unsuccessful" whereas the 1893 editor more positively construes of Evangeline's quest, wherein her "lesson is finally learnt" "when she again meets Gabriel." Still, there seems to be a strong turn-of-the-century reading of *Evangeline* in which 2.1.719 is the thematic center of the poem, the evidence of which is Evangeline's blessing of and love for others in her search for Gabriel.

## *"Gleams of celestial light"*

In an 1890 edition of *Evangeline*, editors H.I. Strang and A.J. Moore take issue with the 2.5 transfiguration passage. Strang and Moore write, "whatever credence we may place in the hallucinations of those on the boundary of the next world, it would seem that the poet has here trenched on the improbable."²⁷ In particular they find the words *gleams* and *splendor* to "scarcely agree with the comparatively subdued character" of a traditional halo.²⁸ Perhaps Strang and Moore are thinking of the faint halos in some medieval and Renaissance paintings. But we have already seen in Hawthorne another possible source for this image—that of the gospel accounts of the Transfiguration of Christ, where the light from Christ's face and clothing shines "like the sun"—hardly a "subdued" image.

In his 1911 edition of *Evangeline*, A.J. Demarest is kinder to these late, light-filled lines of the poem. As Evangeline's "virtues," Demarest writes, "are unfolded by the patience and religious trust with which she passes through her pilgrimage of toil and disappointments, she becomes invested with a beauty as of angels."²⁹ Instead of a Christ-like transfiguration, Demarest sees the heavenly splendor of Evangeline's appearance as an angelic beauty. Further, this beauty suggests to Demarest that some great change has occurred in Evangeline: "The closing scenes, though infused with the deepest pathos, inspire us with sadness, it is true, but at the same time leave behind a calm feeling that the highest aim of her existence has been attained."³⁰ Though he does not use the word *keynote* as the critics before

26. Kingsley and Palmer, *Longfellow's Evangeline*, 61.
27. Strang and Moore, *Longfellow's Evangeline*, 94.
28. Strang and Moore, *Longfellow's Evangeline*, 94.
29. Demarest, *Evangeline*, 148.
30. Demarest, *Evangeline*, 148.

him, Demarest says here a monumental thing; whereas others might speak of Evangeline fulfilling her quest, or finding the object of her earthly love, Demarest says that at the end of the poem Evangeline attains "the highest aim of her existence." Chasles and McCrie turn our attention to the spiritual world of the poem, its logic and its functioning. We might see Demarest's claim as a contribution to the description of *Evangeline*'s spiritual world, for in the final scenes, he argues, we witness the teleological completion of Evangeline, and, perhaps, the model of perfection for all humans. Demarest leaves it to other scholars to elaborate on how or why shining with celestial light is an evidence of this teleological completion. Unfortunately, however, no scholar ever has.

## Theologically Minded Critics of the Twentieth Century

In the second two decades of the twentieth century, as Longfellow's poetic stock was plummeting in the pages of modernist criticism, three critics— Augustus Hopkins Strong, Elmer James Bailey, and Father Richard Hickey— considered at length the theological influences on and theological beliefs of Henry Wadsworth Longfellow. In these three considerations we find several different readings and uses of the religious elements in *Evangeline*.

### *Strong and Bailey*

In 1916 Augustus Hopkins Strong published his *American Poets and Their Theology*, evaluating the major American poets from a theological standpoint similar to that of McCrie a generation earlier. Whereas McCrie seems to have forgiven Longfellow for not being a Calvinist and estimated the poet quite highly, Strong cannot forgive Longfellow his non-Calvinism, explaining at length how great a flaw this is. In Strong's view, Longfellow's "Christianity has no Cross of divine sacrifice, and so furnishes no refuge for the guilty, and no dynamic for the saved."[31] Instead, Longfellow majors on the minors, so to speak:

> His bent was rather toward the mystical element in Christianity . . . He could appropriate, for purposes of poetry, much of the gospel idea of union with Christ, although he would have been unwilling to grant that this Christ is anything more than are other dear friends who have been long departed, but who,

---

31. Strong, *American Poets and Theology*, 246.

> as we love to think, are still invisibly ministering to our good. He was as far from the true Christian mysticism as he was from sheer agnosticism ... Longfellow's faith was simply a faith in the historic value of Christ's human example. This is a minor point in Christian doctrine, yet it is an essential point, as such faith as this, though fragmentary, may have great influence over life and conduct.[32]

For Strong, Longfellow's theology is devoid of what he takes to be the central doctrines of Christianity—human depravity, God's wrath, and substitutionary atonement—but is not wholly without worth in holding up Christ as a loving, moral example.

Strong does not show that this "minor point" can be found in *Evangeline*, but it is easily seen. In 2.5.1287–1288, Evangeline wishes "to follow / Meekly, with reverent steps, the sacred feet of her Savior." If this following in Christ's steps were the only statement describing the content of the Christian life in the poem, Strong would be right. But Father Felician's earlier words in 2.1 go beyond a mere exhortation to follow Christ's moral example. Strong does not mention Felician's "wasted affection" speech, but one assumes that he would find it insufficiently Calvinist. When Strong does mention *Evangeline*, he says nothing at all about religious themes, describing the poem as "an idealization of true love, with its patience and faithfulness."[33] Evangeline is still a model of faithfulness, as she was in the minds of nineteenth-century critics, but this faithfulness is no longer religious, but only erotic. It would be a mistake to dismiss Strong's reading as too focused on Calvinism to be of value. In fact, Strong is in the majority of Longfellow critics in finding few indications that Longfellow believed in or cared much to write about key traditional Christian doctrines, including the Trinity, the atonement, and the depths of human sin.

In his 1922 work Elmer James Bailey, refreshingly not focused on Calvinism, agrees with Strong that Longfellow seemed to have little interest in writing about such doctrines. Bailey goes a step further, arguing that "in the theological sciences of dogmatics and apologetics, [Longfellow] had hardly even the most remote interest, far less indeed, save perhaps Whitman, than has any other American poet. Certainly in the matter of religion Longfellow seems never to have felt himself called upon to make assertions, to seek evidence, or to defend his position."[34] Bailey dedicates his critical research to finding Longfellow's personal theological position nonetheless.

---

32. Strong, *American Poets and Theology*, 238, 242–43.
33. Strong, *American Poets and Theology*, 231.
34. Bailey, *Religious Thought*, 123.

In the course of this search, he dismisses all Longfellow's narrative poems, including *Evangeline*, as unhelpful. Still, he notes that Longfellow was both aware of and used key New Testament passages in *Evangeline*: "One recalls the priest in *Evangeline*, that Father Felician, who stilled the strife and contention of his angry people and led them to utter the forgiving petition of their crucified savior."[35]

Having searched through Longfellow's verse for indications of core theological belief, Bailey lands on a familiar theme: love.

> In the last analysis, the essence of Christ's teaching is love . . . Love, the reflective reader soon perceives, is the great principle underlying the whole of Longfellow's thought. Like faith, it was evidence of things unseen. Through it, he became as one of those whose creed is, not a dead formula of words, but a daily living in the spirit of Christ.[36]

This is not a very different conclusion from the one that Strong comes to about Longfellow's creed. But whereas Strong sees the practical imitation of Christ's love as a minor doctrine of Christianity, Bailey sees it as the "essence of Christ's teaching." While Bailey does not mention it, *Evangeline* is clearly a poem where one finds love championed above all, both in Evangeline's 1.5.559–560 declaration that "if we love one another / Nothing, in truth, can harm us," and in Father Felician's 2.1 "wasted affection" speech.

Unfortunately neither Strong nor Bailey, for all their disagreements and searching for creedal statements, contributes much to the discussion about the spiritual world of *Evangeline*. They address neither the elements of prophesied and realized joy, transfiguration and the attainment of the highest end of human existence, nor the problem of the relationship between God and Gabriel as the dual objects of Evangeline's quest. This is due in part to a loss of interest in *Evangeline* as a created world with its own spiritual logic. Instead, both Strong and Bailey are interested in uncovering what Longfellow himself believed outside the context of his narrative poems.

## Father Hickey

Father Richard Hickey's 1928 *Catholic Influence on Longfellow* takes a different and welcome approach to the religious elements in Longfellow's poetry. Hickey is interested in Longfellow's theological, especially Catholic, sources.

---

35. Bailey, *Religious Thought*, 121. The particular petition referred to is: "Father, forgive them, for they know not what they do." *Luke 23:34 (ESV)*.

36. Bailey, *Religious Thought*, 130–32.

In fact, he calls Longfellow "the first American Protestant to make serious efforts to enter fully into the spirit of the life and practice of Catholicism."[37] Instead of largely ignoring the poem as Strong and Bailey do, Hickey sees *Evangeline* as a major instance of Longfellow's immersion in the Catholic spirit: "The casual reader of *Evangeline* is struck by the note of local and historical color and the profoundly Catholic atmosphere that pervade the whole poem."[38] Hickey sets out to find where Longfellow, a nineteenth-century New England Unitarian, learned about the life and practice of eighteenth-century Canadian Catholics:

> Where then did Longfellow get his information about the history and manner of life of these simple peasant folk with their naïve legends and traditions, with their child-like faith and their religious customs? Thomas Haliburton, *An Historical and Statistical Account of Nova Scotia* . . . was a fruitful source of information for the manners, habits, and history of the French settlers of Acadia. Most of the traditions attributed to the Acadians were common to all the peoples of Europe during the Middle Ages. Longfellow was familiar, no doubt, with several treatises on legends and popular superstitions. But his main authority seems to have been T. Wright: *Essays Connected with the Literature, Popular Superstitions, and History of England in the Middle Ages* . . . Finally, his recollections of the impressions of travels in Catholic countries served him as a gold mine of information when describing the religious customs of Acadians. Minor details were supplied by the poet's vast stock of knowledge, accumulated from years of careful reading.[39]

Not only does Hickey discuss Longfellow's sources on Acadian Catholic life, but he also highlights an essential element of Catholicism—sacrament.

> Of the seven sacraments, that of penance plays the largest role in Longfellow. Evangeline was always "fair to behold", but never so much as when, "down the long street she passed, with her chaplet of beads and her missal . . . " but a "more ethereal beauty" still "Shone on her face and encircled her form, when after confession / Homeward serenely she walked with God's benediction upon her."[40]

---

37. Hickey, *Catholic Influence*, 17.
38. Hickey, *Catholic Influence*, 43.
39. Hickey, *Catholic Influence*, 46.
40. Hickey, *Catholic Influence*, 294.

Here Hickey quotes a passage important not only for its sacramental significance, but also for its foreshadowing of the transfiguration of 2.5, where light again shines from Evangeline's face.

A Catholic priest himself, Hickey is careful in the midst of exploring the Catholic spirit of the poet's verse not to call Longfellow a Catholic. "Perhaps," Hickey writes, "Brownson was not far from right when he wrote 'Evangeline, as a Sister of Charity, is as pure a conception as Protestantism permits.'"[41] Hickey's quotation of Brownson is telling; it represents a return to a more cautious, reserved Catholic attitude toward Longfellow's theological beliefs.[42] In his conclusion, Hickey writes:

> No! There is no use for us Catholics to try to make out of the gentle, sweet, but sentimental Longfellow a Catholic, or even a quasi-Catholic. It is time for us to leave all sentiment aside and look facts coolly in the face. And the simple fact is that he had by nature a deeply religious soul. His education made him tolerant of all creeds and of no creeds . . . He delved deep into the forgotten lore of those glorious ages when all Europe was Catholic. These researches bore fruit in the form of several longer works and many more short poems that have a Catholic theme for their subject. In these works he has given proof that he admired the beautiful, applauded the good, and approved of the true in Catholicism. But he approved, applauded, or admired only inasmuch as what he saw or read appealed to his passing fancy, esthetic sense, or sympathy for his fellow man.[43]

---

41. Hickey, *Catholic Influence*, 59.

42. For those interested in the early Catholic critics who display an eagerness to "Catholicize" Longfellow, see McLaughlin's "Father Livingston on Longfellow" and Eleanor, "Catholic Spirit in Longfellow," 23–31. Though neither McLaughlin nor Eleanor actually claims that Longfellow was a member of the Catholic Church, they both come close. McLaughlin asks, "If not of the body, who can truly say further that Longfellow belonged not to the soul of the [Catholic] church?" McLaughlin, 537. Sister Eleanor lists six major subjects in Longfellow that reveal his Catholic spirit: "Here is the almost puritanical Longfellow, for example, steeping himself in Dante, in Catholic ritual, in medieval monasticism, so as to write his 'Christus'; here is he, descendant of those who taught that faith alone is sufficient, teaching that faith without works is dead; here is he, kin to those who accuse us Catholics of adoring Mary, writing with understanding sympathy of the Incarnation; here is he, amid those who fear everything Romish, calling the Pope the bridge from earth to Heaven and creating priests and nuns who are ideals. Longfellow is only another evidence that poets must turn Catholic when they write of religious themes, for the simple reason that poetry itself is at its best the voice of truth." Eleanor, 24–25.

43. Hickey, *Catholic Influence*, 328–29.

Far from restricting our studies of the religious and theological elements in *Evangeline*, Hickey's warnings free us from the lure of ascribing all theological content in the poem to Longfellow's personal belief, free us from becoming distracted from the text of the poem by the temptation of speculative biography. After all, we are in pursuit of a more detailed picture and a deeper understanding of the spiritual world of *Evangeline* as a poem, especially those elements of the spiritual world that concern Evangeline's journey toward godlikeness. Hickey demonstrates that there is fruit to be found in exploring Longfellow's own research into the Christian past and how that research shaped and influenced *Evangeline*. We will do exactly this in chapters 4–6, where it will be suggested that it was the pre-medieval Church Fathers who exerted a strong influence upon the poet early in his career, and whose doctrines of godlikeness and divine light found their place in the spiritual world of *Evangeline*.

## The Biographers

In the middle decades of the twentieth century, Longfellow was firmly out of critical favor. However, he still held some interest for biographers, perhaps in part because his reputation had taken such a surprising turn for the worse, from the most famous poet in the English-speaking world to something of a national embarrassment. One task all twentieth and twenty-first century biographers have held in common is that of trying to explain just why this happened. Many point to Longfellow's overt wholesomeness, both in his personal life and in his poems. There seemed to be nothing avant-garde, nothing revolutionary, bleak, or twisted about him, and this lack made him the antithesis of what the twentieth-century reading public had come to expect after the works of Eliot, Joyce, Hemingway, and others.[44]

*Evangeline*, somewhat inevitably, became a case in point for the wholesomeness of Longfellow's poetic work. In 1962 Newton Arvin, following the "moral example" interpretation of *Evangeline*, writes: "What characterizes Evangeline is . . . a capacity for passive endurance and long-suffering

---

44. Of course, this lack turned out to be relative. Longfellow was indeed a pioneer in many respects, both in his personal and literary life. Even in *Evangeline* his use of hexameters was seen as daring to the point of foolhardiness. Longfellow helped to invent the study of modern languages in America through his innovative pedagogical methods at both Bowdoin and Harvard and his translation and promotion of Dante's *Divine Comedy*. Charles Calhoun and Christoph Irmscher, discussed below, dedicate their biographies of the poet to the examination of these overlooked aspects of Longfellow's life and work.

patience."⁴⁵ Gone in Arvin is the religiously oriented language of faithfulness or charity. Two years later, Cecil Williams and Edward Hirsh brought a religious flavor back into their descriptions of Evangeline. For Hirsh, Longfellow's "idealization of [his] heroine is closely related to the poem's meaning: Evangeline is increasingly spiritualized by the patiently endured sufferings of her nearly endless journey until she finally emerges as a saint-like figure."⁴⁶ In his use of the term "spiritualized," Hirsh comes the closest of all the twentieth-century biographers to sounding like Hawthorne and Demarest. Hirsh recognizes both the idealization of the heroine and also the reason for such an idealization: Longfellow is creating not just a hero, but a saint.

According to Cecil Williams, who published his biography of Longfellow the same year Hirsh published his, Evangeline is "persistent," possessing "the unassailable defense of a chaste heart."⁴⁷ Further, Williams sees Evangeline as an "embodiment of steadfast human love."⁴⁸ Williams brings the focus back to Evangeline's erotic nature—she loves, and her loving heart is chaste, ever focused only on Gabriel. Even though her chastity is eventually a religious discipline once she becomes a nun, it is first a faithfulness of human eros; she is saving herself for Gabriel, and him alone. Father Felician's "wasted affection" speech in 2.1 is prompted by Evangeline's claim, "Whither my heart has gone, there follows my hand and not elsewhere."⁴⁹ One of the reasons, perhaps, that Evangeline's chastity of heart is "unassailable" is that God blesses Evangeline's singular devotion to Gabriel through Father Felician. "Thy God," her priest tells her, "thus speaketh within thee."⁵⁰ Though Evangeline clearly is a morally admirable character according to these mid-century biographers, she still comes off as rather conventional.

Fortunately, Longfellow's two most recent biographers, Charles Calhoun and Christoph Irmscher, have begun to rethink Evangeline's apparent conventionality, exploring the unique and even radical nature of the heroine's moral example. Irmscher sees Evangeline as an illustration of courage in the face of oppression and displacement:

> In *Evangeline* and *Hiawatha* too, works that both dealt with the destruction of communities and the displacements of a people, Longfellow expertly used the medium of print to circulate stories

---

45. Arvin, *Longfellow*, 101.
46. Hirsh, *Henry Wadsworth Longfellow*, 34.
47. Williams, *Henry Wadsworth Longfellow*, 154.
48. Williams, *Henry Wadsworth Longfellow*, 156.
49. Longfellow, "*Evangeline*," 105.
50. Longfellow, "*Evangeline*," 105.

of courage and resolution in the face of adversity and disorientation that seemed instantly familiar and therefore comforting to his readers, offering them shared, public images to contain their private grief. No wonder that a picture of Longfellow's Evangeline graced many a college dormitory room, as the *Hamilton Literary Monthly* reported.[51]

Irmscher puts Evangeline's moral example in the historical context of the poem. Evangeline becomes the model for how to live in the new America, displaced from the nations and communities of the Old World, displaced—in the case of those who expanded westward—even from the comfort and familiarity of east-coast life. Even the college dorm room becomes a place of exile; interestingly enough, Longfellow's journals while an undergraduate at Bowdoin reveal that he, too, felt displaced there, longing for the comforts of his Portland home twenty-five miles south.

If to Irmscher *Evangeline* is a comfort and courage for the displaced, then to Calhoun *Evangeline* reveals the unique power of women to confront the pain and damage of such displacement:

> Evangeline is not so much a person as an idea in motion: not simply the conventional idea of feminine constancy but the larger idea—which manages to be both personal and political—that it is only a woman who can set things to order again, who can mend that which has been ripped apart, who can heal the wounds men have inflicted. When Evangeline, now a nursing sister, finally meets the dying Gabriel in the Philadelphia charity hospital, their reunion stands for the bringing together again of all the scattered Acadians—indeed, of all exiled peoples—in an imagined world where the Christian charity of women has redeemed the misdeeds of men.[52]

Calhoun here brings us back to the connection between Evangeline's moral example and religion. It is Christian charity that woman uniquely offers in the face of displacement and exile. And Calhoun makes clear that this exile has been caused by "the misdeeds of men"—after all, there are no women among the British soldiers who destroy Grand-Pré, and it is a king, not a queen, who gives the order for their exile. Such a reading, Calhoun suggests, breathes new life into "a poem too often dismissed as a stale endorsement of nineteenth century patriarchy and the importance of female loyalty to a husband."[53] We have already discussed the limitations of such an inter-

---

51. Irmscher, *Longfellow Redux*, 70.
52. Calhoun, *Longfellow: Rediscovered Life*, 187–88.
53. Calhoun, *Longfellow: Rediscovered Life*, 187.

pretation, especially given Evangeline's joining of a monastic order, which problematizes any reading of the poem as a promotion of spousal or maternal domesticity.

Calhoun also sees in *Evangeline* Longfellow's questioning of nineteenth-century notions of manifest destiny. "The great theme of American conquest," he writes, "of marching to destiny's drumbeat ever westward, is subtly undermined by this persistent little Acadian farm girl, who takes on the vast continent and survives, only to return east to her greater destiny."[54] Sadly, Calhoun only characterizes this "greater destiny" as "find[ing] the aged Gabriel" and what this discovery symbolizes politically, not as any sort of realization of joy in Christ-like transfiguration or attainment of the highest end of human existence. For Calhoun, Evangeline's "Christian charity" has no spiritual or eternal repercussions. Instead, it provides hope for the earthly reconciliation of displaced peoples. Thus, for all their contribution to the reassessment of *Evangeline*, Irmscher and Calhoun primarily champion the poem's *political* significance. While this is refreshing and necessary, it stops short of contributing to the conversation about the theological vision of the poet, informed as it was by both Unitarian and patristic doctrine, and how that vision is illustrated in the world of the poem and the experiences of the protagonist.

## CHEVALIER: CHRISTIAN ROMANTICISM

The only book-length treatment of the religious elements in *Evangeline* is Jacques Chevalier's 1990 work *Semiotics, Romanticism, and the Scriptures*. Though Chevalier limits his detailed analysis to *Evangeline* 1.1, he does attempt to describe the spiritual significance of part 1 as a whole. He sees *Evangeline* as a product of Christian Romanticism. In that it is informed by the Christian scriptures, Chevalier explains, *Evangeline* "gravitates round the story of paradise lost, toward tragic memories of the Fall and the mortal redemption through self denial."[55] But, Chevalier warns,

> Longfellow's poem is also the product of a Romantic Movement that challenged the puritanical view of human nature. As such, it must recall lessons from the biblical past with great poetic discretion. The New World narrative emulates the Holy writ while at the same time reappraising central tenets of Yahwism

---

54. Calhoun, *Longfellow: Rediscovered Life*, 188.
55. Chevalier, *Semiotics, Romanticism, Scriptures*, 1–2.

such as the stain of original sin and the depravations of nature worship.[56]

Chevalier is rather up-front about his desire to complicate and deconstruct the text. The first way he does so is to read part 1 both as a story of the fall of the Edenic Grand-Pré, and as a story about the sinless, Adamic state of the Acadians; second, he reads Evangeline's own spiritual journey in 1.1 as "torn between the erotic and the ascetic."[57] He sees in Evangeline a "two sided inclination to betray (reveal and misrepresent) her Edenic ancestry; to recognize her fallen condition while also disavowing her own sinful nature."[58] If Evangeline is an Eve figure and Grand-Pré is Eden, then it would make sense to see Evangeline as responsible for the fall of Grand-Pré, but clearly she is not. She does struggle with worry and sin, as we will see in chapter 5, but Chevalier does not see these flaws as responsible for Grand-Pré's demise.[59]

Though Chevalier does not give detailed analysis of 1.2–1.5, nor of part 2 at all, his most important contribution to the conversation about religion in *Evangeline* is his proposal that we see Evangeline as a woman attempting to embody the ideal of Christian Romanticism, namely "the sacred transgression: closing the distance that separates man from woman, life from death, culture from nature, spirit from body, God from Man, grace from sin, the ascetic from the erotic, the drudgery of fasting from the pleasures of feasting."[60] In essence, Chevalier argues, Evangeline is trying to become the *model woman*, who "distinguishes herself by her ability to feast on fasting. Evangeline's mission has little to do with spiritual denials of bodily wants. Her true task is to translate a woman's play of passion into a model of romantic pathos."[61] If Evangeline succeeds in her task of "feasting on fasting," of not merely giving into erotic indulgence—for then she would become the fallen Eve, or even the wicked woman of the Proverbs—nor throwing away her love for Gabriel—for then she would reject the physical nature that Romanticism so prizes—then she will have achieved the state of the model woman who has united the ascetic and the erotic, and even, Che-

---

56. Chevalier, *Semiotics, Romanticism, Scriptures*, 2.

57. Chevalier, *Semiotics, Romanticism, Scriptures*, 91. Chevalier manages to argue quite convincingly that Evangeline's spiritual journey begins before the fall of Grand-Pré, not only after she loses Gabriel and her father.

58. Chevalier, *Semiotics, Romanticism, Scriptures*, 91.

59. He does, however, see in Evangeline a worry that her own personal sufferings are a result of her sins and shortcomings.

60. Chevalier, *Semiotics, Romanticism, Scriptures*, 113.

61. Chevalier, *Semiotics, Romanticism, Scriptures*, 115.

valier implies, God and man. Despite being complicated by its deconstructionist aims, Chevalier's picture of *Evangeline* is the closest any critic has come to describing the tension and possible resolution between those two objects of Evangeline's faithfulness and love that Whittier described back in 1848. Whereas Brownson sees the reconciliation between the religious and the erotic in *Evangeline* as found in Evangeline's renunciation of Gabriel through monasticism, Chevalier is content to explain in detail a dilemma arising from the poem—that of feasting on fasting, of being a Christian ascetic *and* a romantic heroine.

In the end, Chevalier's work is incomplete, not because he does not give a thorough account of canto 1, but because he gives a thorough account of *only* canto 1, and does not consider whether Evangeline succeeds in her quest to become the model woman of Christian Romanticism; if success is found, it is found not in part 1 but in part 2. I suggest that the explorations of part 2 by Hawthorne and Demarest could be used as starting points from which to evaluate that possible success.

## Pearce and Lewis: Conventional Domesticity

In the 1960s there seemed to be a minor resurgence of critical interest in Longfellow. We have already seen something of this in the work of biographers Newton Arvin and Cecil B. Williams. In addition to these, Roy Harvey Pearce, in his *Continuity of American Poetry*, discusses Longfellow's contribution to the American Renaissance.[62] It is in Pearce and his followers that we find the dismissal of *Evangeline* as patriarchal and domestic, an attitude that Calhoun combats in his biography. Though Pearce finds Longfellow interesting, he concludes that Longfellow is ultimately a poet of the "hearthside" in whom "certitude is wholly domesticated."[63] He contrasts Longfellow's "striving to attain the certitude that life, after all, is not an empty dream" with Poe's striving to "search [life] to its depth."[64] When he turns his eyes to *Evangeline*'s religious elements, he describes the poem as a "story of the rewards of domestic piety, in spite of all the forces which

---

62. In his influential 1941 *American Renaissance* F.O. Matthiessen had largely ignored Longfellow's contribution to American literature. Pearce does some work to set this oversight right, despite his overall negative estimation of Longfellow. Recently, Kerry Larson has called Pearce's book an "ambitious, influential, and still-rewarding study" which does "for American poetry what F.O. Matthiessen's *American Renaissance* had done for prose fiction twenty years before[;] Pearce's book sought to give the modern academy a canon it could respect." Larson, "Introduction," 5.

63. Pearce, *Continuity of American Poetry*, 211.

64. Pearce, *Continuity of American Poetry*, 210.

might work against it."⁶⁵ While most critics have agreed that Evangeline is in some way rewarded for her piety, it is not clear that this piety is primarily *domestic*, nor that domesticity is so negative a thing as Pearce seems to think. Given his interest in characterizing Longfellow as a poet of the home and hearth, it is not surprising that Pearce would find at least some domesticity in *Evangeline*. There are domestic scenes aplenty in part 1, of course, many involving a fireplace. But these domestic scenes cease after the destruction and exile of 1.5, and when Evangeline arrives at a fireside scene in 2.3, she slips out into the garden to escape Basil's happy party. Further, in 2.5 Evangeline takes the quintessentially un-domestic step of becoming a nun, a fact repeatedly ignored by critics from Chasles onward. But perhaps Pearce does not mean that *Evangeline* is a poem about the rewards of stay-at-home motherhood. Instead, Pearce might mean that Evangeline is domestically pious in that she acts the part of a dutiful wife, even though she is not married. As Arvin points out around the same time, Evangeline does somewhat resemble Odysseus in her quest to reunite with a lost beloved with whom she could finally be at home.⁶⁶ Even if we were to find Evangeline to have an Odyssean domestic piety, we would have to conclude that, contrary to Pearce's "rewards of domestic piety," Evangeline's piety, whatever its primary characteristic, is not rewarded by any final domestic bliss.⁶⁷ Unfortunately, Pearce does not describe what he takes "the rewards of domestic piety" in *Evangeline* to be.

Paul Lewis has recently resurrected and intensified Pearce's argument in his essay "Longfellow's Serenity and Poe's Prediction: An Antebellum Turning Point." Attempting to prove once again that Poe is an insightful, original voice, and that Longfellow is a conventional, unoriginal one, Lewis compares *Evangeline* with Poe's "Ligeia":

> Preaching to the converted, [*Evangeline*] follows its eponymous character, a pious, seventeen year old virgin from Grand Pre, Acadie, who is separated on her wedding day from her fiancé,

65. Pearce, *Continuity of American Poetry*, 211.
66. Arvin, *Longfellow*, 100–101.
67. More careful critics have noted that though Longfellow is clearly a poet enamored of hearth and home, *Evangeline* is not a good example of domestic serenity. In his 2000 essay "Longfellow's Place: The Poet and Poetry of Craigie House," Matthew Gartner writes that though Longfellow's domestic lyrics and grand narratives seem *prima facie* serene and untroubled, careful critical attention reveals a contrary undertone: "Longfellow sees fit to bring some of his moodiness, tiredness, and anxiousness into his poetry and to make them emblematic of common emotional states his readers inevitably share . . . Longfellow's longer narrative poems also frequently give voice to these themes, for instance, in *Evangeline* . . . the title character spends her life wandering with increasing weariness across North America." Gartner, "Longfellow's Place," 36n7.

Gabriel Lajeunesse, during the English expulsion of the French from Nova Scotia. To support his pious rendering of a story in which bad things happen to good people, Longfellow must suppress outrage ... Longfellow accomplishes this feat by shielding his undaunted heroine behind the impenetrable armor of faith, evident in her final comment to her soon-to-be-inaccessible betrothed: "Gabriel! Be of good cheer [she says] for nothing can harm those who love each other, no matter what mischances may happen."

"Mischances"? Burning your toast is a "mischance." Losing the love of your life is a cruel joke inflicted randomly in an indifferent universe. Over the ensuing decades, Evangeline searches for Gabriel, resisting suggestions that she settle for another man, pursuing her "work of affection." Thwarted but determined, she brings Christ-like constancy (and pure and simple motives) to the task ... The unwavering loyalty that allows Evangeline calmly to bid her dying beloved adieu marks the height of Longfellow's art, whereas Poe's appears in a terrifying scene [in "Ligeia"] of a literally undying resolve: an all consuming and willful passion.[68]

Lewis here presents an account of what Pearce may have meant by Evangeline's "domestic piety." For Lewis, this piety is a faith that leads, in 2.5, to a "Christ-like constancy" which enables her to bear the death of Gabriel. For Lewis, the death of Gabriel, not Hawthorne's favored transfiguration prior to it, is "the height of Longfellow's art."

What, according to Lewis, does Evangeline have faith in, exactly? Lewis implies that Evangeline's faith is in love itself, and in the ultimate well-being of the lover. Though he mentions the phrase, Lewis does not account for the doctrine presented in Father Felician's 2.1 "work of affection" speech, in which the priest sanctifies Evangeline's erotic doctrine of the hand following the heart by interpreting it as a road to godlikeness. Lewis does mention "Christ-like constancy" as Evangeline's final state; perhaps this is what Pearce meant by the "reward of domestic piety"? Whether or not Pearce would agree with Lewis's assessment of 2.5, we can interpret both writers as approaching *Evangeline* from the same basic perspective, wherein the heroine is a "pious virgin" who ends up being rewarded by God for acting like a dutiful wife.

Neither the word *pious* nor the word *virgin* seems to be used positively in Lewis's account of *Evangeline*. In preferring Poe's Ligeia and Hawthorne's Hester Prynne to Evangeline, Lewis reveals his aesthetic values, which

68. Lewis, "Longfellow's Serenity," 149–50.

include a critical disdain for the Catholic protagonist. Lewis stands in contrast to Chevalier, who sees Evangeline's mission as an attempt to "feast on fasting." Strangely, Lewis misses out on demeaning many characteristically pious aspects of Evangeline's story, including her regular church attendance, her pure and orthoprax relationship with Father Felician, and her taking of monastic orders. Perhaps, in his attempt to paint Longfellow's *Evangeline* as a poem that is "determined to affirm the familiar," he avoids mentioning those aspects of Catholic piety that would have seemed exotic to Longfellow's Protestant readers.

In his concluding statement, Lewis places himself firmly in the camp of Pearce, praising Poe's quest to "destabilize antebellum ideas of piety and domesticity" and lamenting the fact that Longfellow "dedicated his art to producing what Auden called the 'furniture of home.'"[69] Unfortunately neither Lewis nor Pearce convincingly shows that the quality of domesticity is prominent in part 2 of *Evangeline*, nor why domesticity, when it is present, is a negative quality. Further, both fail to mention, let alone theologically account for, Evangeline's transfiguration in 2.5. The only inkling of "godlikeness" in either author's work is the somewhat dismissive "Christ-like constancy" of Evangeline, which is contrasted with the "all consuming and willful passion" of Ligeia. It is easy to see which Lewis assumes will sound more appealing to his readers.

Beyond the problems that the "domestic piety" reading runs into when compared to the complexities of the text of *Evangeline*, a further, more fundamental question emerges: what, after all, is wrong with domesticity? Even if Evangeline were simply a dutiful wife who remained by her husband's hearth throughout the poem, would that be just cause to criticize and reject her? By their dismissal of Evangeline because of her domesticity, Pearce and Lewis not only reveal their failure to closely attend to the text of the poem, but also their adherence to a historically and culturally contingent ideology that prizes the non-domestic over the domestic and transgressive passion over matrimonial bliss.

The aesthetic standard to which Pearce and Lewis hold *Evangeline* is simply foreign to the project of Longfellow, and to expect his poem to meet the criteria of such a standard—and, in so doing, to accord such a standard the status of a universal cultural value—is a critical mistake made all too often by Longfellow's readers. There are many types of poetry with many different conventions and aspirations, and each reader is free to form his or her own preferences. Do not the poetry of domesticity, and the aesthetic

---

69. Lewis, "Longfellow's Serenity," 158. One wonders whether Lewis has read Calhoun's earlier interpretation of *Evangeline* as a destabilizing text both politically and sexually.

achievement of serenity—as opposed to "all consuming passion"—have their own unique appeal? If so, then the aesthetic qualities of the domesticity in Longfellow's poetry—and, for that matter, Jane Austen's novels or Washington Irving's sketches—are real artistic achievements that suffer unjust censure when discarded for failing to elicit the same pleasures that one encounters in Poe or Byron.

## FRANCHOT AND HIGGINS: A CAUTIOUS APPEAL FOR RELIGIOUS TOLERANCE

If Pearce and Lewis find *Evangeline*'s religious elements to be an expression of Longfellow's conservative preference of the familiar and the domestic, then Jenny Franchot and Andrew C. Higgins have found them to be a liberal, Unitarian call to embrace the exotic. In her 1994 *Roads to Rome*, Jenny Franchot advances a new reading of the religious elements of *Evangeline*. For Franchot, Longfellow's positive portrayal of Catholic communities and characters throughout the poem reveals the fascination of Protestant America with Catholic Europe and its exotic atmosphere, an argument somewhat anticipated by Chasles. She also sees Longfellow's Unitarian leanings as leading him to empathize with Evangeline as a Catholic exile.[70] Still, Franchot makes clear that Longfellow's poem is not an apologia for converting to Catholicism, but rather a safe, distanced admiration of a non-maternal woman. In fact, Franchot sees in Evangeline a fortuitous infertility: "This stasis of thwarted desire keeps safely at bay even the possibility of French Catholic reproduction and homebuilding while endowing Evangeline with the sentimental credentials of wifehood. Involuntarily celibate, Evangeline testifies to the transcendent claims of domesticity by virtue of her persistent exclusion from them."[71] Franchot here turns Pearce's theory on its head: *Evangeline* is not about the reward of domestic piety; it is about a piety that is continually denied domesticity, embodied by a woman who loves like a wife, but lives like a nun. We, the readers, remember the bliss of domesticity because that bliss contrasts so sharply with Evangeline's experience. Franchot acknowledges that Longfellow was "enamored of this image of wifely fidelity," but "was also imaginatively preoccupied with evading its reach and frustrating its aspirations."[72] Franchot reads the ascetic and erotic aspects of *Evangeline* from a different angle than does Chevalier. While Chevalier's Longfellow gives his heroine the great task of "feasting on fasting," and thus

70. Franchot, *Roads to Rome*, 203–9.
71. Franchot, *Roads to Rome*, 208.
72. Franchot, *Roads to Rome*, 207.

the chance to marry the ascetic and the erotic, Franchot's Longfellow sounds almost like a malevolent deity not unlike that which Chasles describes, frustrating the erotic heroine with ascetic obstacles imposed from on high.

But Franchot then tones down her characterization of Longfellow, concluding that *Evangeline*'s "author was . . . ideologically committed to the redemptive worth of suffering."[73] Though she does not explicitly connect this idea to Unitarian doctrine, her words might remind us of Channing's concept of suffering as the surest road to godlikeness. Franchot does not use the term *godlikeness*, but does use the term *redemptive* to describe Evangeline's suffering. According to both Chevalier and Franchot, then, in Longfellow's poem suffering is an ascetic activity that fosters spiritual development. But this spiritual development is secondary in Franchot's estimation: "[The poem's] preoccupation is less with Evangeline's deepening religious commitment than with her romantic loss, and it argues, accordingly, that her travels constitute not so much a pilgrimage as a psychological endurance contest."[74]

Though in the above quotation Franchot seems to read *Evangeline* as primarily a story of romance, not of spirituality, she later agrees with Chevalier that Evangeline identifies "the sacred and the romantic,"[75] especially in Father Felician's wholehearted endorsement of Evangeline's erotic quest. Franchot summarizes the end of Evangeline's spiritual journey as follows:

> Swiftly completing her transition from marital pilgrim to religious servant, Evangeline reenters society as a Sister of Mercy who tirelessly nurses the urban poor, dying by the scores in Philadelphia's 1797 yellow fever epidemic. Quite by chance, the aged nun one day discovers her Gabriel among the dying. Embraced for one brief moment after a thirty-eight-year separation, Gabriel slumps back on his pallet and dies. Holding him to her again, Evangeline then bows her head and performs her most stunning devotional surrender, murmuring to God, "Father, I thank thee!" . . . If this concluding embrace satisfyingly joins domesticity and celibacy in the image of the nun who loves, it more disturbingly voices the continuing imperatives of the antebellum Protestant romantic imagination to dissolve the mixtures of human intimacy into the purity of the solitary self.[76]

Franchot is careful, in a manner reminiscent of Chevalier, to avoid a simple theological reading of *Evangeline*; the poem presents Catholics positively,

---

73. Franchot, *Roads to Rome*, 204.
74. Franchot, *Roads to Rome*, 206.
75. Franchot, *Roads to Rome*, 208.
76. Franchot, *Roads to Rome*, 210–11.

but not too positively—Franchot's Longfellow calls for tolerance and empathy, not conversion. Evangeline is neither a full-fledged wife, nor a world-renouncing nun, but a "nun who loves," which seems to Franchot a concept caught between conventional romance and Romantic individualism. Though Franchot is mainly interested in putting *Evangeline* in its context as a careful celebration of exotic Catholic practices, she finds the poem to be as complex and as fraught with competing discourses as Chevalier does. Regrettably, Franchot does not provide any exploration of Father Felician's sanctification of Evangeline's mission through interpreting it as a road to godlikeness, nor does she mention Evangeline's experience of celestial light in 2.5. She does, however, provide a more thoughtful and nuanced reading of the religious elements in *Evangeline* than do Pearce and Lewis, and stands with Chevalier as indicative of the new approach to Longfellow that emerged in the 1990s.[77]

Andrew C. Higgins has recently painted a brighter portrait of the positive portrayal of Catholics in *Evangeline*. Higgins focuses on how this positive portrayal acted as a counter-balance to the anti-Catholic nationalism of mid-nineteenth-century America.[78] He provides a helpful overview of the checkered history of anti-Catholicism in nineteenth-century Philadelphia, Evangeline's final home.

> As important a response to anti-Catholicism as Longfellow's decision to make Evangeline a nun is his decision to end the story in Philadelphia, a city that had become the main flashpoint of anti-Catholicism in the United States. In May and July of 1844, the city was twice wracked with riots between Irish Catholics and nativists. The ostensible cause of the riots was a conflict over whether or not to allow the Catholic Bible into public schools. But the spark occurred when nativists organized a march in a heavily Irish-Catholic ward. After a nativist was killed in the ensuing confrontation, nativists used the death as a rallying cry, and three days of rioting followed. Two months later, three more days of rioting occurred after nativists paraded the dead man's widow and children through the streets. By casting Evangeline as a Sister of Mercy, an Irish-Catholic order founded in 1831 (long after the chronological setting of *Evangeline*), Longfellow ties his story directly to the Irish-Catholic community that suffered at the hands of the nativists.[79]

---

77. Perhaps the most important single essay on Longfellow of the 1990s is Dana Gioia's measured and incisive "Longfellow in the Aftermath of Modernism."

78. Higgins, "Evangeline's Mission," 549.

79. Higgins, "Evangeline's Mission," 561.

In addition to anti-Catholic riots, Higgins describes the popular anti-Catholic literature of Longfellow's day that "exposed," mostly through fabrication, the corruption and debauchery of Catholic nuns and convents. In light of these events, Higgins interprets Evangeline's journey as recasting Catholics, and nuns in particular, in a heroic light.

Higgins argues that this more positive response to Catholicism should not be read as any sort of endorsement of the Catholic creed on Longfellow's part, but of a typical Unitarian tendency to view "America as a Christian multi-culture, where the nation is a synthesis of religious and ethnic groups united by a universal love of and devotion to God."[80] Higgins takes earlier readers and critics to task for ignoring Longfellow's Unitarianism: "Longfellow's faith has often confused readers, especially Christian readers, who tend to overlook the implications of Longfellow's very sincere Unitarianism."[81] Still, Higgins shies away from claiming that Longfellow was a hardline Unitarian in all his beliefs, and reminds his readers that the "details of Longfellow's faith and theology are not fully understood at present."[82] This agnostic approach to Longfellow's personal creed does not hold Higgins back from repeatedly highlighting the Unitarian doctrine that pervades Longfellow's poem:

> The vision of *Evangeline*, then, is not so much an unrealized or aestheticized Catholicism, but rather a Unitarian attempt to evangelize Catholicism itself, to convert it to Unitarian principles and thus tame it to republican politics ... Evangeline may be the most famous Catholic character in nineteenth-century American literature, and she would become the patron saint of Acadian nationalism. But in her heart of hearts, she is a Harvard Unitarian.[83]

Thus Higgins, following Franchot, brings a historical perspective to the Catholic elements of *Evangeline* that Pearce and Lewis are content to ignore. Through their historicizing, Franchot and Higgins highlight what the early Catholic critics and Father Hickey did, namely that *Evangeline* presents a basically Catholic world of sacraments, visions, nuns, and saints, and does so at a time in American history when such a world was unfamiliar and even threatening to the average American reader. Further, Franchot and Higgins attribute Longfellow's interest in positively presenting Catholic subjects to the poet's Unitarian liberalism and ecumenism. Though Franchot and

---

80. Higgins, "Evangeline's Mission," 549.
81. Higgins, "Evangeline's Mission," 563.
82. Higgins, "Evangeline's Mission," 564.
83. Higgins, "Evangeline's Mission," 566.

Higgins, for all their contextual insight, do not explore the keynote passages of 2.1 and 2.5, they provide a theological starting point for such exploration—namely, the doctrines of American Unitarianism.

## The Future of Religious Criticism of Evangeline

If the religious criticism of *Evangeline* in the nineteenth century was characterized by an interest in Evangeline as a moral example, with 2.1 and 2.5 as thematic keynotes, the religious criticism of *Evangeline* in the last century has been characterized by both a dismissal of Evangeline's moral example as uninteresting or outdated and a contrary exploration of the political and cultural resonances of Evangeline's gender and Evangeline's Catholicism. Out of all the literature on *Evangeline* that has emerged over the last two centuries, three concerns of the early critics are particularly ripe for further study, but have been underexplored in recent scholarship: the spiritual world of *Evangeline*, the theological sources of *Evangeline*, and the "keynote" passages in 2.1 and 2.5.

### *The Spiritual World of Evangeline*

In Hawthorne, Brownson, Demarest, and Chevalier there is a clear concern for the spiritual logic of the world described in *Evangeline*. Major questions about the spiritual world of *Evangeline* include: Who is man? Who is God? What is the proper relationship of humans to one another? What is the proper relationship between humans and God? What does true piety look like? What constitutes sin? What, if any, are the earthly rewards of piety? What are the consequences of sin?

Hawthorne sees in the poem a world surprisingly penetrated by light and joy, which are both prophesied to Evangeline in 2.1 and, after virtuous struggle, realized in her in 2.5. Brownson sees in the poem a world wherein consecration to God through monasticism is the road to receiving the earthly joy of reunion with the beloved. Demarest sees in 2.5 an indication that Evangeline has attained the highest end of human existence. And Chevalier sees the world of *Evangeline* caught in a struggle between human eros and Christian ascesis, and Evangeline's quest as an attempt to reconcile within herself these warring contraries. These four authors share in common an interest in describing what takes place in the text at both the level of taught doctrine (mostly from the mouth of Father Felician) and spiritual practice and experience (mostly in the choices, actions, visions, and transfigurations of Evangeline). It could be argued that the reason critics like

Pearce and Lewis fail to give satisfying accounts of the poem is that they have not attended, nor cared to attend, to these doctrines, practices, and experiences; in short, they have not inhabited the world long enough to find out how it works. The patience and labor of Evangeline have not always rubbed off on her critics.

## The Theological Sources of Longfellow

Hickey and Chevalier show great interest in which theological texts Longfellow himself read and drew from in his writing of *Evangeline*. Hickey focuses on Longfellow's research into Acadian custom and his learning of Catholic doctrine and practice from his time in Europe. Chevalier focuses almost solely and at length on Longfellow's use of Scripture, though some of his claims about implied scriptural references strain credulity. Higgins's insistence on *Evangeline* as a Unitarian poem opens the door for examination of Unitarian doctrine in Longfellow's day and where it might show up in the theological teachings and spiritual practices and experiences in the poem. And if the investigation of the poem for Unitarian doctrine has only been suggested by implication, the investigation of *Evangeline* for uniquely Roman Catholic theological doctrines has been virtually unthought-of. Only Sister M. Eleanor has suggested that Longfellow does in fact include doctrines unique to Roman Catholicism in his poems, but she does not explore *Evangeline*.

Thus Longfellow's theological sources—including especially his Unitarian and pre-medieval Christian sources—remain almost wholly unexplored. This is unfortunate, given that Hickey and Chevalier have shown the fruitful and surprising results that occur through the investigation of the poet's theological sources. Major questions about Longfellow's theological sources include: Which texts did Longfellow read? Which theologians and ministers of his own day did Longfellow speak with or hear preach? How did Longfellow change or adapt the theological teachings and spiritual practices and experiences described by theologians in the spiritual world of his own poems?

## The Keynotes: 2.1 and 2.5

The closest readings and most exciting interpretations of *Evangeline* that we have so far encountered have centered on the 2.1 and 2.5 keynote passages. Hawthorne calls 2.1 a prophecy and 2.5 a realization of joy in transfiguration. Kingsley and Palmer find in 2.1 the erotic theme and lesson of the poem, and Demarest finds in 2.5 a description of Evangeline's attainment of the highest end of her existence. But despite the suggestions of Hawthorne, Kingsley, Palmer, and Demarest that 2.1 and 2.5 contain the spiritual and thematic keynotes of the poem, the last century of criticism has ignored these passages. We might wish that Chevalier had tackled the keynotes, for it is likely he would have produced fascinating readings of them.

The critical path before us involves reviving the focus on the keynote passages, bringing to them the two other concerns discussed above—namely, interest in the spiritual world of the poem and in Longfellow's theological sources. No critic yet has combined these interests, but Hawthorne, Demarest, Hickey, and Chevalier have shown how fruitful these interests can be on their own.

An interest in *Evangeline*'s spiritual world, a familiarity with Longfellow's Unitarian and patristic sources, and a renewed interest in the keynotes—these are the starting points from which I will build my reading of *Evangeline*. We have already explored, in the last chapter, the Unitarian theology of William E. Channing and Longfellow's familiarity with it. Though Franchot and Higgins may tempt us to now turn to *Evangeline* and read it—especially the keynotes—through the lens of Channing's Unitarian doctrines, I am not ready to do so. This is because Channing is not Longfellow's only major theological source, nor is he even Longfellow's only major theological source whose doctrine includes the deification of man as a central tenet. The other salient major source is, I suggest, the Church Fathers. In the next chapter, therefore, we will turn to the writings of the Church Fathers of the second through fourth centuries, along with Longfellow's familiarity with them and their early doctrines of deification and divine light. We will then undertake a close reading of the entirety of *Evangeline* with a view to give an account of the spiritual world of the poem, focusing on theological teachings, spiritual practices and experiences, and religious language and allusions. Finally, we will reexamine the keynote passages in light of Longfellow's theological sources and the overall spiritual world of the poem. This will enable us to place Hawthorne's theory of transfiguration and Demarest's theory of the highest human end in their proper theological and narrative contexts, and to explore how, in *Evangeline*, Longfellow presents a unique, light-filled vision of human deification that begins in 2.1 with a theological teaching in line with Unitarian thought, but moves, in 2.5, into a dramatic enactment of a patristic vision of deification.

# 3

# The Doctrines of Deification and Divine Light in the Church Fathers

As WE SAW IN chapter 1, Longfellow lived and wrote in an America newly open to radical visions of the divinity and godlikeness of man. But such visions were far from new, and the Christian doctrine of human deification can be traced back to the early centuries of the church's existence. From the second century through the fourth century, Christian writers of the East and West developed a doctrine of deification wherein the goal of the Christian life was to become like God.[1] After the fourth century, this doctrine became a hallmark of the Christian East, and is regarded today by some as a doctrine that sets apart the theology of the Eastern Orthodox Church, and by others as a doctrine wherein all Christian confessions may, in the future, find common ground.[2]

---

1. The word *doctrine* is fraught with complications, especially in applying it to the concept of deification. Recently Gosta Hallonsten has argued that we should make a distinction between the "theme" of deification and the "doctrine" of deification, reserving the latter term for a fully developed and clearly accepted and taught concept. This caveat will be addressed later in the book. Vladimir Kharlamov is hesitant to use the word *doctrine* for the concept of deification in the early Fathers, writing instead that "The Fathers of the late second to fourth centuries . . . made theosis a major theme." Finlan and Kharlamov, *Theosis*, 5. Norman Russell, on the other hand, names his entire survey of the concept of deification in the Church Fathers from the second century onwards *The Doctrine of Deification in the Greek Patristic Tradition*. I follow Russell in using the word *doctrine* for the concept of deification that the Fathers developed, accepted, and taught.

2. Two recent books that explore the ecumenical possibilities of the doctrine of deification are A.N. Williams, *The Ground of Union: Deification in Aquinas and Palamas*

As the doctrine developed in the early centuries of the church, it became increasingly complex and increasingly integrated into the other major doctrines believed, proclaimed, and taught by the Christian church, as well as into the metaphysical presuppositions of the late classical world. At the risk of oversimplification, we can begin by returning to Norman Russell's categories, noting that the Fathers of the second through fourth centuries tended to take one of two major approaches to the doctrine. The first is the *ethical* approach, according to which deification is a matter of the Christian becoming, in body and soul, like God as much as is possible. Usually the practice of the virtues—those moral qualities perfectly possessed by God—is central in this approach; the deified Christian who has successfully practiced and acquired the virtues is described as "godlike." The second approach is the *realistic* approach, according to which deification consists in the Christian participating in the being and life of God. The sacraments, especially the Eucharist, are often central to this approach; the deified Christian who has eaten the body of Christ in the Eucharist has become god through uniting with God's divine nature.[3] But here a qualification must be kept in view—the Christian becomes god (or becomes like God) only by grace, and never becomes God by nature. In all of the following discussion of the doctrine of deification, a distinction must be maintained between man's becoming god by grace, which the Fathers taught, and becoming God by nature, which according to the Fathers was impossible. It was for the Christians of the second millennium to provide a clear vocabulary for how exactly man participates in God.[4] Nevertheless, it was the Fathers of the fourth century who clearly taught that this participation and this likeness were real and central to Christian faith and experience.

## Deification in Plato and the New Testament

Three passages form the heart of the classical and biblical influence upon the Fathers' doctrine when it comes to deification: the first from the Psalms,

---

and Michael J. Christensen and Jeffrey A. Whittung, *Partakers of the Divine Nature*. For an overview of the recent literature on deification across the Christian spectrum see Gavrilyuk, "Retrieval of Deification," 647–59.

3. I here follow Stephen Finlan and Vladimir Kharlamov in using *god* to refer to the deified Christian, and *God* to refer to the triune being like whom the deified human has become and/or in whom he participates. Finlan and Kharlamov, *Theosis*, 6.

4. St Gregory Palamas gave something of a definitive answer when he wrote that humans participated in the *energies* of God, not the *essence* of God. This has become the standard vocabulary in the East from the fourteenth century onward. See Palamas, *Triads*.

the second from Plato, and the third from 2 Peter.⁵ Together these three passages also represent the two main approaches to describing deification: becoming like god (that is, *ethical* deification) and participating in God (that is, *realistic* deification).

In Psalm 82 the psalmist writes:

> God has taken his place in the divine council;
> in the midst of the gods he holds judgment:
> "How long will you judge unjustly
> and show partiality to the wicked? Selah
>
> Give justice to the weak and the fatherless;
> maintain the right of the afflicted and the destitute.
> Rescue the weak and the needy;
> deliver them from the hand of the wicked."
>
> They have neither knowledge nor understanding,
> they walk about in darkness;
> all the foundations of the earth are shaken.
>
> I said, "You are gods,
> sons of the Most High, all of you;
> nevertheless, like men you shall die,
> and fall like any prince."
>
> Arise, O God, judge the earth;
> for you shall inherit all the nations!⁶

This short psalm is the first place in Scripture where humans are called gods: "I said, 'You are gods.'" The psalm, however, is one of warning; those who are

---

5. An exhaustive list of deification references and allusions in biblical literature alone would be quite long indeed. From time to time scholars have included all of Paul's references to conforming to the image of Christ, being indwelt by the Spirit, and being changed or transformed in any way. Further, sonship language from both testaments has been used as an indication of an underlying doctrine of deification from the Torah through Revelation. Despite this plethora of references, scholars for the last century— and, indeed, most of the early Fathers themselves—have pointed unanimously to Psalm 82:6 and 2 Peter 1:4 as the biblical texts that most clearly teach and give precedent for the Christian doctrine of deification. And because of Plato's massive influence on the Greek neo-Platonic tradition in which most Fathers were educated, it was to Plato's *Theaetetus*, not the Greek mythologies and mysteries of apotheosis, that the Fathers turned to find support for the doctrine in pre-Christian Greek literature.

6. Psalm 82:1–8 (ESV).

called gods are not behaving well, for they "show partiality to the wicked" and are in danger of dying "like men." Despite differing in their exact interpretation of what this means, the Fathers as a whole use this text to prove that the term *gods* can be used of men.

Though Plato was not part of the biblical canon, he was, for the Greek Fathers especially, the pre-eminent philosopher of the classical age. In his dialogue on knowledge, *Theaetetus*, Plato presents a conversation between the philosopher Socrates and his interlocutor Theodorus, in which Socrates describes the aim of those who want to be philosophers:

> We ought to try to escape from earth to the dwelling of the gods as quickly as we can; and to escape is to become like God, as far as this is possible; and to become like God is to become righteous and holy and wise ... God is in no wise and in no manner unrighteous, but utterly and perfectly righteous, and there is nothing so like him as that one of us who in turn becomes most nearly perfect in righteousness.[7]

Here Socrates describes becoming like God as the goal of the philosopher; to accomplish this goal, the philosopher must acquire the ethical qualities of righteousness, holiness, and wisdom, for these are the qualities that God perfectly possesses. But Socrates also includes the qualification "so far as this is possible," which would be used in turn by the Fathers to indicate that complete identity with God by nature—as opposed to becoming godlike by grace—was not possible.

A third key text for the Fathers was 2 Peter 1:4, in which the writer of the epistle explains that true knowledge of God leads Christians to become "partakers of the divine nature":

> His divine power has granted to us all things that pertain to life and godliness, through the knowledge of him who called us to his own glory and excellence, by which he has granted to us his precious and very great promises, so that through them you may become partakers of the divine nature, having escaped from the corruption that is in the world because of sinful desire.[8]

Instead of using the language of likeness to God through acquisition of God's ethical properties, St Peter here speaks of the nature of the human being participating with God's nature through knowledge (*gnosis*) of God. This language of both participation and *gnosis* would become very important

---

7. Plato, *Theaetetus and Sophist*, 176A–C.
8. 2 Peter 1:3–4 (ESV).

for the Alexandrian Fathers, adding epistemological and metaphysical elements to Plato's ethical description of deification.

These texts from antiquity form a rationale for the classically informed Christian to speak in three ways: (1) to apply the word *gods* to men, as long as men meet the criteria for deification; (2) to describe man's acquisition of ethical qualities, such as righteousness or wisdom, as an ethical process of becoming "like god"; and (3) to describe man's deification as a metaphysical union of natures, wherein the human nature participates in the divine nature through knowledge of God. Though they were present in the major texts of antiquity, it took two centuries of Christian reflection and formulation for these three ways of speaking about deification to find full articulation in Christian doctrine. Some Fathers preferred one way of speaking over another, often depending upon how influenced they were by neo-Platonic philosophy. Nevertheless, the rationale for both an ethical and a realistic doctrine of deification are present in the biblical and classical texts inherited by the Fathers. As we will see at the end of this chapter, William Channing rejected the Fathers as credulous and simplistic; however, when he speaks in *Christian Worship* of the Christian's attaining to the likeness of God and participating in the divine nature, he is drawing upon the interpretation of *Theaetetus* and 2 Peter previously set down by the Fathers. We will next turn to seven Fathers who did the most to discover, develop, and articulate the doctrine of deification.[9]

## Justin Martyr

Justin, the great second-century Christian apologist, was the first to use Psalm 82:6 as evidence that the title *gods* may be applied to men. In his

---

9. This list is certainly not exhaustive; still, it represents the Fathers that the major scholars of the last century have agreed are central to the formation of the doctrine of deification in the first three centuries. The scholars consulted include Myrra Lot-Borodine, who was the first twentieth-century writer to investigate seriously the doctrine of deification in the Fathers; Jules Gross, a contemporary of Lot-Borodine, whose *Divinization of the Christian in the Greek Fathers* has become the standard text on deification in the Fathers from the twentieth century; and finally, Norman Russell, whose recent *Doctrine of Deification in the Greek Patristic Tradition* is the newest and most thorough book-length work on the subject, advancing beyond the work of Lot-Borodine and Gross in detail and standardizing vocabulary concerning the differing ways of speaking about deification in the Fathers. Lot-Borodine, Gross, and Russell all agree on the centrality of Justin, Irenaeus, Clement, Origen, Athanasius, and Gregory of Nyssa to the development of the doctrine of deification. Tertullian is not discussed by Lot-Borodine, but is included by both Gross and Russell as an important early Latin voice in the discussion.

*Dialogue with Trypho*, a philosophical dialogue in the style of Plato, Justin argues that Christians hope for nothing less than to "be made, like God, free from suffering and immortal, if they keep his precepts."[10] Justin backs up this extraordinary claim by quoting Psalm 82:6. "By applying this verse to the blessed," Jules Gross explains, "Justin in an equivalent way is saying that the bestowing of incorruptibility is a kind of divinization."[11] We can also recognize in Justin's words Plato's language of acquiring divine attributes, thus becoming "like God." This state of immortality and incorruptibility is not wholly new, for it is the same state that Adam and Eve enjoyed before the Fall.[12] Here begins a tradition of describing deification as a return to a pre-Fall state, a regaining of a likeness to God that was lost in the Fall but is recoverable through Christ.

In his two-part *Apology*, Justin explains that the sacraments of baptism and the Eucharist are the vehicles of human deification. Of baptism Justin writes: "this Baptism is called illumination, because the minds of the catechumens who are thus washed are illuminated; and moreover the Person baptiz'd and illuminated is baptiz'd in the Name of Jesus Christ."[13] A few chapters later, Justin links baptism with the Eucharist:

> This Food we call the eucharist, of which none are allow'd to be Partakers, but such only as are true Believers, and have been baptiz'd in the Laver of Regeneration for the Remission of Sins, and live according to Christ's precepts; for we do not take this as common Bread, and common Wine. But as Jesus Christ our Saviour was made Flesh and Blood for our Salvation, so are we taught that this Food, which the very same Logos blessed by Prayer and thanksgiving, is turn'd into the Nourishment and Substance of our Flesh and Blood; and is in some Sense the Flesh and Blood of the Incarnate Jesus.[14]

Baptism, for Justin, prepares the Christian for the Eucharist by purifying, illuminating, and regenerating the believer. After this new birth into new life, the Eucharist, being the flesh and blood of Christ, nourishes the Christian's own flesh and blood, uniting with it as food and drink. Justin does not use

---

10. Justin Martyr, *Dialogue with Trypho*, 258.

11. Jules Gross, *Divinization of the Christian*, 114.

12. As Kharlamov points out, some scholars have translated Justin's term *apathanatizo* (literally, "becoming immortal") as "deification." Though Justin is clearly on the road to the language of deification, he is not, strictly speaking, using those words—*theosis, theopoesis*, and the like—that literally mean "to become" or "to be made" god that would be used by later Fathers. See Finlan and Kharlamov, *Theosis*, 69.

13. Justin Martyr, "The First Apology," 107.

14. Justin Martyr, "The First Apology," 121–22.

the "partakers of the divine nature" language of 2 Peter, but his description is no less intimate. The Christian is so united with Christ in the Eucharist that God's body becomes, by digestion and by grace, his own.

In Justin's *Apology* we find, at an early date, the incarnation of Christ presented as a prerequisite for man's uniting with and becoming like God. If the incarnation had not occurred, then Justin could claim neither that "our Saviour was made Flesh and Blood for our Salvation," nor that "this Food... is in some Sense the Flesh and Blood of the Incarnate Jesus." We will see in Irenaeus an explicit connection between the incarnation of Christ and the deification of man. Though Justin does not speak explicitly of deification—preferring instead to speak of "illumination," "regeneration," and "becoming immortal and impassible like God"—he lays the groundwork for future theologians, bringing Psalm 82:6 into the conversation, and highlighting the sacraments as avenues by which the Christian can be united with Christ.

## Irenaeus of Lyons

In St Irenaeus we encounter the first use of what scholars call the exchange formula: *x became y, that y might become x*. In his long treatise *Against Heresies*, Irenaeus, after refuting the major heretical schools of his day, turns to a clear explanation of orthodox Christian doctrine. He writes:

> Him alone wilt thou follow, who is the true and Strong Teacher, the Word of God, Jesus Christ our Lord: Who for his immense love's sake was made that which we are, in order that He might perfect us to be what he is.
>
> For in no other way could we learn the things of God, except our Master, being the Word, have been made Man. Because not other but His Word could declare unto us the things of the Father....
>
> And on the other hand, neither could we learn any other way, than by seeing our teacher, and discerning His voice by our hearing: so that we might have communion with Him, becoming both imitators of His deeds and doers of His words; receiving growth from Him Who is perfect, and Who is before the whole creation: we, I say, who are lately made, by Him who is most excellent and good; made by Him Who hath power to give incorruption, to be after His own likeness.[15]

Again we find the language of incorruption and likeness to God that we found in Justin. But Irenaeus has come up with a new formulation: Christ

15. Irenaeus, *Against Heresies*, 449.

"was made that which we are, in order that He might perfect us to be what he is." Norman Russell explains that in this passage from *Against Heresies* "the incarnation is an essential prerequisite for our journey to God."[16] In second-century theology, human nature becomes a meeting point for man and God; God becomes man, meeting man in his own nature, but lifts him up to godlikeness, not just making him better, but "perfect[ing]" him. An implication of this transaction, as later writers will explain, is that deified man and incarnate Christ resemble one another. Both are men, and both are god, though man is god by grace, and Christ is God by nature.[17]

Jules Gross sees in *Against Heresies* not just the language of ethical deification but also the beginnings of a doctrine of deification that involves participation: "In these passages we see a physical or mystical conception of deification beginning to emerge for the first time."[18] Gross, writing many decades before Russell, does not use the term *realistic*, but he uses the word *physical* in a similar way. He points to two passages in particular in Irenaeus to show this new language at work:

> When [the Son of God] was incarnate and made man, He summed up in Himself the long explanations of men, in one brief work achieving salvation for us; that what we had lost in Adam, i.e., our being in the image and likeness of God, that we might recover in Christ Jesus.[19]

> And thus, as we said before, He hath bound and united men to God . . . And except man were united unto God, he could not have partaken of incorruption. Thus it became the mediator between God and man, by His connexion with either side, to gather both into friendship and concord; and while He presented man unto God, to make God known unto men. For how could we be partakers of his adoption of sons, had we not received from Him by the Son, the Communion which is with Him;—had not His Word made Flesh, come into Communion with us? Through which cause also He passed through every age, restoring all to the Communion which is with God.[20]

16. Russell, *Doctrine of Deification*, 106.

17. We can see in this formulation a danger that, in speaking thus, we may accidentally posit that man becomes a member of the Trinity, becomes God in essence. It was not until Gregory Palamas that a strict distinction was made between the uncreated essence of God and the uncreated energies of God, which was used to combat this danger. According to Palamas, the deified man participates in the uncreated energies, not the uncreated essence, of God. See Palamas, *Triads*.

18. Gross, *Divinization of the Christian*, 125.

19. Irenaeus, *Against Heresies*, 275.

20. Irenaeus, *Against Heresies*, 280.

In this first paragraph above (*Against Heresies* 3.18.1), Irenaeus sounds like Justin, saying that in Christ man can regain the image and likeness to God that he lost in the Fall. But in the next paragraph, which is in the same chapter (*Against Heresies* 3.18.7), Irenaeus shows that this restoration of man is nothing less than a uniting of God and man by Christ; as a result of which, through knowledge of God, man partakes in God's adoption. Though Irenaeus does not quote 2 Peter, he does use similar language, and paves the way for later writers (especially Origen) to develop a more metaphysically nuanced description of how man and God are united in man's return to the image and likeness of God.[21]

## Tertullian

Tertullian is not as important to the development of the doctrine of deification as Irenaeus is, but he is worth attending to for his cautious use of language when discussing deification and for the light he sheds on the relationship between the Christian doctrine of deification and pagan doctrines of apotheosis. In his *Apology*, Tertullian largely parodies Greek and Roman apotheosis myths, but nevertheless makes clear that if man could be deified, it would be only the supreme God who could create such a change in man. In his late treatise *Against Hermogenes*, Tertullian uses Psalm 82:6 as a justification for calling men gods:

> Well, then you say, we ourselves at that rate possess nothing of God. But indeed we do, and shall continue to do—only it is from Him that we receive it, and not from ourselves. For we shall be even gods, if we shall deserve to be among those of whom He declared, "I have said ye are gods," and "God standeth in the congregation of the gods." But this comes of His own grace, not from any property in us, because it is He alone who can make gods.[22]

We find here not only a recapitulation of Justin's application of Psalm 82:6 to Christians, but also two common caveats: God is the one who bestows godhood, and those who are made gods are made so by grace, not by nature. Though some may be tempted to call the doctrine of deification a purely Greek invention, Tertullian stands as a witness to the doctrine's sometimes robust presence in the Latin Fathers of the ante-Nicene period.

21. It should be clear by now that I have no desire to put ethical and realistic deification in opposition to one another. The two ways of speaking about man becoming god are compatible and, in Irenaeus, at times inseparable from one another.

22. Tertullian, *Ante-Nicene Fathers*, 3:480.

## Clement of Alexandria

While Tertullian was defending Christianity in the Latin world, Clement was developing Christian doctrine in the neo-Platonic atmosphere of second-century Alexandria. In Clement and his student Origen, both the ethical and realistic descriptions of Christian deification are developed, due in large part to their more drastic incorporation of philosophical vocabulary into theology than in previous Fathers.

Clement uses the exchange formula in the first chapter of his *Protrepticus*: "Yes, I say, the Word of God became man, that thou mayest learn from man how man may become God."[23] Clement makes explicit that what man is made into is God himself. Further, Clement uses the language of learning; Christ teaches man how he may become God. This language of learning is connected to Clement's doctrine of *gnosis*.

This *gnosis* is indeed knowledge of God, but it also goes beyond knowledge. In book 7 of his *Stromata*, Clement explains how the Gnostic, that is, the Christian who acquires true knowledge of God, possesses all the classical virtues: justice, courage, wisdom, and temperance. But, Clement explains,

> The cause of these, then, is love, of all science the most sacred and most sovereign. For by the service of what is best and most exalted, which is characterized by unity, it renders the Gnostic at once friend and son, having in truth grown "a perfect man, up to the measure of full stature." Further, agreement in the same thing is consent, and what is the same is one. And friendship is consummated in likeness; the community lying in oneness. The Gnostic, consequently in virtue of being a lover of the one true God, is the really perfect man and friend of God, and is placed in the rank of son. For these are names of nobility and knowledge, and perfection in the contemplation of God."[24]

True *gnosis* involves the acquiring of all virtues, especially love, the crowning virtue. Through this acquisition and the contemplation of God, man is perfected, united to, and made like God. Jules Gross explains that for Clement, "Gnosis ends in agape . . . [The Gnostics'] love for God causes them to accept suffering and even martyrdom. But the most precious blessing of love consists in the uniting of the soul with Christ and through him, with God."[25] The Gnostic, for Clement, is no serene academic, but rather one

---

23. Clement, *Writings of Clement*, 24.
24. Clement, *Writings of Clement*, 455.
25. Gross, *Divinization of the Christian*, 139.

who undergoes the ascetic activity of "suffering and even martyrdom" in his acquisition and demonstration of love.

Many might mistake the ascetic language of Clement and others as indicative of a strict dualism that rejects all material things as evil. But the goal of ascetic activity according of the early Fathers was not the rejection of all material things, but only of the sinful *passions* of the human soul. Emil Bartos explains that the suffering and martyrdom that the gnostic undergoes, according to Clement's *Stromata*, involves "mastering the passions" in order to "participat[e] in the divine attributes."[26] Clement and the other early Fathers do not use the word *passion* in the contemporary sense, to refer to often laudable deep emotion or commitment, but, as Nonna Verna Harrison argues, to those "unruly emotions" and desires that are the opposite of the virtues, and that, unchecked, lead to sin and death.[27]

Though Clement sees the pinnacle of Christian perfection as active, self-sacrificial love, he brings into the conversation about deification an academic language of *gnosis* and contemplation, according to which Christ is characterized as the ultimate teacher, and Christians are characterized as philosophers. We will see this academic language continue in Origen and the Cappadocians. However, we must also remember that *gnosis*, for Clement and his followers, never means the mere holding of true beliefs or the activities of discursive reasoning; it is the contemplation of God that, through the rejection of sinful passion and acquisition of godlike virtues, leads to intimate union with God in Christ.

## Origen

From Justin to Clement, the Fathers largely used the language of Psalm 82 and *Theaetetus* to describe human deification. They also developed the exchange formula, according to which God's becoming man paved the way for man to be deified, which added a necessary incarnational element to the deification language of Plato and the Psalms. With Origen, the patristic doctrine of deification takes a further step forward, through the use of 2 Peter 1:4, into what Gross calls a physical or mystical doctrine, and Russell calls realistic deification.

In the third book of his treatise *Against Celsus*, Origen explains how human nature is not only capable of becoming like divine nature, but can be "woven together" with it:

---

26. Bartos, *Deification*, 8.
27. Harrison, *God's Many Splendored Image*, 24.

Christians see that with Jesus human and divine nature began to be woven together, so that by fellowship with divinity human nature might become divine, not only in Jesus, but also in all those who believe and go on to undertake the life which Jesus taught, the life which leads everyone who lives according to Jesus's commandments to friendship with God and fellowship with Jesus.[28]

Origen describes a double deification—first, the human nature of Jesus himself is made divine through its union with his divine nature; as Gross says, "The Logos is . . . the archetype of all that have been deified through a participation in the deity."[29] Second, the human nature of the Christian can be made divine through union with God, which is accomplished by living as Christ taught. Gross sees in this passage a retaining of the focus on Christ-as-teacher which we saw previously in Clement: "This passage, where we can believe we are hearing an echo of the physical theory of divinization, clearly shows that for Origen the deification of humankind is the aim of the divine pedagogy, of which the incarnation is the decisive stage."[30] While teaching and learning are still prominent in Origen's doctrine of deification, the goal of Christ's teaching is no longer merely to make believers *like* God, but to create an intimate, participatory union of the human and divine natures within the Christian.

It would be a mistake to conclude that Origen did not care about the language of divine likeness; in fact, he articulates a more nuanced account of the likeness of God than his theological predecessors did. Whereas Justin and Irenaeus spoke of the image and likeness of God as a single attribute or group of attributes that were lost in the Fall but might be regained, Origen, following in the tradition of Clement, distinguishes between the image of God and the likeness of God. It is important, Origen explains, to realize "the difference between man being made in God's image and being made in His likeness, and that though God is recorded to have said 'Let us make man in our image and likeness' God only made man in the image of God, but not as yet in His likeness."[31] Gross explains that for Origen, "if Adam was in the image of God because of his reasoning soul, he still has to acquire the divine likeness by means of his free activity, by the 'imitation of God.'"[32] Origen makes two distinctive claims: first, the image and likeness are two different

---

28. Origen, *Against Celsus*, 146.
29. Gross, *Divinization of the Christian*, 146.
30. Gross, *Divinization of the Christian*, 144–45.
31. Origen, *Against Celsus*, 205.
32. Gross, *Divinization of the Christian*, 143.

attributes; and second, likeness to God is something that Adam did not yet possess. Thus ethical deification, the attainment of likeness to God, is not a mere return to an Edenic state, but a passing beyond the Edenic state into an eschatological state. Further, ethical deification slides into realistic deification, for likeness to God is ultimately a participation in the divine nature, as 2 Peter teaches.

## Athanasius

St Athanasius of Alexandria, the theological giant of the first half of the fourth century, puts the deification of man at the forefront of his theology. He often presents deification as a given, using the axiomatic truth of human deification to prove other doctrines. It is to Athanasius more than any other Father that theologians turn to find clear and succinct summations of the doctrine in its first, mature form.

Athanasius's most famous description of deification is in his early treatise *On the Incarnation*, in which he condenses and particularizes the exchange formulas of Irenaeus and Clement: "He, indeed, assumed humanity that we might become God."[33] In his treatise *Against the Arians*, Athanasius explains this exchange in more detail:

> The Logos is not one of the created beings, but on the contrary the very Demiurge of these. This is why He took the created, human body, that, having renewed it as the Creator, He might divinize it in Himself and usher us all into the kingdom of the heavens, according to the likeness of Him. United with a creature, humankind would not have been divinized again, if the Son was not true God.... This is why the contact was thus made, in order that the human nature might be united with the divine nature and that the salvation and deification of the former might be assured.[34]

Following Origen, Athanasius explains that Christ first deifies his own human body, and secondly deifies "humankind."[35] Once again the incarna-

33. Athanasius, *On the Incarnation*, 93.

34. Athanasius, *Contra Arians*, 2.70, quoted in Gross, *Divinization of the Christian*, 167.

35. Russell interprets the passage as follows: "Here Athanasius moves easily from the deification of a body to the deification of humanity as a whole ... The renewal of the human race is like a second creation carried out by the creator, but this time from within. The unity of humankind, which Athanasius takes for granted, means the whole of human nature is deified in principle when the human nature which the Logos assumed is deified by him." Russell, *Doctrine of Deification*, 172.

tion is necessary for the subsequent deification of man. Further, Athanasius stresses that the Word had to be God in order to deify mankind. If the nature of the Word were something other than divine, we could not properly say that human nature participates in divine nature, as 2 Peter teaches.

Athanasius extends this argument to include the deity of the Holy Spirit in his *Epistle to Serapion*. Using the language of 2 Peter, Athanasius argues:

> It is through the Spirit that we are all said to be partakers of God ... If the Holy Spirit were a creature, we should have no participation of God in him. If indeed we were joined to a creature we should be strangers to the divine nature inasmuch as we did not partake therein. But, as it is, the fact of our being called partakers of Christ and partakers of God shows that the unction and the seal that is in us belong, not to the nature of things originate, but to the nature of the Son who, through the Spirit, who is in him, joins us to the Father ... But if, by participation in the Spirit, we are made "sharers in the divine nature" we should be mad to say that the Spirit has a created nature and not the nature of God.[36]

In this passage Athanasius presents a clear doctrine of deification derived from 2 Peter, but discusses it in a new way. No longer is the doctrine of deification itself being defended. Deification is now a given; it has matured to the point that it is used to defend other doctrines, in this case the doctrine of the Trinity, explaining how each divine person of the Trinity is involved in our salvation. Norman Russell sums up: "To Serapion [Athanasius] declares that all things receive the characteristics of that in which they participate. By participating in the Spirit we become holy; by participating in the Logos we are able to contemplate the Father."[37]

Here we encounter an important principle in the articulation of the doctrine of deification: "all things receive the characteristics of that in which they participate." In Russell's words we find a continuity between the ethical and realistic approaches to deification. If likeness to God means sharing his characteristics, especially his ethical characteristics, and if participating in God allows one to receive God's characteristics, then realistic deification is, simply put, a sure road to ethical deification. Those who want to be like God should seek participatory union with him. Further, the principle that participation leads to shared characteristics will be important for seeing how the doctrine of illumination by divine light is linked to, and, indeed, inseparable

---

36. Athanasius, *Holy Spirit*, 125–26.
37. Russell, *Doctrine of Deification*, 181.

from, the doctrine of deification. For it is in the third and fourth centuries that the Fathers developed and articulated how the deified Christian shines with the light of God. But before exploring the link between deification and divine light, it will be helpful to consider the doctrine of a Father who is regarded as the fourth-century explicator of the doctrine of deification *par excellence*: St Gregory of Nyssa.

## Gregory of Nyssa

Together with his brother, Basil, and Gregory Nazianzus, St Gregory of Nyssa was one of the three great Cappadocian theologians of the fourth century whose theology was to have a great impact on the Ecumenical Council at Constantinople in 381. Though Basil and Gregory Nazianzus speak of deification from time to time, it is Gregory of Nyssa who is currently held above his contemporaries as the grand articulator of deification.

In his treatise *On Virginity*, Gregory considers the state of Adam in Eden, and what was lost at the Fall:

> This reasoning and intelligent creature, man, at once the work and the likeness of the Divine and Imperishable Mind . . . has fallen into the mire of sin and lost the blessing of being an image of the imperishable Deity. He has clothed himself instead with a perishable and foul resemblance to something else.[38]

The divine likeness, however, is neither wholly nor irretrievably lost. In fact,

> this likeness to the divine is not our work at all; it is not the achievement of any faculty of man; it is the great gift of God, bestowed upon our nature at the very moment of our birth; human efforts can only go so far as to clear away the filth of sin, and so cause the buried beauty of the soul to shine forth again.[39]

Thus the divine likeness is always buried in our nature; sin has obscured it, but virtuous living can make it visible, even radiant, again.

What does such living look like? For Gregory the life of virginity, of continually practicing the ascetic disciplines of chastity and celibacy, is a way to regain the Edenic life. "What greater praise of Virginity can there be," Gregory asks, "than thus to be shown in a manner deifying those who share in her pure mysteries, so that they become partakers of His glory Who is in actual truth the only Holy and Blameless One; their purity and their

---

38. Gregory of Nyssa, *Selected Writings*, 357.
39. Gregory of Nyssa, *Selected Writings*, 358.

incorruptibility being the means of bringing them into relationship with Him?"⁴⁰ A life of virginity, Jules Gross explains, is for Gregory that which "frees the soul 'from all that is foreign to it' and brings it back 'to what is proper to it and in accordance with its nature' so that 'the beauty of the soul reappears' and with it, the divine image in its original purity."⁴¹

But virtuous living is not all that is involved in our reclaiming the Edenic life. Christ's incarnation and the sacraments are central. In his *Great Catechism*, Gregory turns again to the exchange formula to explain the necessity of the incarnation for our deification: "He who holds together nature ... was transfused throughout our nature, in order that our nature might by this transfusion of the Divine become itself divine, rescued as it was from death, and put beyond the reach of the caprice of the antagonist."⁴² How is the incarnate Christ transfused into believers? According to Gregory, this takes place through the Eucharist:

> Since the God who was manifested infused Himself into perishable humanity for this purpose, viz. that by this communion with Deity mankind might at the same time be deified, for this end it is that, by dispensation of His grace, He disseminates Himself in every believer through that flesh, whose substance comes from bread and wine, blending Himself with the bodies of believers, to secure that, by this union with the immortal, man, too, may be a sharer in incorruption.⁴³

We saw earlier in Origen an emphasis on the physical body of Christ being deified by its union with the divine nature in the incarnation. Now we see Gregory make explicit the connection between Christ's deified body and the sacramental way of deification: those who consume the bread and wine into which Christ disseminated himself are bodily blended with Christ. This blending makes them incorrupt and immortal. Here we have come full circle back to Justin Martyr, who saw the sacraments as a way to attain the incorruption and immortality lost in the Fall. But now this sacramental road to immortality has been fully integrated into an explicit, mature, and robust doctrine of deification passed down from Irenaeus, Clement, Origen, and especially Athanasius to Gregory of Nyssa in the full bloom of Cappadocian theology. This doctrine would become a standard way of explaining the chief human end in the most influential Fathers of the fifth through

---

40. Gregory of Nyssa, *Selected Writings*, 344.
41. Gross, *Divinization of the Christian*, 182.
42. Gregory of Nyssa, *Selected Writings*, 495.
43. Gregory of Nyssa, *Selected Writings*, 506.

eighth centuries, including Maximus the Confessor, Boethius, and John of Damascus.

While the seven Fathers just examined do not always use the same vocabulary, nor do their doctrines always agree—whether the image and likeness of God are one thing or two, and whether one or both were lost at the Fall, for instance—we can, through a sort of patristic synthesis, determine several key doctrines shared by all. First, we find that all agree that the life of man before the Fall involved a union with and likeness to God that was lost when man sinned. Second, we find that God the Word, who made the world, took on human nature in order to restore fallen man to his former glory. Third, we find that Christ's union with human nature became a model of the Christian's ideal relationship with God, namely a participatory union with the divine nature. Fourth, we find several ways that a man may return to likeness and union with God in response to Christ's work: man may be taught by Christ, and through contemplation of God attain to perfect *gnosis*; man may obey Christ by living a life of virtue and passion-rejecting ascesis; and, finally, man may be physically bound to Christ, and indeed, the whole Trinity, through the sacraments. In brief, the Fathers paint a picture of the entire work of Christ and the Spirit in the Christian's life as one of likening man to God through virtue and dispassion, and uniting man with God through participation in the divine nature. This, then, is the doctrine of deification in the major Fathers of the second through fourth centuries.

## The Doctrine of Divine Light in the Early Fathers

Earlier we paused to examine a statement by Russell that explained Athanasius's metaphysics: "All things receive the characteristics of that in which they participate."[44] Beginning with Justin, the characteristics of God in which Christians sought to participate were God's ethical characteristics (righteousness, holiness, and wisdom) and God's incorruptibility and immortality. To become godlike through participatory, deifying union with the divine nature meant to take on the characteristics of God. All this has been explored in the first section of this chapter. But there is another characteristic of God that humans receive, in addition to those ethical characteristics, that begins to be discussed in the Fathers of the third century: God's divine light. Though the deified human never becomes God by nature, early Fathers argue, he can be illumined by and shine with the rays of God's uncreated glory.

44. Russell, *Doctrine of Deification*, 181.

In comparison with the doctrine of deification, the doctrine of divine light in patristic writings is underexplored. There is not, as there is with deification, a standard list of the most important patristic writings on divine light. Most of the recent writing on divine light in the Fathers is found within commentaries on the Fathers' doctrine of deification.[45] We will look at the doctrine of divine light in seven fathers: Hippolytus, who proves a helpful precursor to Origen; Origen himself, who much more than his predecessors explores the relationship between divine light and the divine nature; Macarius of Egypt, who presents in detail the scriptural warrant for the doctrine of divine light; the three Cappadocian Fathers, who explicate the function of divine light in trinitarian relationships and human salvation; and John Chrysostom, who explores the sacramental and Edenic aspects of the doctrine of divine light.

## Divine Light in Hippolytus

An older contemporary of Origen, Hippolytus does not yet portray the metaphysics of participation that Origen would bring into the discussion of deification. Nevertheless, Hippolytus makes clear that deification is indeed the goal of all who repent and live the Christian life. In the conclusion of his *Refutation of All Heresies*, he draws heavily on Psalm 82 to describe this deified state:

> For thou hast become God: for whatever sufferings thou didst undergo while being a man, these He gave to thee, because thou was of mortal mould, but whatever it is consistent with God to impart, these God has promised to bestow upon thee, because thou hast been deified, and begotten unto immortality . . . For Christ is the God above all, and He has arranged to wash away sin from human beings, rendering regenerate the old man. And God called man His likeness from the beginning, and has evinced in a figure His love towards thee. And provided thou obeyest His solemn injunctions, and becomest a faithful follower of Him who is good, thou shalt resemble Him, inasmuch as thou shall have honour conferred upon thee by Him. For the deity (by condescension) does not diminish aught of the dignity of his divine perfection; having made thee even God unto his glory![46]

---

45. While Jules Gross highlights John Chrysostom's writings on divine light, Norman Russell highlights instead the writings of Hippolytus, Origen, and the Cappadocians. In his influential *Mystical Theology of the Eastern Church*, Vladimir Lossky uses Macarius as the primary Father through whom to present the doctrine of divine light.

46. Hippolytus, *Ante-Nicene Fathers*, 5:153.

Hippolytus provides us with a description of ethical deification well balanced between the incredible claim that man can, though obedience, become god, and the Tertullian-esque reminder that God himself is the only dispenser of divinity. But in the final two sentences we also see the beginnings of a doctrine of divine light; first, Hippolytus says that the deified Christian will "resemble" God—a shift in from the language of "becoming" in the first sentence. Then, Hippolytus says that God has made the Christian "even God unto his glory." This may at first glance seem like a rhetorical flourish, a sort of tacked on *soli deo gloria*, but Norman Russell calls it a promise that "this attainment of likeness to God will manifest itself as participation in the glory of God."[47]

Though Hippolytus does not use the language of participation, he does use the language of resemblance, and it is in this passage that we can begin to see the budding of a doctrine: that one of the ways in which deified man resembles God is that he receives God's glory. To see in detail what this glory is, we must turn again to Hippolytus's younger contemporary, Origen.

## *Divine Light in Origen*

Origen's doctrine of the divine light of God's glory is closely tied to his doctrine of the human intellect and how it is deified. In his commentary on John, he describes the deification of the intellect, and uses Moses as a model of the deified intellect:

> An intellect which has been purified and has transcended all material things is deified by what it contemplates in order that it may perfect the contemplation of God. Such a state may be said to be the glorification of the face of him who has contemplated God and conversed with him and spent time in such a vision, since this is represented figuratively by the glorified face of Moses, when his intellect had been deified by God.[48]

Origen describes several stages in the deification of the intellect: it is purified, it transcends the material world, it contemplates God, and it is, through contemplation, deified by God. He then says that this deification of the intellect could be called, figuratively, the "glorification of the face." In Exodus, Moses talks with God face to face on Mount Sinai and descends the mountain with a shining face. Origen interprets this figuratively—it is not that those who contemplate and converse with God will emit physical light

---

47. Russell, *Doctrine of Deification*, 111.
48. Origen, *Commentary on John*, 32.27, quoted in Russell, *Doctrine of Deification*, 143–44.

from their face, but rather that the intellect will be illumined by the metaphysical glory of God. As Russell describes it, "The way in which deification is manifested is through participation in divine glory, which may begin even in this life. This is a theme which Origen develops in his Commentary on John."[49] It is important, especially for our study of *Evangeline*, to note that the participation in the glory of God does indeed, for Origen, begin in *this* life. Moses is very much alive, and even relatively young, when he first shines with the light of God.

Origen explains in more detail the connection between God's glory and God's divine nature in *Against Celsus*. Origen discusses the glory of God in connection with three major events in the life of Christ. First, Origen says that the pre-incarnate Christ existed in the "Realms of Light and Glory," which he left "to come down into this miserable and sinful world."[50] For Origen, heaven is the natural realm of God's glory, contrasted with earth, which does not sound glorious at all. Second, when Christ is transfigured on mount Tabor, he reveals to his disciples "the Glory of his Raiment, and the Heav'nly lustre of Moses, and Elias, who were to discourse with him."[51] In the Transfiguration, Christ shows his disciples that he is clothed in glory, which had heretofore been hid from them; further, the disciples see that Moses and Elijah are also shining with the light of heaven. Thus, according to Origen, that transfiguration which would be mentioned centuries later by Hawthorne in his review of *Evangeline* is an event in which we see not just the transfiguration of Christ, but also the transfiguration of two human Christ-followers, Elijah and Moses. Third, Origen describes Christ shining with divine light after his resurrection: "For after he had honourably, and happily accomplished the Work of our Redemption, we have Reason to believe, that his Divinity shone with much brighter rays, thro' the Glass, if I may so say, of his Humane Nature."[52] Origen makes clear that the light with which Christ shines is the light of his *divinity*. Several times throughout Book 2 of *Against Celsus* he refers to this light: "the bright rays of his divinity";[53] "the Bright rays, or ev'n the least glimmerings of his Deity, was what exceeded the capacity of the Generality of Men. I speak now of his Humane and Divine Nature."[54] Thus, Origen repeatedly makes clear that Christ's divine nature shines with heavenly glory, a glory which shines

49. Russell, *Doctrine of Deification*, 143.

50. Origen, *Against Celsus*, 181.

51. Origen, *Against Celsus*. This idea of a "glorious raiment" can also be found in Clement. See Carroll, "Being clothed in righteousness."

52. Origen, *Against Celsus*, 162.

53. Origen, *Against Celsus*, 168.

54. Origen, *Against Celsus*, 177.

through his human nature, and is the same glory with which the saints in heaven shine, and with which the intellects of those who contemplate God in this life may be illumined.

## Divine Light in Macarius of Egypt

Macarius, a fourth-century monk of the Egyptian desert, gives a wide ranging overview in his homilies of where and how the divine light of God has worked in humans throughout history. In his fifth homily he explains that the glory of God is something with which Christians can indeed be clothed beginning in this life:

> Let us then strive by faith and virtuous living to gain here that clothing, that when we put off the body we may not be found naked, and there be nothing in that day to glorify our flesh. For in proportion as any one has been permitted to become through faith and diligence a partaker of the Holy Ghost, his body also shall be glorified in that day. What the soul has now stored up within shall then be revealed and displayed outwardly in the body.[55]

In this passage Macarius uses the language of participation; it is through faith that men partake of the Spirit and, through such partaking, are glorified. This glorification of the soul can then be "revealed and displayed" through the body, just as Christ's divinity, as Origen describes, shone out from his deified body.

Macarius gives many scriptural examples of such glorification in his twenty-fifth homily, characterizing the divine light as a heavenly fire:

> The immaterial divine fire has the effect of enlightening souls and trying them, like unalloyed gold in the furnace, but of consuming iniquity, like thorns or stubble; *for our God is a consuming fire, taking vengeance on them that know Him not in flaming fire, and on them that obey not His gospel*. It was this fire that worked in the apostles, when they spoke with fiery tongues. It was this fire which shone by the voice round St. Paul, enlightening his mind, but blinding his sense of sight; for not without the flesh did he see the power of that light. It was this fire which appeared to Moses in the bush. This fire, in the shape of a chariot, caught up Elias from the earth . . . So the angels and ministering spirits partake of the shining of this fire, according to what is said, *Who maketh his angels spirits, and His ministers a flaming fire*. It is this fire which burns up the beam that is in the inward

55. Macarius, *Fifty Spiritual Homilies*, 52.

eye, making the mind clear, that recovering its natural power of penetration, it may see without interruption the wonderful things of God . . . This fire drives away devils, and destroys sin; but it is the power of resurrection, and the effectual working of immortality, the illumination of holy souls, and the strengthening of rational powers. Let us pray that this fire may reach us also, that always walking in light, we may never for a moment *dash our feet against a stone, but shining as light in the world, may hold forth the word of everlasting life.*[56]

This long and Scripture-filled passage develops the doctrine of divine light further than Origen had. No longer is the language about humans shining with light a figurative description of a glorified intellect. Instead, there is a fire that is immaterial and divine, which nevertheless can be literally seen by the physical eyes. But, Macarius warns, those who are full of sin, like devils, are burned and banished by this light. The unrepentant Saul, soon to be St Paul, is blinded by it. Holy Christians, on the other hand, who have been purified by the light of God, can both see and interact with this light. The apostles in Acts preach by its power; Elijah rides a chariot made of this light; and, most importantly for our argument, both angels and men can "partake of the shining of this fire." Further, this fire has several marvelous effects upon the one who partakes of it, purifying, illumining, and strengthening: it purifies the intellect, making "the mind clear" so that it may see "the wonderful things of God"; it illumines "holy souls"; and it strengthens "rational powers."

In his essay on divine light in *The Mystical Theology of the Eastern Church*, Vladimir Lossky describes the Macarian metaphysics of this light. He writes:

> this light or effulgence can be defined as the visible quality of the divinity, of the energies or grace in which God makes Himself known. It is not a reality of the intellectual order, as the illumination of the intellect, taken in its allegorical and abstract sense, sometimes is. Nor is it a reality of the sensible order. This light is a light which fills at the same time both intellect and senses, revealing itself to the whole man, and not only to one of his faculties. The divine light, being given in mystical experience, surpasses at the same time both sense and intellect.[57]

Thus Lossky and Macarius, drawing on Origen, but surpassing him in detail, show that the divine light is both intellectually and physically apprehended, but is beyond the nature of both. It is, simply put, *divine*, and in being so,

56. Macarius, *Fifty Spiritual Homilies*, 183–84.
57. Lossky, *Mystical Theology*, 221.

is the origin of both the created intellect and the created body, and can be given to humans in mystical experience.

## *Divine Light in the Cappadocians*

In that it is divine, the light of God is one of those characteristics of God that the deified human receives. The theology of the fourth-century Cappadocian Fathers, drawing on the doctrines they received from Ireneaus, Clement, Origen, and Athanasius, includes many descriptions of this reception of the light of God. We have already seen in the first chapter of Gregory of Nyssa's *On Virginity* that the ascetic purity of the virgin life causes Christians to "become partakers of His glory."[58] We can now see that such a statement implies a participation in the divine light of God on the part of the one who is being deified through virginity. Further, we have seen that for Gregory the likeness of God is a "buried beauty" of the soul that will "shine forth" from those who cleanse themselves of sin.

In the treatise *On the Holy Spirit*, by Gregory's elder brother, St Basil the Great, we find a description of the illuminating and deifying power of the Holy Spirit:

> He, like the sun, will by the aid of thy purified eye show thee in Himself the image of the invisible, and in the Blessed spectacle of the image thou shalt behold the unspeakable beauty of the archetype. Through His aid hearts are lifted up, the weak are held by the hand, and they who are advancing are brought to perfection. Shining upon those that are cleansed from every spot, He makes them spiritual by fellowship with himself. Just as when a sunbeam falls on bright and transparent bodies, they themselves become brilliant too, and shed forth a fresh brightness from themselves, so souls wherein the Spirit dwells, illuminated by the Spirit, themselves become spiritual, and send forth their grace to others. Hence comes . . . joy without end, abiding in God, the being made like God, and, highest of all, the being made God.[59]

Basil uses the sun's shining on and reflecting through a transparent object as an analogy for the Spirit's relationship with the human soul. The Spirit both illumines and shines out from the purified soul, perfecting it, making it like God, deifying it. And this light of the Spirit also illumines any others who are around the illumined soul. As Russell explains, Basil's imagery here

58. Gregory of Nyssa, *Selected Writings*, 344.
59. Basil, *Nicene and Post-Nicene Fathers*, 8:15–16.

"is more spiritualized and more Platonic [than Athanasius's] as souls . . . are lifted up, suffused with light, to the likeness of God."[60]

St Gregory Nazianzus, sometime best friend of Basil, also speaks of illumination by divine light as an element in human deification. He explains this doctrine in his oration on Athanasius:

> Whoever has been permitted to escape by reason and contemplation from matter and this fleshly cloud or veil (whichever it should be called) and to hold communion with God, and be associated, as far as man's nature can attain, with the purest light, blessed is he, both from his ascent from hence, and for his deification there, which is conferred by true philosophy.[61]

This is a good instance of Gregory's characteristically academic language concerning deification and divine light; man ascends to God through "reason and contemplation," associates "with the purest light," and is deified though the "true philosophy" of heaven. And Gregory is careful to add the phrase "as far as man's nature can attain." In all, Gregory's description of divine light, in addition to his academic tone, is a development of the theological approach of Origen, a Father whom Gregory loved and from whose works he drank deeply.

Though Gregory Nazianzus is the most explicit, each of the Cappadocians owes to Origen and the Alexandrian theological tradition the language of participation found in 2 Peter, in which the human nature that participates in the divine nature receives the characteristics of God, including divine light. It is from the Cappadocian Fathers that the later Fathers of the fifth through eighth centuries—especially Maximus the Confessor, Dionysius the Areopagite, and John of Damascus—take their basic doctrines of theology and economy. The five theological orations of Gregory Nazianzus, especially, form the heart of all subsequent Greek theology concerning the nature and relationships of the Holy Trinity. The Cappadocians, then, form a pinnacle of Greek theology, a culmination of all that had come before them, and a model for all who would come after.

## *Divine Light in John Chrysostom*

The Cappadocians, however, are not the final stop in our survey of the fourth-century doctrine of divine light. St John Chrysostom, the great preacher and Bishop of Constantinople, stands as a late-fourth-century

---

60. Russell, *Doctrine of Deification*, 209.
61. Gregory Nazianzus, *Nicene and Post-Nicene Fathers*, 7:270.

model of non-Alexandrian theology. Chrysostom does not take up Origen's participatory model of deification, instead opting for a more purely ethical doctrine of deification and divine light.[62]

Chrysostom's doctrine of divine light begins in his explication of Genesis, where he explains that before the Fall, Adam and Eve "did not know they were naked; moreover, they were not naked, for the glory from above covered them more than any garment"; when they sinned, however, "they were deprived of the glory which surrounded them."[63] Thus the original state of man is one of being clothed in glory, as Moses was on Sinai, and as Christ, Moses, and Elijah were in their transfiguration on Tabor.

Humans can return to this state, according to Chrysostom, through an ethical deification enacted by a life of virtue and participation in the sacraments. In his commentary on the Psalms, Chrysostom echoes the language of *Theaetetus*: "Here is the peak of highest virtue and what helps arrive at the very summit of benefits: to make ourselves like God as much as is possible for us."[64] Such a life will necessarily involve the sacraments. The blood of Christ, imbibed in the Eucharistic wine,

> revives the flower of the royal image in us; . . . it is the salvation of our souls; by it the soul is purified, beautified, ignited; by it, our nous becomes brighter than fire, our soul more magnificent than gold. This blood has been shed and has opened heaven for us . . . Let us suppose, as if it were possible, that someone plunges a hand or tongue into molten gold; it would suddenly be gilded. As great, perhaps even greater still are the effect which the present gifts have upon the soul.[65]

Chrysostom characterizes the sacrament-partaking soul as shining, molten, brightened by the fire of Christ, and ushered, as it were, into heaven, which Christ has "opened . . . for us." Though he does not use the language of participation, Chrysostom does describe an intimate union between God and man in the sacraments that borders on an ecstatic eroticism—Chrysostom writes, speaking in the voice of Christ,

---

62. In fact, Chrysostom's doctrine of deification is so different from that of the Alexandrian school of Clement, Origen, Athanasius, and their Cappadocian inheritors that Russell does not include Chrysostom at all in his long and otherwise thorough *Doctrine of Deification*. However, earlier writers, including Lot-Borodine and Gross, do include Chrysostom in their surveys of the doctrine of deification in the early Fathers.

63. John Chrysostom, *Homilies on Genesis*, 16.5, quoted in Gross, *Divinization of the Christian*, 201–2.

64. John Chrysostom, *Commentary on the Psalms*, 134.7, quoted in Gross, *Divinization of the Christian*, 205.

65. John Chrysostom, *Commentary on John*, 44.3, quoted in Gross, *Divinization of the Christian*, 204.

I also descended to earth, not only to mingle myself with you, but to intertwine myself with you; I am eaten, I am broken in pieces, in order that the mingling, the blending, the union may be profound. These things which one unites remain—each in itself; I, even I, as if one tissue with you. I no longer want anything between the two of us: I desire that the two may be one.[66]

Here Chrysostom makes clear that the sacraments create an indissoluble and unmediated union between Christ and the believer. Though he avoids the language of Alexandrian theology, Chrysostom does not shy away from preaching the mystical doctrine of divine-human union. And he makes clear that through a life of virtue and partaking in the sacraments, the Christian may regain the likeness of God and the garment of glory lost in the Fall.

Chrysostom, a preacher who lived to see the dawn of the fifth century, stands as the final Father of our investigation, not just because he chronologically closes out the fourth century, but because he is a model of a clear and moderate doctrine of deification. Without recourse to the neo-Platonic metaphysics of the Alexandrians, Chrysostom clearly presents godlikeness as the goal of virtuous living, and the re-glorification of the *nous* with divine light as the goal of partaking in the sacraments. His language parallels that of Macarius, characterizing glory as visible, but of a higher nature than visible things, as receivable by the *nous*, but as originating from the uncreated source of the *nous* itself.

The seven Fathers surveyed above take various approaches to describing divine light and how it relates to the human being deified. It is spoken of as "surrounding," "illuminating," and "suffusing," as "falling on," "catching up," and being "sent forth" from the human person. These many participles and prepositions can easily lead to confusion about what exactly the Fathers see as the relationship between divine light and the human person. For this reason, we will limit our descriptors of this relationship to three main phrases: *illumined by*, *shining with*, and *transfiguration*. First, we may speak of the human being *illumined by* divine light; this refers to the process of divine light coming from God to the human soul, body, or both. Divine light, according to the Fathers, always originates with God, and shines from God upon the human. The second phrase describes a further step. The human in the process of deification is not only illumined by divine light, but also *shines with* divine light. The preposition *with* is most appropriate to describe this shining, for it is a participation in the light of God such that it is no longer just a quality of God—though it always remains so—but also becomes a quality of the deified human, the prime example of which, for

66. John Chrysostom, *Commentary on 1 Timothy*, 15.4, quoted in Gross, *Divinization of the Christian*, 203–4.

our purposes, is Evangeline. It is *her* light, too, for once she is illumined, it is sent forth from her, as Basil describes.

Thus the light that the deified human sends forth has a double source: God, ultimately, but also the deified human, mediately. When we use the term "shine with," it is this that we mean: that divine light has been received from God, has filled the human, and now is sent forth from her. The deified become "co-shiners" with God. The final term we will use in this study is *transfiguration*, which will be used to refer to the whole process of being illumined by and shining with divine light.[67]

## Deification in the Fathers and Channing

Recent theological debate has developed over which theologians may be rightly said to possess a doctrine of deification. For instance, when Finnish scholars in the latter part of the twentieth century began a conversation about whether one could speak of deification in the theology of Martin Luther, this inspired others to search for the doctrine of deification in theologians ranging from Thomas Aquinas and John Calvin to John Wesley and Karl Rahner. In his essay "*Theosis* in Recent Research: A Renewal of Interest and a Need for Clarity"[68] Gosta Hallonsten calls for an attitude of extreme caution in ascribing to any theologian a doctrine of deification, especially theologians in those traditions, like Roman Catholicism and Protestantism, which explicitly reject major philosophical and theological tenets upon which the Greek Fathers based their thought and doctrine.

Because the rest of this book is concerned with whether we can speak of a doctrine of deification and divine light in Longfellow's *Evangeline*, it will be helpful to clarify the similarities and differences between the doctrines of Longfellow's two major theological influences—Channing and the Fathers—concerning three concepts: ethical deification, realistic deification, and divine light.

### *Ethical Deification in the Fathers and Channing*

The Fathers speak of man's original state as one of likeness with god, and of the goal of human beings on this earth as becoming godlike through virtuous living, ascetic practices such as virginity, and partaking in the

---

67. Note, of course, that this is "transfiguration" with a lowercase *t*, distinguishing it from "the Transfiguration" which properly refers to the particular event of Christ's transfiguration on Mount Tabor.

68. Hallonsten, "*Theosis* in Recent Research," 281–93.

sacraments. If another writer speaks thus, we can conclude that these ideas are in line with a basic patristic doctrine of ethical deification, as found especially in Justin Martyr, Clement, and John Chrysostom.

When compared with the Fathers' writings, Channing's doctrine of ethical deification—according to which man develops the latent divine characteristics within him through virtuous living and thus regains the divine likeness—is compatible with statements of Clement and Gregory of Nyssa concerning man's innate likeness to God, which must be revealed and developed through virtuous living. Further, Channing's focus on the benefit of trials and ascetic struggle are also compatible with the ascetic focus found in Clement and in Gregory's treatise *On Virginity*. Where Channing differs from the Fathers is in the complete absence of the sacraments from his discussion of godlike living. This is largely due to what could be called Channing's dual non-sacramentalism; for Channing, Christ and the Spirit are not present in the Eucharist nor in Baptism; further, since neither Christ nor the Spirit is God himself according to Channing, their presence in the sacramental elements would not create any participatory unity with God in the sacrament-partaker anyway.

It would be tempting to say that Channing is most in line with early Fathers like Justin Martyr and Tertullian whose deification language is much simpler and more strictly ethical than that of the later Fathers, stressing simple godlike living and God the Father's gracious bestowal of godhood. But, as we will see in more detail in the next chapter, even this would be going too far. Justin and Tertullian were staunch supporters of Christ's divinity, and Justin stressed the central role of the sacraments in the ethical deification of the believer.

## *Realistic Deification in the Fathers and Channing*

The Fathers speak of Jesus Christ, the second person of the Trinity, becoming incarnate, uniting the divine nature with human nature, in order to deify fallen humans through creating a relationship of participatory union between their human nature and his divine nature. At the same time, the Fathers maintain a distinction between a human's becoming god by grace and Christ's being God by nature. If another writer speaks thus, we can conclude that their ideas are in line with a basic, patristic doctrine of realistic deification, as found especially in Origen, Athanasius, and Gregory of Nyssa.

The denial of the divinity of both the Son and the Spirit creates an incompatibility between Channing's theology and the Fathers' concept of realistic deification. Because for Channing, God did not become man in the first place, no formula of exchange is possible. Instead, Channing's theology suggests a different formula—namely, that Christ became godlike and participated in divine nature so that man may become godlike and participate in divine nature. Christ is not involved in man's deification in any other way than as an example of a man who experiences ethical and realistic deification. However, the realistic deification that Christ did and humans can experience, according to Channing, lacks any concept of the incarnation, the key tenet that the Fathers teach makes realistic deification possible. Thus, for the Unitarian, the uniting of man to God through participatory union with the divine nature is wholly a gracious act of the Father. Here is a deification stripped of all its trinitarian and incarnational content; it can no more be called patristic than can Socrates's teachings about deification in *Theaetetus*.

## Divine Light in the Fathers and Channing

The Fathers speak of the deified human—whether ethically or realistically deified or both—receiving and shining with the immaterial light of God through the illuminating work of God the Spirit and/or Christ. Because descriptions of bright faces and shining figures are so common in literature, it is important to keep in mind that the Fathers make a clear distinction between earthly, created, physical light, and the heavenly, divine, immaterial glory by which the godlike human is illumined and with which she shines. If a writer speaks thus, we can conclude that their ideas are in line with a basic, patristic doctrine of divine light as found in Origen, the Cappadocians, and John Chrysostom.

The major problem with comparing Channing's theology to the Fathers' doctrine of divine light is that Channing speaks very seldom of light or glory at all, and has nothing like a clearly taught doctrine of light, whether earthly or divine. Nevertheless, he does offer two provocative hints. The first, as we saw in chapter 1, is in "Objections to Unitarian Christianity Considered," where Channing calls virtue "a ray of God's brightness." He does not, however, give any further explanation of what God's brightness is, nor does he say that the Christian who participates in the divine nature will shine with the divine characteristic of heavenly light. The closest he comes to any statement like this is in "Christian Worship," in which God's "bright image" in the believer will reveal the Father to others. Though this is not incompatible with a patristic doctrine of divine light, it lacks the metaphysical underpinnings found in Origen and John Chrysostom. Thus we can conclude that while Channing's descriptions of divine light are not incompatible with patristic doctrine, they are underdeveloped. Further, the non-sacramental, non-incarnational, non-trinitarian stance of Channing makes it unlikely that he would agree with any of Origen's statements about divine light in relation to Christ's human and divine natures, nor any of Chrysostom's statements about divine light in relation to the Eucharist.

## Channing's Rejection of the Fathers

Though this book is not primarily about Channing, his clear influence upon Longfellow makes it important for us to provide something of a categorization of his doctrine of deification in relation to the Fathers. Given the aforementioned major incompatibilities between the doctrine of Channing and that of the Fathers, it is safest to say that Channing teaches a doctrine of deification that is closest in nature to the doctrine described by Socrates in *Theaeteus*. Both Channing's language of ascent to God and his language of becoming like God through virtue, in addition to his lack of a doctrine of incarnation, are compatible with a Platonic universe of vice-laden humans, a transcendent deity, and philosophical salvation through right thought and ethical living.

This Platonic note in Channing is supported by Channing scholarship. Dorrien, as we have seen, calls Channing a "spiritualizing neo-platonist,"[69] and D.H. Meyer has pointed out that Channing was a student of Plato who developed the Greek philosopher's ethical ideas.[70] Thus, if we are to conclude anything about Channing and the Fathers, it is that Channing rejected fundamental doctrines of the Fathers from Justin through Chrysostom, but that he was familiar with and influenced by the same texts of antiquity as the Fathers, especially Plato and 2 Peter. Channing developed his doctrines of ethical and realistic deification along different lines than the Fathers did, using strictly Unitarian principles derived from Plato and a biblical scholarship divorced from the interpretive traditions of the patristic, medieval, and Reformation eras.

Given Channing's avid anti-trinitarianism, it is not surprising that the Fathers do not factor into his theological writings. The few times he mentions the Fathers it is to dismiss them. In his advice to the blue-collar Christian, he writes: "I do not expect the laborer to study theology in the ancient languages, in the writings of the Fathers, in the history of sects; nor is this needful. All theology, scattered as it is through countless volumes, is summed up in the idea of God."[71] Likewise, in his essay extolling Milton, he writes,

69. Dorrien, *American Liberal Theology*, 24.
70. Meyer, "The Saint as Hero," 175.
71. Channing, *Selected Discourses and Essays*, 264.

> The earliest Fathers, as we learn form their works, were not receptive of large communications of truth. Their writings abound in puerilities and marks of childish credulity, and betray that indistinctness of vision, which is experienced by men who issue from thick darkness into the light of day. In the ages of barbarism that followed the fall of the Roman empire, Christianity, though it answered wise purposes of Providence, was more and more disfigured and obscured . . . How vain, then, was Milton's search for "the mangled Osiris," for "the lovely form and immortal features of Truth," in the history of the church![72]

Perhaps this lack of interest in the Fathers and disdain for their works comes from the fact that Channing received the patristic doctrines of the Trinity and the incarnation primarily through the Puritan tradition, not through the writings of the Fathers themselves. He seems wholly uninterested in studying the Fathers' writings, and even dissuades others from doing so. The Christian writers of the past whom Channing champions are instead Enlightenment writers like John Milton, John Locke, Isaac Newton, and Samuel Clarke—all Unitarians, Channing says, who were "able and illustrious defenders of the truth of Christianity."[73]

In a strange historical twist, it was Henry Wadsworth Longfellow himself who, more than both his Unitarian and Transcendental contemporaries, familiarized himself with the writings of the Church Fathers of the second through fourth centuries, and who encountered there the patristic doctrines of ethical and realistic deification and divine light. Even as he read and was edified by Channing, Longfellow was also reading and writing about Justin, Origen, Chrysostom, and others, taking them seriously as writers of both aesthetically pleasing literature and forceful arguments for the faith. In the next chapter we will explore Longfellow's hitherto ignored writings about the Fathers, and delineate which of the major texts and doctrines of the Fathers previously discussed made their way into Longfellow's library and Longfellow's writings. We will then be ready to turn our eyes to *Evangeline* itself, reading it with both Longfellow's Unitarian and patristic influences in mind, with an eye to understand and interpret the doctrines of deification and divine light therein.

---

72. Channing, *Works*, 66–67.
73. Channing, *Selected Discourses and Essays*, 81.

# 4

# The Christian Fathers in Longfellow

RECENT CRITICS, ESPECIALLY FRANCHOT and Higgins, have highlighted the Unitarian influence on Longfellow and stressed the importance of understanding Unitarian viewpoints in order to interpret Longfellow's poetry properly. But there exist in the critical literature on Longfellow hints of another influence—that of the early Church Fathers. These hints begin in the biography of Longfellow written by his brother Samuel. In his 1886 *Life of Henry Wadsworth Longfellow*, Samuel writes that the poet composed a series of lectures on literary history for his students at Bowdoin College in 1832, "beginning with the Christian Fathers and coming down to the origin of modern languages."[1] In his 1955 biography of the poet, Edward Wagenknecht also mentions Longfellow's interest in the Fathers and quotes one of the lectures that Samuel mentions, "The Literary History of the Middle Ages," where the poet writes, "the eloquence of the Christian Fathers flowed from a purer fountain than the streams of classic poetry ... bright with the glories of revelation, and radiant with a more than earthly splendor."[2] Wagenknecht reveals here not only Longfellow's interest in the Fathers, but also his estimation of the Fathers above the writers of classical antiquity.

The evidence for the Fathers' influence on Longfellow expands when we look to Longfellow's published works. In his first book, the 1835 *Outre Mer: A Pilgrimage Beyond the Sea*, we find Longfellow quoting the writings of Justin Martyr, Tertullian, and Marcus Minutius Felix, and mentioning John Chrysostom in passing. In his 1846 journals again Longfellow mentions

1. Longfellow, *Life of Longfellow*, 1:188–89
2. Wagenknecht, *Longfellow: Full Length Portrait*, 290.

John Chrysostom, and in his 1849 novella *Kavanagh* both Chrysostom and Athanasius make an appearance. The next year, Gregory Nazianzus shows up in Longfellow's notes on *The Golden Legend*. Lastly, there is a final flowering of commentary on the Fathers in Longfellow's 1867 notes on *The Divine Comedy*, in which Longfellow includes hagiographies of Jerome, John Chrysostom, and Macarius of Egypt, among others, and generously quotes from Tertullian, Augustine, Dionysius the Areopagite, Boethius, and, again, Chrysostom.

Despite this patristic undercurrent in Longfellow's published prose and notes, Samuel Longfellow and Edward Wagenknecht alone among Longfellow's commentators note the poet's interest in the Fathers. This is somewhat understandable—after all, Longfellow only mentions the Fathers in passing in his published prose, and the patristic references in his critical notes all serve to illuminate non-patristic texts. But if we take a cue from Samuel Longfellow and Wagenknecht and look not to Longfellow's published works, but instead to his early, unpublished lectures, an exciting discovery awaits us.

Housed in the Houghton Library at Harvard University alongside most of Longfellow's other unpublished manuscripts are two handwritten lectures titled "The Christian Fathers." It is in these unpublished and heretofore overlooked manuscripts that Longfellow discusses the early Church Fathers in their own right, embracing them as skilled creative writers, forceful apologists, and thinkers who laid the groundwork for the history of western philosophy and literature. In these lectures Longfellow not only reveals which Fathers he read, but even provides some of the names of the translations and secondary sources he used in his early research on the patristic era. These neglected lectures bear witness to Longfellow's detailed knowledge of the Church Fathers and provide an indispensable resource for any investigation of Longfellow's theological concerns. They also, more particularly, cast light upon the keynote passages of *Evangeline*—for they show that in the years before he wrote the poem, Longfellow consulted and meditated on theologians who wrote about human godlikeness and transfiguration in divine light.

In this chapter we will first place the "Christian Fathers" lectures in their context within the whole of Longfellow's writings on the Fathers, and then examine the doctrines of deification and divine light as they appear in the patristic texts that Longfellow read. Through our chronological exploration of Longfellow's relationship with the Fathers, we will see that there are three interrelated doctrines that Longfellow learned from the early Fathers: first, that human nature and divine nature can be and have been united in Christ; second, that the final destiny of the Christian is a likeness to and unity with divine nature—in other words, those doctrines we have come to know as ethical and realistic deification—and third, that mature and exemplary Christians, such as martyrs, are illumined by and shine with a light of heavenly origin, which is God himself. These three doctrines are not wholly incompatible with those that Longfellow found in Channing. In fact, a clear doctrine of ethical deification, as we have discussed in chapters 1 and 3, is found in Channing's "Christian Worship." It is the Fathers' detailed doctrines of the incarnation and of divine light that Channing lacks, and which, in their connection with the doctrine of deification in the text of *Evangeline*, will reveal that that poem, especially the transfiguration scene of 2.5, cannot be seen merely as a product of Unitarian theology, but rather as a work of art that culminates in a characteristically patristic vision of deification and divine light.

## The Fathers in Outre-Mer

In 1835, Longfellow published a memoir, *Outre-Mer: A Pilgrimage Beyond the Sea*, which recounts his early encounters with the Church Fathers on his first trip to Europe. The first mention of the Fathers is in "The Baptism of Fire," a chapter in which Longfellow describes the martyrdom of the Huguenot Anne Du Bourg. We first meet Du Bourg in prison awaiting execution, where he reads and takes comfort in Tertullian's *Apology*. Longfellow describes Tertullian as "the oldest and ablest writer of the Latin Church,"[3] and quotes what is perhaps the most rhetorically dazzling section of the *Apology*: "When we are thus begirt and dressed about with fire, we are then in our most illustrious apparel. These are our victorious palms and robes of glory; and, mounted on our funeral pile, we look upon ourselves as in our triumphal chariot."[4] When Du Bourg is approached by his Catholic captor and offered a bribe to recant, he refuses, supporting his decision with another early Christian text—the *Apology* of Justin Martyr:

> "Had the apostles and martyrs of the early Christian Church listened to such paltry bribes as these, where were now the faith in which we trust? These holy men of old shall answer in earnest for me. Hear what Justin Martyr says, in his earnest appeal to Antonine the Pious, in behalf of the Christians who in his day were unjustly loaded with public odium and oppression."
>
> He opened the volume before him and read:
> "'I could wish you would take this also into consideration, that what we say is really for your own good; for it is in our

---

3. Longfellow, *Outre-Mer and Driftwood*, 102.
4. Longfellow, *Outre-Mer and Driftwood*, 102–3.

power at any time to escape your torments by denying the faith, when you question us about it; but we scorn to purchase life at the expense of a lie; for our souls are winged with a desire of a life of eternal duration and purity, of an immediate conversation with God, the Father and Maker of all things. We are in haste to be confessing and finishing our faith; being fully persuaded that we shall arrive at this blessed state, if we approve ourselves to God by our works, and by our obedience express our passion for that divine life which is never interrupted by any clashing evil."[5]

Longfellow clearly intends his audience to be inspired by the words of Justin and Tertullian, as well as by Du Bourg's use of them in the face of the "odium and oppression" of his own day. Still, there is a note of frustration in the story, for Longfellow writes, "The Catholic and Huguenot reasoned long and earnestly together, but they reasoned in vain. Each was firm in his belief, and they parted to meet no more on earth."[6] Here we can begin to see a theme in Longfellow that has often been noted—namely, the futility of sectarian arguments. But there is also a contrary note of admiration of Du Bourg's refusal to abandon his particular, Huguenot beliefs, and the Church Fathers are used to both inspire and support Du Borg's perseverance in these beliefs.

Toward the end of *Outre-Mer*, Longfellow recounts his time at a Capuchin Monastery in La Riccia, Italy, where he meets a monk who sets him straight about the relationship between pagan antiquity and early Christian culture:

"From my youth up I have been a disciple of Chrysostom, who often slept with the comedies of Aristophanes beneath his pillow; and yet I confess that the classic associations of Roman history and fable are not the most thrilling which this scene awakens in my mind . . . The town of Ostia, which lies before us on the sea shore, is renowned . . . Marcus Minutius Felix, a Roman lawyer, who flourished in the third century, a convert to our blessed faith, and one of the purest writers of the Latin Church, here places the scene of his 'Octavius.' This work has probably never fallen into your hands, for your are too young to have pushed your studies into the dusty tomes of the early Christian Fathers."

I replied that I have never so much as heard the book mentioned before.[7]

---

5. Longfellow, *Outre-Mer and Driftwood*, 104–6.
6. Longfellow, *Outre-Mer and Driftwood*, 106.
7. Longfellow, *Outre-Mer and Driftwood*, 261–62.

The monk then reads his favorite passages, leaving Longfellow with "a parting injunction to read the 'Octavius' of Minutius Felix as soon as [he] should return to Rome."[8] Though this passage centers around Felix, Chrysostom is mentioned in passing, and of this we should take note, for of all the Church Fathers it is St John Chrysostom who most often appears in Longfellow's writings.

It is unclear whether Longfellow followed the monk's advice and procured for himself a Latin copy of Felix's *Octavius* while in Rome. What is certain is that by the time he began teaching at Bowdoin, Longfellow had found a copy of the *Octavius* in English translation. The text in which he found and read the *Octavius* was *The Apologies of Justin Martyr, Tertullian and Minutius Felix in Defence of the Christian Religion with the Commonitory of Vincentius Lirinensis Concerning the Primitive Rule of Faith*, translated by William Reeves, an Anglican priest, in the early eighteenth century. It is from this collection of translations that Longfellow garners all his quotations from the Fathers in *Outre-Mer*, including those from Tertullian and Justin Martyr as well as from Felix's *Octavius*.

## The Fathers in Longfellow's "The Christian Fathers" Lectures

Reeves's translation of the *Apologies* plays a important part in Longfellow's two, hitherto ignored "Christian Fathers" lectures, which have the potential to augment our picture of Longfellow's reading and lecturing habits, and refine our understanding of his theological mind. As mentioned before, these lectures currently sit unpublished in the Houghton Library collections at Harvard University along with the rest of Longfellow's lectures. The lectures are handwritten in Longfellow's lovely cursive and bound in two slim notebooks, with one loose leaf appended to the first.

The "Christian Fathers" lectures cover the first three centuries of church history, beginning with Justin Martyr and ending with the fourth-century ante-Nicene Fathers. The first lecture discusses the biographies and major works of Justin Martyr, Tertullian, Minutius Felix, and Origen. Given Longfellow's familiarity with Reeves's translations of the *Apologies*, it is not surprising that he begins with Justin, Tertullian, and Felix. In fact, Longfellow quotes exclusively from Reeves's translations in his sections on Justin, Tertullian, and Minutius Felix.

Longfellow's comments on these first three Fathers are in line with what he heard from the Capuchin monk at La Riccia. He describes Justin Martyr

---

8. Longfellow, *Outre-Mer and Driftwood*, 264.

as "a man of profound erudition, being skilled in Heathen Philosophy and knowledge of the Scriptures," whose *Apology* "possesses all the nervous and forcible eloquence of simple truth."[9] Tertullian is "a dark and rugged writer ... full of energy and fire" who nevertheless is "so much absorbed by what he has to say, that he thinks little of the manner in which he shall say it."[10] Felix has "more grace, but ... less power than Tertullian. He has more of the studied grace of the scholar than the bold Spirit of the martyr: more of the Roman Orator, than of the Christian Father."[11] We can see in the quotations from Felix's *Octavius* Longfellow's interest in the rhetorical flourishes and pastoral passages of the Fathers. For instance, Longfellow quotes an image-filled passage about the sea shore which includes the strange and delightful phrase "the crisping frizzly waves," which, according to *Outre Mer*, is the same passage the monk read him in La Riccia.

Longfellow links Origen to Justin, Tertullian, and Felix by highlighting Origen's apologetic writings from *Against Celsus*. For his quotations from Origen, Longfellow relies on an English edition of *Against Celsus* translated by James Bellamy, which only includes the first two books of Origen's original five. Longfellow esteems Origen as "perhaps the most remarkable of the Christian Fathers of the 3rd Century,"[12] and summarizes some of his major teachings. "Being master of the Platonic Philosophy," Longfellow writes, "[Origen] brought its principles to the explanation of the scriptures: and maintained that they were to be interpreted in the same allegorical manner in which the Platonists explained the history of their gods. He maintains that the scriptures not only possessed a literal sense, conformable to the outward letter, but also a certain misterious [sic] or hidden sense, in pursuit of which his lively imagination constantly pursues throughout his commentaries."[13] In a rather debatable claim, Longfellow writes that Origen's theory of the interpretation of Scripture "seems to have been the origin of the Scholastic Theology, which ... enlisted so much talent in vain subtelties and useless enquiries."[14]

One of the more curious aspects of the first lecture is a quotation from John Chrysostom, in Latin, which comes at the end of the first lecture, just after the section on Origen, and is written on the aforementioned

---

9. Longfellow, "The Christian Fathers," 6–8.
10. Longfellow, "The Christian Fathers," 18–20.
11. Longfellow, "The Christian Fathers," 34–35.
12. Longfellow, "The Christian Fathers," 49.
13. Longfellow, "The Christian Fathers," 53–54.
14. Longfellow, "The Christian Fathers," 55–56.

loose leaf.[15] While this quotation is out of place chronologically, given that Chrysostom does not fit within the time period of the other Fathers discussed, it suggests that Longfellow familiarized himself early on with the post-Nicene Fathers, and read some of the Fathers in Latin. The quotation is from the first paragraph of Chrysostom's panegyric on the martyrs Juventinus and Maximinus, and bears some resemblance to the Tertullian quotation about the glory of the martyrs which is cited in both *Outre Mer* and the first "The Christian Fathers" lecture. Both Chrysostom and Tertullian speak of the martyrs as shining with light; Tertullian characterizes this light as the fire that burns the martyrs, calling it "illustrious apparel," while Chrysostom characterizes it as heavenly light, "the glory of their innate brilliance."[16] Whether it is the beauty of the Italian seashore, or the beauty of the perseverant martyrs, Longfellow seems quite interested in the aesthetic qualities of the Father's writings.

In the second "Christian Fathers" lecture, which is shorter than the first, Longfellow discusses St Cyprian of Carthage, Arnobius, and Lactantius. Whereas in the first "Christian Fathers" lecture Longfellow carefully noted which English translations of the Fathers he used, the poet includes none of this sort of information in the second lecture, and we are left to guess at which translations he used, or whether he translated any of the quoted passages himself.

Longfellow devotes most of the second "Christian Fathers" lecture to the third-century bishop of Carthage, St Cyprian, quoting from three of his works: "To Donatus," "On the Lord's Prayer," and the "Tract to Demetrian." Longfellow gives considerable space to the comparison between Cyprian's argument in the "Tract to Demetrian" that the Christians are not responsible for natural disasters and social upheavals—as some pagans alleged—to

---

15. The quotation is as follows, retaining Longfellow's spellings: "Eorum flor neque languescit, neque defluit tempore. Nescit vetustatis rubiginem splendoris istius natura. Temporis accessione, opes que ad corpora spectant, facile intereunt, vestimenta absumuntur, domus destruuntur et aurum rubigine consumitur: et in Summa, omnium sensibilium facultatem natura, tempore tandum aboletur et intercidit. At non sic se res habet in spiritualibus thesauris de martyribus inquam, qui semper in eodem manent vigore, semper in eodem juventutis flore sunt, semper suae gloriae fulgoreni emittunt et radios." A contemporary translator renders it thus: "'Their bloom doesn't fade, it doesn't flow away with time. By nature this brilliance doesn't succumb to age's rust. For whereas physical riches fade and pass away with the passage of time—indeed, clothes wear out and houses collapse and jewelry rusts, and with time the entire essence of these riches we see and touch perishes and vanishes—in the case of the spiritual treasures it is not like this. Rather, the martyrs always and perpetually remain brilliant in equal vigor and youth, brightly reflecting the glory of their innate brilliance." John Chrysostom, "Juventinus and Maximinus," 92.

16. John Chrysostom, "Juventinus and Maximinus," 92.

a similar argument in the writings of Arnobius. St Cyprian gives a wide-ranging and vivid description of the decay of the natural and social orders:

> The seasons of the year are not the same as formerly: the winter-rains descend not in sufficient quantity to cherish the seeds which are lodged in the ground; the summer sun gives not its usual heat; the temprature [sic] of the spring hath not its accustomed gaiety, nor doth autumn abound as formerly, in plenty of fruits. The mountains produce less marble, the mines less gold and silver than heretofore: the veins of ore become daily impoverished and exhausted, and there is everywhere an universal failure . . . It is imaginable, think you, that the world grown old, should retain its powers in the same state of activity and vigour which in its youth belonged to them? They must needs be lessened as their end approaches. . . . This is the general law of the world: and of all the things in it: appointed for it and them, by a decree of providence: that whatever rises must set, whatever has a beginning must have an end.[17]

Longfellow then compares Cyprian's image-filled argument that the world is naturally decaying to Arnobius's argument that, in fact, the world is still getting on quite nicely, and has not been troubled at all by the advent of Christianity:

> And first of all in faire and familiar speech this we demand of these men: since the name of Christian religion began to [be] in the world, what uncouth, what unusual things, what against the lawes instituted at the beginning hath nature, as they term and call her either felt or suffered? . . . Hath this wheeling about of heaven, swerving from the rule of its primitive motion, either begun to creepe more slowly, or to be carried with headlong volubility? Doe the stars begin to raise themselves up in the west, and the signes to incline towards the east? The Prince of Stars, the sun whose light coloreth, and heat quickeneth all things, doth hee cease to be hot, is he waxen cooler, and hath he corrupted the temper of his wonted moderation into contrary habits? . . . Have the winds breathed forth their spirits, as having spent their blasts? Is not the aire straitned into clouds, and doth not the field being moistened with showres wax fruitful? Doth the earth refuse to receive the seeds cast into her? . . . These things, therefore, being so, and that no noveltie hath broken in to interrupt the perpetuall tenor of things by swerving and discontinuing them: what is it that they say, confusion is brought

---

17. Longfellow, "The Christian Fathers," 14–17.

upon the world since Christian religion entered into it, and discovered the misteries of hidden veritie?[18]

In both St Cyprian and Arnobius, Longfellow seems as much impressed by the colorful catalogs of natural phenomena as by the arguments of the writers. But he does, nevertheless, present these passages as reasonable arguments by "active and vigorous defender[s] of the Christian religion,"[19] not as naturalistic dabblings by merely lyrical essayists.

Though Longfellow places primary source quotations front and center in these lectures, he also shows himself, in his secondary source quotations and footnotes, to be a wide-reading student of seventeenth- and eighteenth-century ecclesiastical history. His main secondary source for the history of the early church is Louis Dupin, a controversial French Catholic writer of the late seventeenth century whose ecumenical streak may have been attractive to the schism-averse Longfellow.[20] But Longfellow also consulted and quotes from Johann Mosheim, a German Lutheran, as well as the Anglicans Adam Clarke and the aforementioned William Reeves. What unites these four historians is their overall estimation of the early Fathers as representative of a pure, primitive Christian faith, uncorrupted by later sectarianism caused by both medieval innovation and Enlightenment materialism.[21] How different this view must have seemed from Channing's low estimation of the early patristic era as one of puerility, barbarism, and credulity. One perspective that Longfellow does not draw upon, save for a quotation from Richard Baxter, is that of the Calvinist Puritans, whose determinism Longfellow more than once pronounced off-putting. Longfellow uses two ancient sources of ecclesiastical history in these lectures as well: Eusebius's *Ecclesiastical History* and the *Commonitory* of St Vincent of Lerins (called by Longfellow and Reeves "Vincentius Lirienesis"), an English translation of which was included in Reeves's collection.

---

18. Longfellow, "The Christian Fathers," 20–23.

19. Longfellow, "The Christian Fathers," 19.

20. Dupin allegedly called for reunion between his own French Catholic Church and both the Church of England and the Greek Orthodox Church. See Lejay, "Louis Ellies Dupin."

21. Mosheim sums up this view well in his description of the Fathers of the second century: "The Christian system, as it was hitherto taught, preserved its native and beautiful simplicity ... This will not by no means appear surprising to those who consider that, at this time, there was not the least controversy about those capital doctrines of Christianity which were afterward so keenly debated in the church; and who reflect, that the bishops of these primitive times were, for the most part, plain and illiterate men, remarkable rather for their piety and zeal than for their learning and eloquence." Mosheim, *Ecclesiastical History*, 149–50.

An obvious question arises at this point: why would a New England Unitarian, raised on the sermons of William Ellery Channing and hired to teach *modern* languages, devote his research and classroom time to obscure theologians from the dawn of ecclesiastical history? In Wagenknecht's quotation from the "Literary History of the Middle Ages" we have already seen a possible answer to this question: "The eloquence of the Christian Fathers flowed from a purer fountain than the streams of classic poetry... bright with the glories of revelation, and radiant with a more than earthly splendor."[22] Three things are significant about this quotation. First, it is a bold step away from Channing's historical views. Second, it seems to be an intensification of the same principle that Longfellow heard from the Capuchin Monk at La Riccia—namely, that the Christian Fathers are "more thrilling" than classical sources. If Longfellow did indeed see the writings of the Fathers as more worthy of attention than those of pagan Greece and Rome, then this might explain why he began his course with an overview of their works and lives. Third, and perhaps most excitingly, in this quotation Longfellow uses the language of divine light to describe the Fathers' writings. Not only is the Fathers' eloquence "purer" than classical poetry, but it is also "bright with ... glories, and radiant with a more than earthly splendor." Intentionally or not, Longfellow defends the Fathers using luminous imagery reminiscent of Origen's language in *Against Celsus* and Chrysostom's in his "Homily of Praise on the holy martyrs Juventinus and Maximinus."

## Longfellow's 1830's Boethius Translations

Sometime in the 1830s, while he was still teaching at Bowdoin, Longfellow translated, presumably for his modern languages students, selections from *The Consolation of Philosophy*, a philosophical text from the sixth-century Christian theologian and philosopher Boethius.[23] Boethius wrote this famous text while awaiting execution by the Arian King of Rome Theodoric, who persecuted the Roman community of Nicene Christians to which Boethius belonged. In *The Consolation*, Boethius dramatizes an encounter between himself and Lady Philosophy, who consoles the imprisoned narrator in both verse and prose, reminding him that true happiness lies not in

---

22. Wagenknecht, *Longfellow: Full Length Portrait*, 290.

23. Curiously, Longfellow's translation is not from Boethius's original Latin, but from the Anglo-Saxon translation attributed to King Alfred the Great. Like the "Christian Fathers" lectures, these translations exist only in manuscript form in the Houghton Library at Harvard under "Handbook of the Anglo-Saxon tongue. Selections from King Alfred's version of Boethius with an interlineary translation."

worldly success, but in a virtuous life lived in pursuit of God, the source of all goodness and divinity. Through the eleven sections he translated, we can see that Longfellow was drawn to the passages in verse where Lady Philosophy describes the natural world and God's providential rule over it.

## The Fathers in the 1846 Journals and Kavanagh

After the "Christian Fathers" lectures and the Boethius translations, the Fathers continue to appear sporadically in Longfellow's work over the next few decades. Chrysostom is his favorite Father to reference offhand. After hearing Emerson's lecture on Goethe in January 1846, Longfellow notes in his journal that "there is a great charm about [Emerson], the Chrysostom ... of the day."[24] And in November 1846, he praises the Unitarian preacher John Weiss thus: "Weiss Preached. I told him after church that I felt like applauding him, as the people of old did St. Chrysostom."[25] Longfellow uses the same anecdote in his 1849 novel *Kavanagh*, describing the state of the churches of New England: "In modern times no applause is permitted in our churches, however moved that audience may be, and consequently, no one dares wave his hat and shout,—'Orthodox Chrysostom! Thirteenth Apostle! Worthy the Priesthood'—as was done in the days of the Christian Fathers."[26]

Of course, these brief references to Chrysostom and applause hardly indicate a particularly thorough knowledge of Chrysostom's theology on Longfellow's part. But Longfellow is not finished with the Church Fathers in *Kavanagh*. He describes the spiritual journey of the protagonist, the preacher Arthur Kavanagh, from Catholicism to Protestantism, including a description of Kavanagh's own perspective on the Fathers:

> The study of philosophy and theology was congenial to his mind. Indeed, he often laid aside Homer for Parmenides, and turned from the odes of Pindar and Horace to the mystic hymns of Cleanthes and Synesius ... Moreover, the study of ecclesiastical history awoke within him many strange and dubious thoughts. The books taught him more than their writers meant to teach. It was impossible to read of Athanasius without reading also of Arius; it was impossible to hear of Calvin without hearing of Servetus. Reason began more energetically to vindicate itself; that reason, which is a light in darkness, not that which is "a thorn

---

24. Longfellow, *Life of Longfellow*, 2:30.
25. Longfellow, *Life of Longfellow*, 2:64.
26. Longfellow, *Prose Works*, 2:333.

in Revelation's side." The search after Truth and Freedom, both intellectual and spiritual, became a passion in his soul, and he pursued it until he had left far behind him many dusky dogmas, many antique superstitions, many time-honored observances . . . By slow degrees, and not by violent spiritual conflicts, he became a Protestant . . . Out of his old faith he brought with him all he had found in it that was holy and pure and of good report. Not its bigotry, and fanaticism, and intolerance; but its zeal, its self-devotion, its heavenly aspirations, its human sympathies, its endless deeds of charity.[27]

What exactly is Arthur Kavanagh's view of the Fathers in this passage? Apparently, he prefers the mystic hymns of the fourth-century neo-Platonist bishop Synesius to the writings of pagan writers like Horace, but he seems to be dissuaded from the arguments of Athanasius by the existence of Arius. Conveniently, Kavanagh retains only positive-sounding qualities of church tradition, with no doctrinal details given. All we are told is that he ends up a Protestant, of unknown denomination. Here Longfellow slyly avoids sectarian controversy by letting his readers decide for themselves which "fanaticisms" Kavanagh has rejected, and which "aspirations" he has surely retained.

Still, the knowledge of ecclesiastical history, including the Fathers in particular, is a central element in Kavanagh's development of what we are meant to see as mature and reasonable religious beliefs.[28] Further, we have some reason to believe that Longfellow's development, contrary to Kavanagh's, was one of moving from the liberal religion of American Unitarianism toward the ancient church and the teaching of the Fathers, if not in his creed, at least in his academic attentions and creative considerations. We have already seen how the young Longfellow, raised on Channing and Goethe, is introduced to the Fathers in Italy, and how they quickly become an integral part of his teaching curriculum at Bowdoin. And though Longfellow's protagonist in *Kavanagh* is a liberal Protestant preacher, he still follows the Capuchin monk's estimation of early Christian writings over the pagan classics, for Kavanagh prefers Synesius to Horace and Homer.[29]

27. Longfellow, *Prose Works*, 2:352–55.

28. Though *Kavanagh* is the closest Longfellow gets to Channing's skepticism about the early church, it still recommends the study of the Fathers as instructive for the theologically minded Christian. Compare this to Channing's dismissal of the fathers as unnecessary for the Christian layman quoted in the previous chapter.

29. This is a big claim coming from Longfellow, who loved Horace quite a lot, calling him "my favorite classic." Longfellow, *Life of Longfellow*, 1:320. Further, scholars have credited Longfellow's early translations of Horace with winning him the notice of Bowdoin College officials in their search for a new language professor. See Prichard,

## The Fathers in Longfellow's Work after 1849

If there is a work in which Longfellow seems most ambivalent about the Fathers, it is *Kavanagh*. Even so, the Fathers come out of *Kavanagh* looking more dignified and valuable than they ever do in Channing's work. Lest we think that Longfellow's interest in the Fathers waned after the 1840s, it is worthwhile to look at the two appearances of the Fathers in Longfellow's post-1849 work, where there is evidence of Longfellow's continued interest in patristic subjects and texts.

After *Kavanagh*, Longfellow returned to verse, but not to lyric. Instead he composed the verse play *The Golden Legend*, a retelling of a Faust-like medieval legend. In a note on the origin of the medieval mystery plays, Longfellow mentions Gregory Nazianzus: "The earliest religious play which has been preserved is the *Christos Paschon* of Gregory Nazianzen, written in Greek, in the fourth century."[30] Apparently Longfellow was familiar with not only the theological writings of the early Fathers, but also their dramatic endeavors. Such a familiarity with the *Christus Paschon*, one of the most obscure and controversial of the works associated with Gregory Nazianzus, further suggests that Longfellow was more knowledgeable about the Fathers and their works than has been hitherto acknowledged.

After the "Christian Fathers" lectures themselves, the treasure-trove of patristic references in Longfellow's oeuvre is his 1867 notes on Dante's *Divine Comedy*. Though they primarily serve to illuminate Dante's text, these notes also reveal Longfellow's ongoing interest in the Fathers. Here we find again Felix's "crisping frizzly waves" from the *Ocatvius*,[31] as well as two quotations from Tertullian,[32] and John Chrysostom's remarks on applause in church.[33] But the most oft-quoted fathers here are Boethius, Augustine, and Dionysius the Areopagite, whose influence upon both Dante and St Thomas Aquinas are explored and illustrated. Longfellow also presents the hagiographies of several early Fathers, including St Benedict, Dionysius, St Jerome, St Macarius of Egypt, St Nicholas, and, of course, St John Chrysostom, whose "whole life," Longfellow writes, "is more like a romance than a narrative of facts."[34]

---

"Horatian Influence upon Longfellow," 23.

30. Longfellow, *Christus: A Mystery*, 444. Though this note concerns the mystery play that Longfellow depicts in *The Golden Legend*, interesting research could be conducted comparing St Gregory's *Christos Paschon* and Longfellow's play about the life of Christ, *The Divine Tragedy*.

31. Longfellow, *Divine Comedy*, 367–68.

32. Longfellow, *Divine Comedy*, 676, 694.

33. Longfellow, *Divine Comedy*, 706–7.

34. Longfellow, Divine Comedy, 648.

As we saw in chapter 2, some scholars, chief among them Augustus Hopkins Strong,[35] have criticized Longfellow for an alleged ignorance concerning key Christian doctrines of sin, salvation, and the nature of God. But it is in the *Divine Comedy* notes, especially those expounding Dante's use of patristic theology, that we see in Longfellow a clear and even impressive understanding of Christian doctrine. The doctrines Longfellow expounds in his notes are not just those vaguely associated with Dante, but those of Athanasian trinitarianism and Christology,[36] Boethian compatibilism,[37] Dionysian doctrines of angelic hierarchy and divine light,[38] and even St John Damascene's theology of icons.[39] Whatever Longfellow himself believed, it cannot be maintained that he was ignorant of or unable to articulate the fundamental Christian doctrines of the patristic or medieval eras, and the *Divine Comedy* notes illustrate that over thirty years after the "Christian Fathers" lectures, Longfellow was as familiar as ever with the Fathers, their lives, and their ideas.

## Longfellow's Fathers

What, then, should be our general conclusions, having briefly considered the place of the Church Fathers in the writings of Longfellow? In the first place, it is plain that Longfellow was interested in and inspired by the writings of the Fathers. This interest and inspiration has prominent aesthetic dimensions—in Longfellow's words the Fathers are variously "pure," "radiant," and "rugged," and their lives and writings are filled with "grace," "eloquence," "energy," and "fire." In the second place, Longfellow saw the Fathers as more important than the writers of pagan antiquity for the proper understanding of subsequent western literature and the proper formation of reasonable and mature religious beliefs. Third, Longfellow attributes much of the early Fathers' aesthetic and literary importance to their admirable defense of a pure, primitive faith, untainted by sectarianism.

The phrase *Longfellow's Fathers* will be used henceforth to describe those Fathers with whom Longfellow was clearly familiar, as evidenced by those citations and quotations in *Outre Mer*, "The Christian Fathers," and *Kavanagh* previously discussed. These include the following:

35. See Strong, *American Poets and Theology*, 235–41.
36. Longfellow, *Divine Comedy*, 652.
37. Longfellow, *Divine Comedy*, 409–10.
38. Longfellow, *Divine Comedy*, 703–4.
39. Longfellow, *Divine Comedy*, 712–13.

1. The *Apologies* of Justin and Tertullian, the *Octavius* of Felix, and the *Commonitory* of St Vincent, all of which Longfellow read in Reeves's English translation, and from which he quotes in *Outre Mer* and "The Christian Fathers."

2. The first two books of Origen's *Against Celsus*, translated by James Bellamy, quoted by Longfellow in "The Christian Fathers." It is possible that Longfellow read the rest of *Against Celsus* in some other translation, but this possibility remains unconfirmed, as Bellamy only translated and annotated the first two books of *Against Celsus*, and Bellamy's translation is the only one Longfellow references.

3. St Cyprian's "To Donatus," "On The Lord's Prayer," and "Tract to Demetrian."[40]

4. St John Chrysostom's "Homily of Praise on the holy martyrs Juventinus and Maximinus," in Latin translation, from which Longfellow quotes in "The Christian Fathers."

5. The *Hymns* of Synesius, to which Longfellow refers in *Kavanagh*.[41]

6. *The Consolation of Philosophy* by Boethius, which Longfellow read in Anglo-Saxon in the 1830s.

This list would be much more sparse were it not for the discovery of the "Christian Fathers" lectures, which bring to light a wealth of detailed information about Longfellow's knowledge of Origen, Cyprian, Chrysostom, and Mosheim, and are an invaluable resource for understanding the theological mindset that Longfellow brought to the writing of *Evangeline*.

There is some evidence that Longfellow was also familiar with the writings of Athanasius in the 1840s, but he does not actually cite or quote any of the Alexandrian bishop's specific works until the Dante notes of the 1860s, and even then he quotes only the Athanasian Creed, the authorship of which Longfellow himself calls into question. Athanasius, then, is a *possible* source for the doctrines that we will discuss in this chapter, but not as sure a source as Justin, Tertullian, Felix, Cyprian, Origen, Chrysostom,

40. As mentioned above, Longfellow does not note which translation of Cyprian's work he read. Though it is possible that Longfellow prepared his own translations of Cyprian's works, the archaic spellings of many words in his quotations from Cyprian lead me to believe that he was using an eighteenth-century translation. Further research into which translation of Cyprian, Lactantius, and Arnobius Longfellow used is needed and could prove fruitful.

41. Of course, Arnobius and Lactantius are also among Longfellow's Fathers. They will feature less prominently in this chapter, partly because Longfellow does not discuss them in depth, and also because the writings by these two Fathers that Longfellow cites do not deal specifically with incarnation, deification, or divine light.

Synesius, or Boethius. Finally, as Longfellow shows in "The Christian Fathers," his interpretation of these Fathers was somewhat influenced by those notes and annotations he found accompanying the translations by Reeves and Bellamy, as well as in the ecclesiastical histories of Clark, Dupin, and, most importantly, Mosheim.

Looking at the list of Longfellow's Fathers, we can immediately see that the poet was familiar with some, but not all, of the major proponents of the doctrines of deification and divine light in the second through fourth century. Notably missing are Clement and the Cappadocians. Further, in the case of Cyprian, Synesius, and Boethius, he was familiar with Fathers who have not traditionally been seen as important to the development of the doctrines of deification and divine light, but nevertheless do, as we will see, include discussions of those doctrines in their work. In the following section we will explore the doctrines of incarnation, deification, and divine light as they appear in Longfellow's Fathers, with a view to show that, even though Longfellow did not read—and most likely did not have access to—all of the Fathers discussed in the last chapter, he did read enough of the Fathers to get a clear picture of the patristic doctrines of ethical and, to some extent, realistic deification, and divine light, grounded in the context of a clear trinitarian, incarnational, and sacramental theology.

## Christ's Unification of Divine and Human Natures in Longfellow's Fathers

If there is one doctrine on which all of Longfellow's Fathers agree, it is that Jesus Christ possesses both a human and a divine nature, which were united in the incarnation. This unity of natures in Christ is not just a byproduct of Christ's work of the salvation of man, but it central to it. Though Longfellow's Fathers do not all use the same terminology to describe this salvific unification of natures, they do all agree that Christ is both divine and human, and that this unity of the divine and human in Christ is a *saving* union.

Justin is the first of Longfellow's Fathers to describe this saving union. In book 1 of his *Apology* he writes: "Jesus Christ our Saviour was made Flesh by the *Logos* of God and had real Flesh and Blood for our Salvation."[42] Justin describes the divinity of Christ in the language of the Gospel of John 1, by calling Christ the "Logos" of God, which, according to St John, is "*with* God" and "*is* God."[43] Justin describes the humanity of Christ as "Flesh and Blood." This again echoes the Gospel of John, for St John writes, "The Word

---

42. Justin, "First Apology," 121.
43. John 1:1 (ESV); emphasis mine.

became flesh and dwelt among us."⁴⁴ This unity of the Logos with Flesh and Blood is "for our Salvation," and this union is accomplished by the Logos himself, not by the flesh and blood. Thus the divinity of Christ, for Justin, is the active agent in the unification of divinity and humanity in Christ.

In his own *Apology*, Tertullian presents a more narrative and philosophical description of this saving union of the divine and human:

> The Logos that is come forth from God is both God and the Son of God, and those Two are one . . . This Ray of God then descended, as it was foretold, upon a certain virgin, and in her Womb was incarnated, and being there fully formed the God-man, was born into the world, the divine and human nature making up this Person, as Soul and Body does one man. The flesh being wrought and perfected by a divine spirit, was nurs'd and grew up to the Stature of a Man, and then addressed the Jews and preached and work'd miracles among them; and this is the Christ, the God of the Christians.⁴⁵

In this passage Tertullian explains the relationship between the Logos and God in an even more explicitly Johannine way than Justin does. The Logos is "from God," "is . . . God," and is "the Son of God" who is "one" with God. Tertullian also describes the Logos as a "Ray" of God, which is incarnated within the Virgin Mary. Christ is not just the Logos-become-Flesh-and-Blood, as he was in Justin, but is now a God-man, who is one person with two natures, "human and divine." In accordance with Justin, Tertullian also sees the divine nature of Christ as the active agent in the incarnation, "perfect[ing]" the flesh, or human nature, of Christ. It is in Tertullian that we first find, among Longfellow's Fathers, the standard, patristic description of Christ as one *person* with two *natures*. This formulation will continue through the rest of the Fathers we examine here.

In the second book of *Against Celsus*, as we saw in the previous chapter, Origen describes the relationship between Christ's human and divine natures after Christ's saving work: "For after he had honorably, and happily accomplished the Work of our Redemption, we have Reason to believe, that his Divinity shone with much brighter rays, thro' the Glass, if I may so say, of his Humane Nature."⁴⁶ As noted before, this is a description of a further development in the union of the divine and human natures after the events in Christ's life described by Tertullian. After the resurrection, Origen explains, the divinity of Christ is more apparent, more "bright," shining more clearly than before his passion, death, and resurrection.

---

44. John 1:14 (ESV).
45. Tertullian, "Apology," 258–59.
46. Origen, *Against Celsus*, 162.

In his *Commonitory*, St Vincent of Lerins sets out the orthodox view of Christ, distinguishing it from various heresies of the first four hundred years of Christology. He spends much of his time explaining exactly why Christ can be said to possess both divinity and humanity (which he calls "Substances" as well as "Natures"), but is still only one person:

> But how then in our Savior is there one and another Thing, but not one and another Person? Because there is one Substance of his Divinity, and another of his Humanity . . . Thus in one and the same Christ there are two Substances, but one Divine, the other Human; one from God the Father, the other from the Virgin-Mother; one Co-eternal, and equal to the Father, the other Temporary and inferior to the Father . . . As God, he has Divinity in Perfection; as Man, he had complete Humanity; I say, a complete Humanity, as containing in it both Soul and Flesh . . . But he is one, not by a strange Mixture and Confusion of the Divinity and Humanity together, but by one entire and individual Unity of Person: For that Conjunction of two different Natures made no Conversion or Change of the one into the other, (which is proper Arianism) but rather compacted both into one in such a manner that the Propriety of each Nature remains for ever distinct in one and the same single Person of Christ; so that the Divinity shall never commence Body, nor that which was once Corporeal, ever cease to be Corporeal.[47]

St Vincent here presents a wealth of patristic Christology in concise summary. For our purposes, we will single out several important details. St Vincent stresses, as did Tertullian before him, that Christ is one person, not two people. The incarnation, wherein the human and divine natures were united, did not result in a twin personhood in Christ; Christ does not have what we would call multiple personalities. Following the metaphysics of Tertullian and Origen, Vincent makes clear that one person may, by the work of God, be made both human and divine, and that Christ is the prototype of this. Vincent also explains that the union of the human and divine natures in Christ does not mix nor essentially change either nature. In Christ the human and divine natures are both full and complete; neither diminishes the other. If anything, Vincent shows, the union of the natures is what makes human nature complete. This echoes Tertullian's earlier dictum that the "flesh [is] perfected by the divine."

Thus, Longfellow's Fathers make clear three things about the incarnation of Christ. First, the Logos, the second person of the triune God, existed

---

47. Vincent, "Commonitory," 297–303.

before his incarnation. Second, the Logos descended into the womb of a human, Mary, where his divine nature was united with the human nature of Mary. The resulting child was one person with two united but unharmed natures. Third, the human nature of Christ was perfected by the divine nature, and—after Christ's saving passion, death, and resurrection—clearly reflected forth Christ's divine nature, as a glass reveals the light behind it. Each of these doctrines—so central to all patristic theology—was rejected by Channing as unbiblical, and each was encountered by Longfellow in his early investigation of the Fathers.

## The Deification of the Human in Longfellow's Fathers

If Christ is the God who becomes man, uniting in his one person both the divine nature and the human nature, and if, further, Christ saves man from his sin by giving him the opportunity to be Christ-like, then an implication of these doctrines is that the mature Christian will be united, eventually, with the divine nature, just as Christ was united with the human nature. The Word made flesh enables the flesh to become Word. This doctrine of deification, in its ethical and realistic forms, was discussed at length in the last chapter. We will now consider the presence of deification in Longfellow's Fathers, showing that Longfellow was familiar with patristic notions of deification when he set out to write *Evangeline*.

We have already encountered an early description of deification in the quotation from St Justin Martyr in *Outre-Mer*:

> We scorn to purchase life at the expense of a lie; for our souls are winged with a desire of a life of eternal duration and purity, of an immediate conversation with God, the Father and Maker of all things. We are in haste to be confessing and finishing our faith; being fully persuaded that we shall arrive at this blessed state, if we approve ourselves to God by our Works, and by our obedience express our passion for that divine life which is never interrupted by any clashing evil."[48]

Justin characterizes the life of the mature or perfected Christian as one of "eternal duration and purity," in which conversation with God is "immediate." This life is no longer merely human life, but "divine life." Though Justin does not use a language of the union of *natures*, as Origen would, he does expect that the final state of Christians will be a new and different kind of

---

48. Longfellow, *Outre-Mer and Driftwood*, 106.

life, in which there is no more mediation between God and man, and human life has become divine.

In his *Doctrine of Deification*, Norman Russell focuses on Tertullian's descriptions of deification in *Against Hermogenes*. Longfellow, however, gives no indication that he was familiar with this work. We will turn, then, to the work with which Longfellow was familiar, Tertullian's *Apology*, where we find a surprisingly thoughtful early description of deification in a polemic directed at the pagans of the Roman Empire:

> Because you have not the Hardiness to deny, but that your Gods were once Men, and yet stand up for Posthumous Divinities, or dead Men turn'd into Gods, I shall now consider the Reasons for such an Imagination. In the first place, then, you will be forc'd to grant some superior God who auctions out his Divinity; and upon good Consideration makes Gods of Men; for Men cannot naturalize themselves into Gods; nor can anyone else bestow the Divine Nature upon 'em but him who is the Proprietor of it. But now, if the supreme Power itself cannot make Gods, you then presume in vain upon made Gods without a Maker. Certainly if Men could deifie themselves, they would never have taken up with a humane being, when a divine one was in their power. Upon supposition, therefore, that there is one who is able to make Gods, I will examine the Reasons for making 'em; and upon consideration I can find none, unless it be that the supreme God has too much business upon his Hands to manage as it should be, without some Sub-gods to assist him.[49]

Though largely a mockery of Roman mythology, this passage does lay down hypothetical rules for the deification of man. Human beings, Tertullian explains, could not "naturalize" themselves into gods, for, after all, they do not possess a divine nature on their own. Therefore only the proprietor of divine nature, the "supreme God," can "bestow" a divine nature upon man. Further on in the passage, Tertullian supposes that a God may bestow divine nature upon man for virtue, but he finds little virtue in those god-men worshipped by the pagans:

> Say that this conferring of Godships was intended for the rewarding of virtue. From hence, I suppose, you'll grant the God-making God himself to be virtuous in Perfection, and consequently not to dispense these honours at Sixes and Sevens, without having any Respect to the Merits of the Persons. I desire you to sum up the Merits of those you worship as Gods, and

---

49. Tertullian, "Apology," 214–15.

judge whether they are likely to lift men up to heaven, or not rather press 'em down to the very Bottom of Hell.[50]

Here Tertullian extends his hypothetical doctrine of deification. If there is a "God-making God"—that is, a perfect deity who is capable of bestowing divine nature upon men—then he will not randomly hand out the divine nature, but rather only bestow it upon those who, through virtue, become worthy of it. Though Tertullian does not seem to be taking these hypothetical doctrines very seriously, his descriptions of the deification of man are metaphysically compatible with his description of Christ's incarnation, in which God, the Logos, unites human and Divine nature in one person. Further, this is the very language he uses more seriously when discussing deification in *Against Hermogenes*, and which later Fathers, including Origen and Athanasius, would use to describe the deification of the Christian.

Thus far the first "Christian Fathers" lecture has proved extremely helpful in revealing that Longfellow was familiar with several key patristic works of the second and third centuries wherein the Fathers discuss incarnation and deification. But the second "Christian Fathers" lecture also proves valuable, for in it Longfellow reveals his familiarity with St Cyprian of Carthage, whose language of deification has much in common with Channing's, and, as we will see, shows up in *Evangeline* itself.

In Cyprian's third-century treatise "On the Lord's Prayer," Longfellow encountered an early, Latin description of ethical deification. In his exegesis of the phrase "thy will be done on earth as it is in heaven," Cyprian turns his attention to the new, heavenly nature of the disciples of Christ:

> Since the disciples are not now called by [Christ] earth, but the salt of the earth, and the apostle designates the first man as being from the dust of the earth, but the second from heaven, we reasonably, who ought to be like God our Father, who maketh His sun to rise upon the good and the bad, and sends rain upon the just and the unjust, so pray for the salvation of all men; that as in heaven—that is, in us by our faith—the will of God as been done, that we might be of heaven; so also in earth, that is, in those who believe not—God's will may be done, that they who as yet are by their first birth of earth, may, being born of water and of the Spirit, begin to be of heaven.[51]

Cyprian uses the language of ethical deification, that we "ought to be like God our Father," and, like Justin, describes the sacrament of baptism as

---

50. Tertullian, "Apology," 217.
51. Cyprian, *Treatises*, 410.

leading humans to divine life. "Being born of water and of the Spirit," the newly baptized Christian "begin[s] to be of heaven." As in Justin, the Cappadocians, and others, Cyprian shows that the Spirit, the third person of the Trinity, is involved in this ethical deification of individual Christians. But Cyprian does not forget about Christ and the Eucharist; in the next paragraph, he explains that "our daily bread" is, in fact, the sacrament of the Eucharist, wherein Christ becomes "the bread of those who are in union with his body."[52] Just as the Spirit begins to make us, through baptism, "of heaven," so Christ, the second person of the Trinity, unites us with his deified body in the Eucharist. Thus in Cyprian, Longfellow found a sacramental, trinitarian approach to deification. This deification is explicitly ethical, and in Cyprian's language of "union" begins to anticipate the realistic doctrine of Origen.

Origen was one of the first to formulate a serious and nuanced description of the realistic deification of the Christian, but the passage in which he does this is not contained in Longfellow's Fathers. That famous first use of 2 Peter in book 3 of *Against Celsus* was not included in the translation by Bellamy that Longfellow read. Still, within Bellamy's translation of Origen's *Against Celsus*, we do find a passage that uses the language of 2 Peter to explain the spiritual perception of the prophets and saints:

> But one who dives to the Bottom of Things, will find, that, according to the Account, we have, in Holy Writ, there is a certain, Divine Knowledge, which none, but a few, happy Persons have . . . and that the several Branches of it, are such as follow; *viz*. A Sight, adapted to the Contemplation of Objects, that are beyond the Sphere of *unassisted Nature*, such as Cherubims, and Seraphims; a Hearing suited to the Perception of Sounds, vastly different from those, which are form'd in the Air, a Tast[e], that can relish the living Bread, that came down from Heaven; a Smell, that can distinguish that Heavenly Perfume, of which, as the Apostle speaks, when he says, *We are unto God a sweet Savour in Christ*; and a Touch, of which St John, speaks, when he says, *Our Hands have handl'd of the Word of Life*.
>
> The Blessed Prophets, being Partakers of these Divine Sensations, and seeing, hearing, tasting, and smelling, in a Way that is perfectly supernatural we must understand these Things, in the same Sense, in which we must take that Place in Ezekiel, where he's said, to have eat the Book that was deliver'd him.[53]

---

52. Cyprian, *Treatises*, 410.
53. Origen, *Against Celsus*, 157–58.

In employing the phrase "Partakers of these Divine Sensations" Origen seems to be building up, here, to his book 3 use of 2 Peter to describe union with God. Before he gets there, he uses 2 Peter's language to refer to a more minor (but no less miraculous) stage of the human journey to God—namely, the apprehension with the physical senses of metaphysical truths. Just as Cyprian and Arnobius discern truths about God and man from observing the cosmos around them, Origen does not cast away the body and its senses in his characterization of the Christian life, but instead shows how they begin to partake in a new kind of sensation, wherein created nature is the avenue through which God is known.

Elsewhere in book 2, Origen speaks of the life of the Christian in a way similar to Justin:

> So that we plainly see, that from the very Infancy of Christianity they who embrac'd it, were effectually taught by it, to despise the gaudy Vanities of the present life (which the greatest part of mankind imagine to be so charming, and agreeable) and to have the sincere Desires of their souls most vehemently carry'd out, after another Life, which is far more excellent, and in a word, is every way worthy of a God.[54]

Here again the mature Christian seeks a life different from the present one, a life that is "worthy of a God." For Origen, the rejection of the sinful passions of the human soul is one of the great benefits of the Christian's pursuit of this divine life:

> Now they, who find fault with the Christian Religion, do willfully Neglect, to consider, how many unruly Passions are successfully govern'd by it, what a stop it puts to that rapid Torrent of Vice, and Immorality, which is too visible in the world . . . yet they must confess that it conduces very much to the true interest of Mankind, and which is more, has an Immediate, and Principal Regard to their better, and Immortal part.[55]

Origen's language here is in line with that of Justin and Cyprian—the Christian life is one that seeks to be divine, immortal, godlike; and this is accomplished through the suppression of passion, vice, and the "Vanities of the present life." Still, though realistic deification may be implied here, it has not yet been made explicit.

The explicit descriptions of realistic deification in Longfellow's Fathers are found in the *Hymns* of Synesius of Cyrene, the *Consolation* of Boethius,

---

54. Origen, *Against Celsus*, 114.
55. Origen, *Against Celsus*, 205.

and the commentary on Origen provided by Johann Mosheim, one of Longfellow's main secondary sources for the patristic era in the "Christian Fathers" lectures.

Synesius of Cyrene is a controversial figure. Living at the end of the fourth century, he is an example of a thoroughly neo-Platonic Christian. The legend goes that he only agreed to be ordained a bishop if he could retain his neo-Platonic belief in the preexistence of the human soul. Scholars still debate whether he should be considered primarily a neo-Platonist or a Christian writer.[56] One thing is sure: he wrote striking and enduring works of literature. His letters in particular are considered as exemplary in the Greek epistolary tradition. What interests us, however, are the "mystic hymns" of which Longfellow's Arthur Kavanagh was so fond. In "Hymn 1," Synesius describes the life of the Christian as a difficult journey that ends in deification. In the final lines of the poem, the speaker calls his soul to mount up and unite with God himself:

> Come, my soul, that you may drink from
> Heaven, greatest of all fountains.
> Now entreat the one who made you;
> He it is who gave you life. O
> Leave to earth this earthly worship.
> Quick, unite now with the Father:
> Thus shall God with God go dancing.[57]

We hear an echo of both Justin and Origen in Synesius's call to "leave to earth this earthly worship" and ascend to a heavenly or divine life. But what Justin and Origen imply, Synesius (echoing Clement and Gregory of Nyssa) makes explicit. As the early-twentieth-century commentator W.S. Crawford writes, "the elevation and deification of the intelligence" is man's "supreme aim" according to Synesius.[58] In the penultimate line of "Hymn 1," this deification is characterized as a unification of the soul of the Christian with God the Father. In the final line the Christian is even described as "God." In fact, it is unclear, in both the Greek and the literal English translation, which "God" is which. The last line in Greek reads *"theos en theo choreuseis,"*[59]

56. Two good sources on Synesius's biography and the controversy surrounding him are the introductions by Fitzgerald in *Essays and Hymns of Synesius*, vol. 1, and Stevenson in *Ten Hymns of Synesius*.

57. Synesius of Cyrene, "Hymn 1," ll. 128–34. The translation is my own, wherein I have attempted to preserve both the literal meaning and the approximate line length of the original. For the Greek text of the poem, see Synésios de Cyrene, *Hymnes*, 40.

58. Crawford, *Synesius the Hellene*, 206.

59. Synésios de Cyrene, *Hymnes*, 105.

literally, *God with God dancing*. Some translators have tried to distinguish the two Gods more clearly than Synesius does, by reading the second word for God, *theo*, as *theio*, meaning a "divine" or "godlike" being.[60] Fitzgerald's prose translation of the last two lines reads: "in unison with the Father thou mayest perchance move in harmony with God, thyself divine."[61] Alan Stevenson's verse translation opts for the ethical deification term *godlike*:

> ... with earnest prayer entreat
> Thy Father! Halt not—leave this earthly mount,
> For godlike thou shalt be—in God complete.[62]

Both Fitzgerald and Stevenson attempt to explain the state of the Christian once union with God has taken place. Echoing Justin, Fitzgerald says that the Christian is now "divine," and, in a language of ethical deification that we will find used by Longfellow himself in *Evangeline*, Stevenson calls the perfected Christian "godlike." In Synesius, then, we find an explicitly stated doctrine of deification, both ethical and realistic. The soul of the human, no longer desiring an earthly life, ascends to God the Father, unites with him, and, now divine and godlike, enjoys that immediate communion with God for which Justin longs, which Synesius characterizes as a dance. In his 1982 study of Syneisus, Jay Bregman suggests that Synesius's portrait of the "'gnostic' [who] aspires to the life of the Nous, the truly divine life," is also akin to Origen's conception of the "saintly and deified natures" of those fortunate persons who achieve "direct contact with the Nous."[63] Thus Synesius stands as a writer who ably illustrates in his hymns an Alexandrian portrait of the deified human.

Coming a century after Synesius, Boethius inherited a well-developed metaphysics and soteriology from his Nicene forebearers. In Book III of the *Consolation*, Lady Philosophy explains true happiness as a sort of realistic deification:

> Since it is through the possession of happiness that people become happy, and since happiness is in fact divinity, it is clear that it is through the possession of divinity that they become happy.

---

60. Evidence points to Longfellow's familiarity with the Greek text—not English translations—of Synesius's hymns. He encountered discussion of Synesius's biography and major works in Clark, Dupin, and Mosheim, and most likely read Synesius's hymns in the course of his Greek poetry reading project in autumn 1839. Longfellow, *Life of Longfellow*, 1:342–43.

61. Synesius, *Essays and Hymns*, 2:374.

62. Synesius, *Ten Hymns of Synesius*, 4.

63. Bregman, *Synesius: Philosopher-Bishop*, 114.

> ... So those who possess divinity necessarily become divine. While God is so by nature, as many as you like may become so by participation.[64]

Here is a standard, late patristic description of deification as participation in divinity, using the language inherited from 2 Peter, Origen, and the Cappadocians.

In Johann Mosheim's *Ecclesiastical History* we find the most explicit description of deification in Longfellow's secondary sources on the Fathers. Though Mosheim is clearly skeptical of them, he describes in detail those doctrines of Origen and his followers that he calls "mystical theology." In his explanation of mystical theology, Mosheim includes not only a description of the union of the human soul with God, but also the practical steps that the mystics took in order to unite with the divine nature:

> Origen and his disciples [taught] that the divine nature was diffused through all human souls; or, in other words, that the faculty of reason, from which proceeds the health and vigour of the mind, was a emanation from God into the human soul and comprehended in it the principles and elements of all truth, human and divine. They denied that men could, by labour or study, excite this celestial flame in their breasts; and therefore, they disapproved highly of the attempts of those who, by definitions, abstract theorem, and profound speculations, endeavored to form distinct notions of truth, and to discover its hidden nature. On the contrary, they maintained that silence, tranquility, repose, and solitude, accompanied with such acts of mortification as might tend to extenuate and exhaust the body, were the means by which the hidden and internal word was excited to produce its latent virtues, and to instruct men in the knowledge of divine things. For this they reasoned; "they who behold with a noble contempt all human affairs, who turn away their eyes from terrestrial vanities, and shut all the avenues of the outward senses against the contagious influences of a material world, must necessarily return to God when the spirit is thus disengaged from the impediments that prevented that happy union. And in this blessed frame, they not only enjoy inexpressible raptures from their communion with the Supreme Being, but also are invested with the inestimable privilege of contemplating truth undisguised and uncorrupted in its natural purity, while others behold it in a vitiated and delusive form."[65]

---

64. Boethius, *Consolation of Philosophy*, 71.
65. Mosheim, *Ecclesiastical History*, 215–16.

Mosheim summarizes several of the main doctrines we have already seen in Longfellow's Fathers and adds a few new ones. The "happy union" with God is the destiny of the "mystical" Christian, in which the human communes with God and knows truth in an immediate way. This union with God necessitates a prior renunciation of the earth and earthly life—so far Justin, Origen, and Synesius. But Mosheim goes further and describes the mystic way as one that spurns all academic study and speculation in favor of active ascesis—"silence . . . solitude . . . mortification as might extenuate and exhaust the body." This ascesis, if successful, does not bring man into a wholly new state, but into his original, natural state of union with God. For, Mosheim explains, man was created with a spark or flame of the divine nature within him, which is rediscovered and kindled through active ascesis. Thus it is natural, according to Origen's mystical theology, to be united with God and know truth in purity. It is the earthly life of human nature disconnected from the divine nature that is unnatural. Though Mosheim is most directly attributing these views to Origen, we have seen that they also appear in Clement and Gregory of Nyssa, especially the latter's writings on virginity.[66] Of course, Mosheim is deeply skeptical of this ascetic road to deification as followed by the Christian mystics. But of all Longfellow's secondary sources it is he who explains it in the most depth. And it is understandable that such a spiritual road—of active service and worship, as opposed to academic speculation—struck the same chord in Longfellow that he had articulated in *Kavanagh*: a strong suspicion of "dusky dogmas [and] antique superstition" and a preference for "endless deeds of charity."

In summary, two important doctrines found in Longfellow's Fathers are the unification of the human and divine natures in Christ, and the eventual unification of the Christian's human nature with God's divine nature, resulting in a deified state. This final state is a state of being "worthy of God" in Origen, a state of "divine life" in Justin, a state of being "like God" in Cyprian, a state of "happy union" with God in Mosheim, and, in Synesius, a state in which the Christian may even be called "theo"—*god*. As we have seen, it is unclear whether Longfellow was familiar with the most major texts on deification of the third and fourth century, chief among them Origen's *Against Celsus*, Book 3; Athanasius's *On the Incarnation*; and the writings of

---

66. One might find it odd that Mosheim attributes an actively anti-academic mysticism to Origen when scholars like Gross and Russell credit Origen with the most intellectual and academic of the approaches to deification of the early Fathers. See Gross, *Divinization of the Christian*, 194; and Russell, *Doctrine of Deification*, 143–44. While Mosheim provided Longfellow with a good summary of a Patristic doctrine of deification, he arguably fails to adequately describe Origen's view, and provides a description more in line with the theology of Gregory of Nyssa.

the Cappadocian Fathers. Still, we may conclude that Longfellow at the very least read around the edges of these major texts, finding rudimentary descriptions of ethical deification in Justin, Tertullian, and Cyprian, and very explicit, post-Nicene descriptions of realistic deification in Synesius, Boethius, and Mosheim. But there is one final doctrine, related to the doctrines of incarnation and deification, that is quite explicit in Longfellow's Fathers, and to which he himself is clearly drawn, given the passages he quotes in his writings on the Fathers: the doctrine of divine light.

## The Doctrine of Divine Light in Longfellow's Fathers

The patristic doctrine of divine light may be summarized as follows: there is a type of light, wholly different from the visible light we experience on earth, which becomes manifest to men's eyes and intellects when they encounter the divine nature, whether of Christ or in some other holy person. This light is variously referred to as "divine light," "celestial light," "heavenly light," or, often, "glory." Most interestingly, this light cannot be described as a created thing, but is, in Lossky's words, "the visible aspect of God Himself." Finally, those who receive the characteristics of God through deification are illumined by and shine with this light.

First among Longfellow's Fathers, Justin describes this light in a passage of his *Apology* about the second coming of Christ. Christ, he explains, "shall come in his own form, encircled in celestial glory."[67] Christ's "own form" most likely refers to the form of his divine nature, and this divine nature naturally shines with the light of "celestial glory." In Bellamy's translation of *Against Celsus*, Origen presents a similar description, in which the resurrected Christ's "Divinity shone with much brighter rays, thro' the Glass, if I may so say, of his Humane Nature."[68] Further, Origen speaks of "the bright rays of [Christ's] divinity" and warns that "the Bright rays, or ev'n the least Glimmerings of his Deity, was what exceeded the capacity of the Generality of Men. I speak now of his Humane and Divine Nature."[69] Divine light's exceeding of man's natural capacity is also mentioned by Cyprian in the passage of "To Donatus" that Longfellow quotes in the second "Christian Fathers" lecture: "His essence is too bright and dazzling to be visible, too pure and spiritual to be perceived by contact."[70]

67. Justin, "First Apology," 91.
68. Origen, *Against Celsus*, 162.
69. Origen, *Against Celsus*, 168; 177.
70. Cyprian, "To Donatus," quoted in Longfellow, "The Christian Fathers," 21.

THE CHRISTIAN FATHERS IN LONGFELLOW 131

Moreover, to those who might doubt that the light of which the Fathers speak is indeed God himself, Origen writes: "We endeavor to form our scheme of divinity upon this most excellent model, who sometimes tells us, that *God is light, and in him is no Darkness at all.*"[71] Among Longfellow's Fathers, Justin, Cyprian, and Origen seem to agree that there is a light that shines from, and is, God himself. Further, they explain that Christ's ultimate form, once he has accomplished the work of redemption, is one wherein the divine nature can clearly be seen, and what is seen is *light*. Finally, they warn that this light can be overpowering for those who are not prepared to see it. God's essence may even be too dazzling to be seen at all.

Though divine light is spoken of as belonging to and identical with God, Longfellow's Fathers make clear that it is something with which human beings may shine too, if properly united with God through passion-rejecting ascesis on earth or perfection in heaven. When discussing the Transfiguration in *Against Celsus*, Origen not only writes, as we have seen, that Christ then "display[ed] the Glory of his Raiment," but also that "Moses and Elijah" shone with "Heavenly Lustre" as well when they conversed with the transfigured Christ on the mountaintop.[72] For Origen, then, the Transfiguration is something of a meeting point of the doctrines of incarnation, deification, and divine light. First, the divine light with which Christ shines on the mountain reveals his twofold natures: he possesses a human nature that is united to a glorious divine nature. The divine light with which Moses and Elijah shine on the mountain reveals the highest end of human nature—to be united to and shine with that same divine nature that belongs to Christ. It is no small claim that Hawthorne makes when he says that Longfellow's true triumph is the "transfiguration" of Evangeline, whether or not he was aware, as we now are, of Longfellow's familiarity with the doctrine of divine light in the Fathers.

St Cyprian, too, thinks that divine light can be perceived by and shine forth from some humans. In "On the Lord's Prayer," he writes, "Christ is the true sun and the true day, as the worldly sun and the worldly day depart, when we pray for the advent of Christ, which shall give us the grace of everlasting light."[73] By the grace of God, Christians may be given an "everlasting light" that is distinct from the "worldly sun and worldly day." This light, given by grace, will make it so that "the children of light have the day even in the night."[74] Further on in the same passage, in a phrase

71. Origen, *Against Celsus*, 178.
72. Origen, *Against Celsus*, 163.
73. Cyprian, *Treatises*, 422.
74. Cyprian, *Treatises*, 422.

reminiscent of ethical deification described earlier in the treatise, Cyprian writes, "New-Created and new-born of the Spirit by the mercy of God, let us imitate what we shall one day be. Since in the kingdom we shall possess day alone, without intervention of night, let us so watch in the night as if in the daylight."[75] Even those who have not yet been fully illumined by everlasting light should act as if they were, for one day they shall be so illumined. As a scriptural support for this language of light and illumination, Cyprian quotes the book of Isaiah:

> By Isaiah the Lord also reminds us and teaches us similar things, saying, "Loosen every knot of iniquity, release the oppressions of contracts which have no power, let the troubled go into peace, and break every unjust engagement. Break thy bread to the hungry, and bring the poor that are without shelter into thy house. When thou seest the naked, clothe him; and despise not those of the same family and race of thyself. Then shall thy light break forth in season, and thy raiment shall spring forth speedily; and righteousness shall go before thee, and the glory of God shall surround thee."[76]

According to Cyprian, deeds of kindness and mercy, especially to the poor and needy, lead to being illumined with and clothed in divine light. This biblically derived doctrine of divine light, and how to receive it, will be central to our explication of the second keynote passage of *Evangeline*: the transfiguration scene in 2.5.

St John Chrysostom also writes of the heavenly light of the saints in his "Homily of Praise on the holy martyrs Juventinus and Maximinus," which Longfellow quotes in Latin at the end of part 1 of "The Christian Fathers." Chrysostom begins this homily by contrasting the incorrupt, eternal treasures of the saints with earthly, perishing things:

> Of such a nature is the Church's treasure, containing young and old pearls. But the beauty of all of them is one and the same. Their bloom doesn't fade, it doesn't flow away with time. By nature this brilliance doesn't succumb to age's rust. For whereas physical riches fade and pass away with the passage of time—indeed, clothes wear out and houses collapse and jewelry rusts, and with time the entire essence of these riches we see and touch perishes and vanishes—in the case of the spiritual treasures it is not like this. Rather, the martyrs always and perpetually remain brilliant in equal vigor and youth, brightly reflecting the glory of their innate brilliance.[77]

---

75. Cyprian, *Treatises*, 423.
76. Cyprian, *Treatises*, 420.
77. John Chrysostom, "Juventinus and Maximinus," 91–92.

Central to this passage is Chrysostom's description of the "brilliance" of the martyrs whom he is praising. This brilliance is unchanged by time, perpetually remains, and is, in fact, "innate" to the martyrs, reflected from within them. Thus, according to Chrysostom, the saints shine with the heavenly glory that Origen describes as shining from Christ's divine nature. Of course, this should not surprise us, having examined the doctrine of deification in Longfellow's Fathers. If humans can be united with the divine nature, and if the divine nature shines with celestial light, then the deified human will, like Christ, shine with celestial light as well. It is important to stress that Chrysostom calls this brilliance of the saints "innate." It is reflected from them because it is innate to them—the divine light is now, in a sense, *theirs*, for they have been united to God through their ascesis of martyrdom, and now shine with his light.

The above paragraph, which Longfellow directly quotes, in Latin, in "The Christian Fathers," is not the only description of the divine light of the martyrs in the sermon. In his description of the martyrdom of Juventinus and Maximinus, Chrysostom writes, "in thick darkness the light-sources were escorted out and beheaded."[78] The Martyrs are now "light-sources," and Chrysostom goes on to explain why they are worthy of the title: "It is fitting to address them together as pillars, and lookouts, and guard towers, and light sources, and bulls. For . . . like light-sources they drove away the darkness of impiety."[79] Though "light-source" is one of several metaphors he uses for the martyrs, it is the only one that has a literal analogue, given Chrysostom's description of the innate, celestial brilliance of the martyrs in the first paragraph of the homily.

In Longfellow's Fathers divine light shines from God's nature; it is seen in Christ because of his divine nature; and it can be participated in by, and shine out from, those Christians who are united to the divine nature through martyrdom, care for the poor and needy, or some other ascetic activity. Longfellow's Fathers never describe immature Christians or non-Christians shining in this way.

There is one final way that divine light is described in Longfellow's Fathers: as a guide to the Christian who is journeying toward union with God. Such a description is found in Synesius's "Hymn 1" before the final scene of deification through divine union that we examined earlier. Synesius writes:

> Happy is the one who, after
> Fate and labor, after bitter
> Anxious cares of earthly living,

---

78. John Chrysostom, "Juventinus and Maximinus," 98.
79. John Chrysostom, "Juventinus and Maximinus," 99.

> Lets noetic impulse lead him
> To deep seas seen in light divine.
> Toil it is to rise above all
> On the pinions of the heart, led
> Ever upward, ever praying.
> By a sudden leap the *nous*, the
> Rushing intellect, can mount, but
> Only if Another lights his
> Way and strengthens his affections.
> For, unbroken sunbeams shining
> On the path laid out before you,
> You will fly to that noetic
> Country, to the source of Beauty.
> Come, my soul, that you may drink from
> Heaven, greatest of all fountains.
> Now entreat the one who made you;
> He it is who gave you life. O
> Leave to earth this earthly worship.
> Quick, unite now with the Father:
> Thus shall God with God go dancing.[80]

Synesius describes divine light in two ways: first, it is that by which, in the fifth line, the intellect, or *nous*, can see the inviting "deep seas" of the heavenly realms. Thus, for Synesius, divine light is to heaven what visible light is to earth: it is that by which the objects in that realm are seen. But divine light can also shine down from heaven to lead the Christian on the path to heaven: "unbroken sunbeams" illuminate "the path laid out before" the ascending *nous*. Given the context of this quotation, we can see that these are no mere earthly sunbeams, for they are provided by "Another," God, who "lights [the] way" to divine union and deification.[81] The human that Synesius describes, though not deified until the final lines, is already quite mature; he or she has gone through "Fate," "labor," and "the bitter / Anxious

---

80. Synesius, "Hymn 1," ll. 112–34, my translation.

81. Synesius's "Homily 2" provides a helpful description of this "light divine": "It is a holy night that brings light to those that are accursed, a light greater than that wherewith the sun has ever illumined the day. Lo, it is not holy that even the fairest thing upon the earth should be compared to the Creator; but that light which illumines souls and lit up the perceptible sun is no piece of Creation [*oude demiourgema*, literally 'not a demiurge-made thing']. It exists through the harmony of its present blessedness, that will bless us in the future." Synesius, *Essays and Hymns*, 2:370.

cares of earthly living." When we examine *Evangeline*, we will see that Longfellow's descriptions of the protagonist's struggles and her encounters with celestial light are quite similar to those we find in these final lines of Synesisus's hymn.

For Longfellow's Fathers, then, divine light is God, and shines from his divine nature wherever it may be found—it shines from Christ's divine nature, from the divine nature of the deified human, and from heaven itself in order to lead the journeying Christian to God. And this illumination of the mature Christian by divine light is made possible by two previous metaphysical doctrines: first, the doctrine of the incarnation, according to which Christ united human and divine natures in his single person, becoming an archetype of proper divine-human union; and second, the doctrine of deification, wherein the sinful human turns to Christ, is purified, strengthened, and perfected by the sacraments and a life of godlike virtue, and at last unites with divine nature and receives the characteristics of God, which is her proper end. It is only because of Christ's incarnation that she can be deified, and it is only because she has been deified that the light with which she shines can properly be called divine, heavenly, or celestial light.[82]

## Deification and Divine Light in Longfellow's Dante Notes and John Endicott

In order to show that Longfellow was indeed aware of and capable of articulating the doctrines discussed in this chapter, it will be helpful to examine two places where these doctrines show up in Longfellow's non-patristic, post-1840s work. In Longfellow's 1867 notes on the *Divine Comedy* we find a clear description of deification and divine light. Longfellow begins his translation of the first canto of *Paradiso* thus:

> The glory of him who moveth everything
> Doth penetrate the universe, and shine
> In one part more and in another less.

---

82. We have already examined in chapter 3 why these three doctrines are so interrelated. It is important to note that there are longstanding theological and philosophical traditions that dismiss Christ's incarnation from the mix, and preach the doctrines of human deification and divine light on their own. However, these traditions are not, in the strict sense, *Christian* traditions. Though the Christian tradition—in which Longfellow's Fathers are firmly entrenched—does teach, as Mosheim has described, that all men partake in God's nature insofar as they are made in his image and likeness, the Christian tradition also teaches that man's corruption and sin make any sort of Christless deification impossible. This is made most clear, as discussed earlier, by Athanasius in his *On the Incarnation*, a text that may or may not have been familiar to Longfellow.

> Within that heaven which most his light receives
> Was I...[83]

In this first canto concerning the glory-filled, heavenly realm, Dante describes a process of "transhumanization" wherein Beatrice and he are illumined and lifted by God's light:

> But I beheld [the sun] sparkle round about
> Like iron that comes molten from the fire;
> And suddenly it seemed that day to day
> Was added, as if He who has the power
> Had with another sun the heaven adorned.
> With eyes upon the everlasting wheels
> Stood Beatrice all intent, and I, on her
> Fixing my vision from above removed....
> To represent transhumanise in words
> Impossible were; the example, then, suffice
> Him for whom Grace the experience reserves.
> If I was merely what of me thou newly
> Createdst, Love who governest the heaven,
>   Thou knowest, who didst lift me with thy light.[84]

In his note on line 141 of this remarkable canto, Longfellow quotes from Dante's *Convito*, III. 2:

> The human soul, ennobled by the highest power, that is by reason, partakes of the divine nature in the manner of an eternal Intelligence; because the soul is so ennobled by that sovereign power, and denuded of matter, that the divine light shines in it as in an angel; and therefore man has been called by the philosophers a divine animal.[85]

In this quotation, which alludes to 2 Peter, we can discern the basic doctrines of deification and divine light. The human soul, through reason, "partakes of the divine nature," and, consequently, shines with divine light like an angel, like the resurrected Christ described by Origen, or like the martyrs described by Chrysostom. While this is not a description of these doctrines in Longfellow's own words, it is a philosophical quotation selected

---

83. Longfellow, *Divine Comedy*, 493.
84. Longfellow, *Divine Comedy*, 494.
85. Longfellow, *Divine Comedy*, 611.

by Longfellow himself to help his readers understand Dante's description of the shining souls in paradise. At the very least, this shows that Longfellow was, late in life, still familiar with Christian texts that described deification and divine light, and still offered such texts to his readers as helpful for their understanding of a master like Dante. Also in this quotation we can discern a more scholastic, contemplative approach to deification. It is by "reason," Dante says—not by the active ascesis that Cyprian, Chrysostom, and Mosheim describe—that the soul can partake in the divine nature and thus be illumined by divine light.

Soon after Longfellow translated Dante's *Divine Comedy*, he published a play that he had been working on for many years, *John Endicott*, which dramatizes the clash between Quakers and Puritans in colonial New England. Longfellow returns to the language of 2 Peter in a scene where the fiery Quaker Edith encourages her persecuted companions by quoting the martyr William Leddra:

> I am persuaded that God's armor of Light,
> As it is loved and lived in, will preserve you . . .
> And as the flowing of the ocean fills
> Each creek and branch thereof, and then retires,
> Leaving behind a sweet and wholesome savor;
> So doth the virtue and the life of God
> Flow evermore into the hearts of those
> Whom he hath made partakers of his nature.[86]

Here again Longfellow joins the deification language of 2 Peter with the language of divine light. According to Leddra, God both preserves his followers in "the armor of Light," and sends his own virtue and life into those who participate in his nature. He uses two figures to describe this light: the ebbing and "flowing of the ocean," and "a sweet and wholesome savor." In Leddra's words we may discern a principle similar to that of Russell in chapter 3, namely that one receives the characteristics—in this case light, virtue, and life—of that in which one participates. Dante says that it is "impossible" "to represent transhumanise in words," but following Cyprian, Arnobius, and Origen before him, Longfellow uses natural imagery to help his readers discern divine experiences. Thus we see that Longfellow retained his interest in deification and divine light late into his career, placing deification language in both his critical notes and his dramatic works.

---

86. Longfellow, *Works*, 7:313.

We will see in our examination of *Evangeline* in the next two chapters that the path that Evangeline takes to deification and illumination is not the path of reason or academic speculation, but instead that of the ascetic activity of "labor and patience;" the rejection of sinful passion; the miraculous partaking in divine sensations that help her discern, through nature, the right path; and the active charity of her "work of affection." In the spiritual world of *Evangeline*, deification and illumination with divine light are the goal of the Christian life, and the path to deification and illumination is the "mystical" path described by Cyprian, Origen, Chrysostom, Mosheim, and, to an extent, Channing, not the academic path of Dante's *Convito*. Before we connect *Evangeline* back to Longfellow's theological sources, we will examine in depth the theological teachings, the spiritual practices and experiences, and the religious language in *Evangeline*. We will then be ready to discern in these doctrines, experiences, and language the influences first of Channing and, at the poem's culmination, of the unique vision of the Fathers.[87]

---

87. In using the word "influence," I inevitably must mention Harold Bloom's famous theory of poetic influence. Bloom gives a helpful history of the changing meaning of the word "influence" in the history of criticism, from Johnson's more basic definition to his own complex understanding of influence as necessarily involving a misreading of the influencing precursor. I do not intend to follow Bloom into positing this necessary misreading, but find his description of Johnson's theory of influence an apt description of the Fathers' influence on Longfellow. "Johnson," Bloom writes, "in 1755 defines influence as being either astral or moral, saying of the latter 'Ascendant power; power of directing or modifying.'" Bloom, *Anxiety of Influence*, 27. As we will see in more detail in chapter 6, it was the doctrine of divine light in the Fathers that especially directed and modified Longfellow's language about the illumination of his heroine.

# 5

# The Religious Elements of *Evangeline*

Now that we have explored in depth the two major theological influences on Longfellow—American Unitarianism and patristic theology—we are finally in a position to give our undivided attention to *Evangeline*. Our ultimate goal is to present a new interpretation of the keynote passages in light of the Unitarian and patristic doctrines of deification and divine light. This interpretation will be undertaken in chapter 6. First of all, however, it will be helpful to explore the religious elements of *Evangeline* as a whole, which will enable us to present an account of the spiritual world of *Evangeline*, focusing on the spiritual logic and basic soteriology at work in *Evangeline*'s cosmos. This larger context will then inform our interpretation of the keynote passages.

We can break the religious elements of the poem into three major categories: (1) theological teachings, in which the narrator or a character within the narrative presents clear religious propositions, often in homiletic form; (2) spiritual practices and experiences, wherein a character's physical, emotional, or intellectual adherence to the teachings of the church, along with the experience of spiritual consolation or frustration, often mediated miraculously through nature, are described; and (3) religious language, including allusion and figuration, wherein the narrator or characters use religious terms or figures in their descriptions of phenomena.

## Theological Teaching in Part 1

Though the theological teachings in part 2 will concern us more in the course of this chapter than those in part 1, those teachings that are presented in part 1 are precursors of those in part 2, not so much in content, but in how they influence those to whom they are taught. There are three major theological sections of part 1: the theology of the narrator in the introduction, of the notary in 1.3, and in the sermon of Father Felician in 1.4. Together these last two passages reveal the typical theological beliefs of the Acadians.

In the last stanza of the introduction, the narrator addresses his readers:

> Ye who believe in affection that hopes, and endures, and is patient,
> Ye who believe in the beauty and strength of a woman's devotion,
> List to the mournful tradition, still sung by the pines of the forest;
> List to a tale of love in Acadie, home of the happy.[1]

The teaching here is not so much argued for as it is implied and even assumed. Further, Longfellow tells us for whom this story is told. It is for those who "believe in affection that hopes, and endures, and is patient"—in other words, for those who are familiar with and convinced of the words of St Paul in 1 Corinthians 13, that love "is patient . . . hopes all things, endures all things."[2] And it is, further and more specifically, for those who "believe in the beauty and strength of a woman's devotion." In these lines Longfellow reveals both what the narrative will be about, and what teaching will be presented—it will be about a woman who is devoted, whose affection hopes, endures, and is patient. Further, it will teach that such affection is admirable, and that such devotion is both beautiful and strong. In assuming that the ideal reader already believes these two things, the poem does not attempt to convince, but seeks instead to explore and reinforce these teachings. Longfellow also puts himself squarely in the Romantic camp at the outset in that he presents nature as the mediator of these teachings, for it is "the pines of the forest" that sing the "tradition" of *Evangeline*.

The next two instances of theological teaching are presented not by the narrator, but by the characters themselves. In 1.3, René Leblanc, the notary, is introduced:

> Father of twenty children was he, and more than a hundred
> Children's children rode on his knee, and heard his great watch tick.
> Four long years in the times of war had he languished a captive,
> Suffering much in an old French fort as the friend of the English.
> Now, though warier grown, without all guile or suspicion,
> Ripe in wisdom was he, but patient, and simple, and childlike.

---

1. Longfellow, "Evangeline," ll. 16–19.
2. 1 Corinthians 13:4, 7 (ESV).

> He was beloved by all, and most of all by the children;
> For he told the tales of the Loup-garou in the forest,
> And of the goblin that came in the night to water the horses,
> . . .
> With whatever else was writ in the lore of the village.[3]

When this storyteller and lore-keeper is asked to contribute to the conversation of Basil and Benedict about the British ships, Leblanc replies:

> "Gossip enough have I heard, yet am never the wiser,
> And what their errand be I know not better than others.
> Yet am I not of those who imagine some evil intention
> Brings them here, for we are at peace, and why then molest us?"
> "God's name!" shouted the hasty and somewhat irascible blacksmith,
> "Must we in all things look for the how, and the why, and the wherefore?
> Daily injustice is done, and might is the right of the strongest!"
> But without heeding his warmth, continued the notary public,—
> "Man is unjust, but God is just; and finally justice
> Triumphs; and well I remember a story, that often consoled me,
> When as a captive I lay in the old French fort at Port Royal."
> This was the old man's favorite tale, and he loved to repeat it
> When his neighbors complained that any injustice was done them.[4]

Leblanc presents the "moral" of his story, namely that "God is just; and finally justice / Triumphs," before he recounts the narrative, which is about a servant who is falsely accused and hanged for stealing her mistress's pearls. The girl is hanged in front of a great statue of lady Justice, and just as she dies, lighting strikes the statue and knocks loose its left hand, which, when examined, is found to contain a bird's nest into which the real thief, a magpie, has woven the pearls.[5] Thus the second major teaching of the poem is presented, namely that justice will triumph, but not necessarily before injustice destroys the life of the innocent.

The next major theological teaching in part 1 is found in Father Felician's sermon in part 1, canto 4, preached to quell the violent confrontation between Basil the blacksmith and the British soldiers:

> In the midst of the strife and tumult of angry confusion,
> Lo! the door of the chancel opened, and Father Felician

---

3. Longfellow, "Evangeline," ll. 273–81, 287.
4. Longfellow, "Evangeline," ll. 293–305.
5. Longfellow, "Evangeline," ll. 313–25.

> Entered, with serious mien, and ascended the steps of the altar.
> Raising his reverent hand, with a gesture he awed into silence
> All that clamorous throng; and thus he spake to his people;
> Deep were his tones, and solemn, in accent measure and mournful
> Spake he, as, after the tocsin's alarum, distinctly the clock strikes;
> "What is this that ye do, my children? what madness has seized you?
> Forty years of my life have I labored among you, and taught you,
> Not in word alone, but in deed, to love one another!
> Is this the fruit of my toils, of my vigils and prayers and privations?
> Have you so soon forgotten all lessons of love and forgiveness?
> This is the house of the prince of Peace, and would you profane it
> Thus with violent deed and hearts overflowing with hatred?
> Lo! where the crucified Christ from his cross is gazing upon you!
> See! In those sorrowful eyes what meekness and holy compassion!
> Hark! How those lips still repeat the prayer, 'O Father forgive them!'
> Let us repeat that prayer in the hour when the wicked assail us,
> Let us repeat it now, and say, 'O Father, forgive them!'"[6]

Father Felician's message is as simple as Leblanc's, but more immediate and practical. It is a simple lesson "of love and forgiveness" which teaches the Acadians to "repeat the prayer" of Christ on the cross "in the hour when the wicked assail" them. Though this teaching prescribes more action than Leblanc's did, it assumes the same principle of non-resistance to oppression and injustice. Nowhere in the theology of the elders of Grand-Pré is there a revolutionary or violent spirit.

## Spiritual Practice and Experience in Part 1

The spiritual practices described in part 1 of *Evangeline* are largely those of a typical Roman Catholic community in the eighteenth century. The descriptions of these practices begin in 1.1, when Father Felician passes "down the street . . . and the children / paused in their play to kiss the hand he extended to bless them."[7] As these gestures of respect to the priest are being performed, "from the belfry / softly the Angelus sounded."[8] This opening scene, where the "simple Acadian farmers" dwell together "in the love of

---

6. Longfellow, "Evangeline," ll. 460–78.
7. Longfellow, "Evangeline," ll. 33–34.
8. Longfellow, "Evangeline," ll. 48–49.

God and man,"⁹ is one that is organized around the priest as the central authority figure and the church as the central institution of village life. Further, even the time-keeping of the village is here ecclesially centered, for it is not the village clock that sounds out the hour, but the church belfry which sounds the Angelus, the evening prayer in honor of the Annunciation. Chevalier insightfully ties the presence of the Angelus early on in the poem with what will be a recurrent theme: Evangeline as the "model woman," just as Mary was the model woman. Further, the words of the Angelus are the words of Gabriel the archangel, announcing the good news, or "evangel," to Mary. In the Angelus, then, according to Chevalier, both the names of Gabriel and Evangeline are implied and anticipated.[10]

When we meet Evangeline in canto 1, we find that she is fully integrated into the Catholic practices of the village. As she walks home from church on "Sunday morn," Evangeline carries "her chaplet of beads and her missal," physical representations of Catholic devotion.[11] She is dressed in a "kirtle of blue" as well, a color that associates her, again, with Mary.[12] Not only her possessions, but also her body itself reveals her devotion:

> But a celestial brightness—a more ethereal beauty—
> Shone on her face and encircled her form, when, after confession
> Homeward serenely she walked with God's benediction upon her.
> When she had passed, it seemed like the ceasing of exquisite music.[13]

First, we are shown that Evangeline carries beads and a missal, indicators of her involvement in personal prayer and communal worship, respectively. Then, we are shown that her "face" and "form" themselves are indicators of her devotion, particularly of her participation in the sacrament of confession. This is the first time in the poem that we are introduced to "celestial brightness," or "celestial light," which will appear several times throughout the poem, most prominently in part 2, canto 5, the exact "opposite side" of the poem. Chevalier sees parallels between Evangeline's celestial brightness and the promise in Revelation 22:16 that the "righteous [shall] shine forth as the sun." Chevalier warns, however, that in canto 1 Longfellow describes not an eschatological scene of final perfection, but an Edenic purity soon to experience a Fall.[14]

9. Longfellow, "Evangeline," ll. 52–53.
10. Chevalier, *Semiotics, Romanticism, and Scriptures*, 148.
11. Longfellow, "Evangeline," ll. 71–74.
12. Longfellow, "Evangeline," 1. 75.
13. Longfellow, "Evangeline," ll. 78–81.
14. Chevalier, *Semiotics, Romanticism, and Scriptures*, 184–86.

While the word "encircled" gives a clear enough image, there is a prepositional ambiguity in the phrase "shone on her face." Is the light something that comes from without and rests upon Evangeline, as "God's benediction" does in the next line, or is it a light that emanates from within Evangeline herself?[15] The preposition "on" neither excludes nor enforces a sense of emanation; it will not be until part 2 that Longfellow will clarify how exactly celestial light is related to Evangeline's body and soul. To return to our terminology from chapter 3, we can at least say that Evangeline here is visibly *illumined by* divine light, whether or not she *shines with* it. Whatever the case, it is important to establish that the part 1, canto 1, experience of celestial light encircling the face and form is directly related to the participation in the sacrament under the authority of the Roman Catholic ecclesiastical hierarchy.[16] In other words, Evangeline is revealed here as a good Catholic who experiences an exceptional effect of her orthopraxy—illumination by celestial light.

Later in 1.1 we find the next instance of spiritual practices and experiences, this time of a more humorous and less orthodox variety:

> Many a youth, as he knelt in church and opened his missal
> Fixed his eyes upon [Evangeline] as the saint of his deepest devotion;
> Happy was he who might touch her hand or the hem of her garment.[17]

Here we find a mildly erotic spiritual practice carried out by the youths of the village,[18] wherein they gaze upon Evangeline, instead of the saints, with "deepest devotion." Evangeline, who has been associated with Mary at least twice before in the poem, is now treated like Mary by her peers. Further, she is treated like Jesus, as her admirers wish to "touch . . . the hem of her

---

15. We will see this ambiguity and interplay between within/without language throughout the narrative, not only in relation to light, but also in relation to love.

16. Higgins has pointed out that though Longfellow is careful to keep the Catholic traditions and hierarchical structure intact from the priest downward, there is a curious lack of mention of any bishop. To what authority, we might ask, does Father Felician answer? Though Felician is clearly a Roman Catholic priest, the upper echelons of ecclesiastical authority are effectively absent from the poem. See Higgins, "Evangeline's Mission," 547.

17. Longfellow, "Evangeline," ll. 105–7.

18. Chevalier says of this passage that "the scene under discussion shows no evidence of . . . virtuous conduct." Chevalier, *Semiotics, Romanticism, and Scriptures*, 235. Though it is clear that Evangeline is proving a distraction to these youths in church, Longfellow has already given his readers reason to think that Evangeline shows promise for sainthood; after all, she shines with "celestial brightness" and "ethereal beauty" even at a young age. And we will see in "Evangeline" 2.1 that Evangeline rejects the "devotion" of those youths who once idolized her.

garment," just as the woman with the issue of blood touches Jesus's garment in the Gospel of John. And, more distantly, we might hear an echo of Dante's young pilgrim pining for Beatrice with a love that leads at last, as we learn in the *Commedia*, to Paradise.

Evangeline again is associated with light in canto 3, as she readies her house and herself for sleep:

> Carefully then were covered the embers that glowed on the hearthstone,
> And on the oaken stairs resounded the tread of the farmer.
> Soon with soundless step the foot of Evangeline followed.
> Up the staircase moved a luminous space in the darkness,
> Lighted less by the lamp than the shining face of the maiden.[19]

If there were any doubt that Evangeline herself was being described as shining with light in canto 1, here things are made more clear: she outshines even the lamp she holds in the darkness.

The singing of religious songs is another important spiritual practice in Grand-Pré. Father Felician teaches the children "the hymns of the church and the plain song,"[20] there is "music" and "dance" at the "joyous feast of the Patron Saint of the village,"[21] and Benedict Bellafontaine sings "Carols of Christmas"[22] with Evangeline by the winter hearth. Additionally, after Father Felician preaches his sermon of love and forgiveness to the men imprisoned in the church, he leads them in an "evening service" in which they sing the "Ave Maria."[23] Finally, as the men are led out of the church to the shore in 1.5, they sing:

> with tremulous lips a chant of the Catholic Missions:—
> "Sacred heart of the Savior! O inexhaustible fountain!
> Fill our hearts this day with strength and submission and patience!"[24]

Though it is not always an explicitly religious practice, submission and obedience to one's elders is a prominent practice in part 1 of *Evangeline*, and is followed by positive results. We have already seen that submission to her priest in the sacrament of confession results in Evangeline's being illumined by celestial light. In part 1, canto 4, Evangeline also finds great consolation

---

19. Longfellow, "Evangeline," ll. 358–61.
20. Longfellow, "Evangeline," l. 122.
21. Longfellow, "Evangeline," ll. 111–13.
22. Longfellow, "Evangeline," l. 207.
23. Longfellow, "Evangeline," ll. 482–84.
24. Longfellow, "Evangeline," ll. 547–49.

in ministering to others and heeding the notary's words about justice as she waits for the release of the men from the church:

> Thus did Evangeline wait at her Father's door, as the sunset
> Threw the long shadows of trees o'er the broad ambrosial meadows.
> Ah! On her spirit within a deeper shadow had fallen,
> And from the fields of her soul a fragrance celestial ascended,—
> Charity, meekness, love, and hope, and forgiveness, and patience!
> Then, all forgetful of self, she wandered into the village,
> Cheering with looks and words the mournful hearts of the women. . . .
>
> In the dead of night, she heard the disconsolate rain fall
> Loud on the withered leaves of the sycamore tree by the window.
> Keenly the lightning flashed; and the voice of the echoing thunder
> Told her that God was in heaven, and governed the world he created!
> Then she remembered the tales she had heard of the justice of Heaven;
> Soothed was her troubled soul, and she peacefully slumbered till morning.[25]

In the first stanza, Evangeline—despite her fear—draws on her inner virtues, which Longfellow calls a "celestial fragrance," and ministers to the women of the village, over whom the "shadow of fear" has fallen. But in the second stanza, Evangeline is worried. However, she receives, in the dead of night, consolation from nature itself, which reinforces the theological teaching presented to her the night before by the notary—namely, that the justice of Heaven will triumph. Evangeline's "troubled soul" is "soothed" and she sleeps "peacefully" at remembering this teaching. There is no hint of doubt in her, or of questioning God's plan or goodness. This spirit in Evangeline matches that of her earlier serenity while walking home from confession.

This is hardly the only time in the poem that Evangeline is consoled or otherwise taught spiritual truths through nature. In canto 1, Evangeline and Gabriel together admire Basil at work, and see a spiritual truth in the sparks that fly from his forge:

> Oft on autumnal eves, when without in the gathering darkness
> Bursting with light seemed the smithy, through every cranny and crevice,
> Warm by the forge within they watched the laboring bellows,
> And as its panting ceased, and the sparks expired in the ashes,
> Merrily laughed, and said they were nuns going into the chapel.[26]

25. Longfellow, "Evangeline," ll. 496–503, 518–23.
26. Longfellow, "Evangeline," ll. 129–33.

This description of the sparks is an allusion to the apocryphal book of the Wisdom of Solomon, which, in chapter 3, says that "the souls of the righteous . . . will shine forth and they will run about like sparks through straw."[27] Implied here is an association of the devout nun, "going into the chapel," with the shining forth promised in Wisdom of Solomon, a subtle foreshadowing of Evangeline's own shining with celestial light, while a nun, in the 2.5 keynote.

Evangeline is not the only character who finds consolation and strength through submission and obedience to an elder. This is also seen in the reaction of the imprisoned men to Father Felician's sermon in part 1, canto 4:

> Few were his words of rebuke, but deep in the heart of his people
> Sank they, and sobs of contrition succeeded the passionate outbreak,
> While they repeated his prayer, and said, "O Father, forgive them!"
>
> Then came the evening service. The tapers gleamed from the altar.
> Fervent and deep was the voice of the priest, and the people responded,
> Not with their lips alone, but their hearts; and the Ave Maria
> Sang they, and fell on their knees, and their souls, with devotion translated
> Rose on the ardor of prayer, like Elijah ascending to heaven.[28]

Thus, in canto 4 we see two rather climactic instances of Acadians submitting to and obeying the guidance of their elders and their pastor. These acts of submission and obedience, far from leading to confusion, doubt, or apathy, quickly have the desired results; when an elder's words of consolation are heeded, consolation is soon found. When one is told to repent and forgive, "contrition," forgiveness, and "devotion" immediately follow. Simply put, in the Grand-Pré of *Evangeline* part 1, spiritual practices *work*.

## Religious Language in Part 1

Before moving on to part 2 of *Evangeline*, it behooves us to look for a moment at religious language in part 1. Most of this language occurs within similes made by either the narrator or the characters. The first simile of this kind is found in the first stanza of the introduction:

> This is the forest primeval. The murmuring pines and the hemlocks
> Bearded with moss, and in garments green, indistinct in the twilight,

---

27. Wisdom of Solomon 3:1–7 (Orthodox Study Bible).
28. Longfellow, "Evangeline," ll. 479–86.

> Stand like druids of Eld, with voices sad and prophetic,
> Stand like harpers hoar, with beards that rest on their bosoms.[29]

This is one of the only instances in part 1 where an object is compared in a simile to a non-Judeo-Christian subject. Still, it is among Longfellow's most famous images, and casts a shadow over the entire work, for the "pines of the forest"[30] sing Evangeline's whole story. All that comes after the introduction is placed in the mouths of the trees that appear like pagan druids, not Christian saints or prophets.[31]

Most of the Judeo-Christian figures appear in descriptions of village life. The Acadians' lives are "like rivers that water the woodlands . . . reflecting an image of heaven."[32] The "columns of blue smoke" which rise "over the roofs of the village" are like "clouds of incense ascending."[33] On Sunday morning, the "holy sounds" of "the bell" are "sprinkled [in] the air, as the priest with his hyssop / Sprinkles the congregation."[34] Even the Bellefontaines' beehives are

> overhung by a penthouse
> Such as the traveller sees in regions remote by the roadside
> Built o'er a box for the poor, or the blessed image of Mary.[35]

Finally, the stars at which the young lovers gaze are "the forget-me-nots of the angels."[36] In these figures of the smoke, hives, and stars we see Longfellow give religious significance to even the natural objects in and around Grand-Pré. And the narrator is not alone in comparing non-religious objects to religious ones. The villagers call the light of Evangeline's face "the sunshine of Saint Eulalie,"[37] and, as seen above, Evangeline and Gabriel

---

29. Longfellow, "Evangeline," ll. 1–4.
30. Longfellow, "Evangeline," l. 18.
31. It is upon similes like this that Chevalier bases his argument that Longfellow mixes the Romantic worship of nature with Christian imagery, thus complicating and creating tension in the poem at a deep semiotic level. Whether or not there is a tension between the love of nature and the love of Christ is debatable. Dante provides a good example of a poet who, through his use of the *via affirmativa*, portrays Christian doctrine and the natural world as in league to lead the human soul to God.
32. Longfellow, "Evangeline," ll. 10–11.
33. Longfellow, "Evangeline," ll. 49–50.
34. Longfellow, "Evangeline," ll. 71–73.
35. Longfellow, "Evangeline," ll. 87–89.
36. Longfellow, "Evangeline," l. 351. The metaphor of stars as flowers is a recurring one in Longfellow's poetry. It is first seen in the poem "Flowers" in Longfellow's 1839 collection *Voices of the Night*.
37. Longfellow, "Evangeline," l. 144.

allude to the Wisdom of Solomon in their comparison of the "sparks" from Basil's forge that "expire ... in the ashes" to "nuns going into the chapel."[38] Thus in part 1, Longfellow not only describes Evangeline as shining with celestial light, but puts in her mouth passages from scripture that describe such illumination.

Old Testament figures are prominent in part 1. At the beginning of canto 2, the "wild winds of September / Wrestle ... the trees of the forest, as Jacob of old with the angel."[39] As Evangeline looks into the night sky at the end of 1.3, she sees

> serenely the moon pass
> Forth from the folds of a cloud, and one star follow her footsteps,
> As out of Abraham's tent young Ishmael wandered with Hagar.[40]

At the end of canto 4, as Evangeline waits for the men imprisoned in the church, she watches the sunset:

> Down sank the great red sun, and in golden, glimmering vapors
> Veiled the light of his face, like the Prophet descending from Sinai.[41]

This is the third simile in so many cantos that compares natural phenomena to the actions of Old Testament characters. The last two of these metaphors also implicate Evangeline herself in their symbolism; the moon which "serenely ... pass[es]" mimics the earlier action and demeanor of Evangeline after confession, who "serenely ... walk[s]" homeward. The sun, which resembles the prophet Moses in that both have shining faces, also resembles Evangeline, whose face, too, sometimes shines with "celestial light." It should by now be clear that light, both earthly and celestial, is central to the overall imagery of *Evangeline*. Though Evangeline uniquely shines with celestial light, the people and phenomena around her often shine, glimmer, and spark with earthly light as well.

There is one New Testament figure at the end of 1.5, wherein Father Felician on the shore is compared to St Paul:

> Onward from fire to fire, as from hearth to hearth in his parish,
> Wandered the faithful priest, consoling and blessing and cheering,
> Like unto shipwrecked Paul on Melita's desolate sea-shore.[42]

---

38. Longfellow, "Evangeline," ll. 132–33.
39. Longfellow, "Evangeline," ll. 153–54.
40. Longfellow, "Evangeline," ll. 379–81.
41. Longfellow, "Evangeline," ll. 506–7.
42. Longfellow, "Evangeline," ll. 595–97.

The penultimate religious figure in part 1 is an image from early church history, wherein the burning village appears as a martyr in the pyre:

> Columns of shining smoke uprose, and flashes of flame were
> Thrust through their folds and withdrawn, like the quivering hands of a martyr.[43]

Finally, as the remaining villagers bury Benedict Bellefontaine, and Father Felician intones "the service of sorrow,"

> Lo, with a mournful sound, like the voice of a vast congregation,
> Solemnly answered the sea, and mingled its roar with the dirges.[44]

So ends part 1, and so ends the story of Grand-Pré, as the ocean itself sings along with the villagers, now exiles, who, as we will see in the next section, find a world less friendly to their spiritual strivings than was the land of Acadie.

## Theological Teaching in Part 2

While there are several major theological sections of part 1, part 2 contains only two major theological teachings, the truth of which are tested by Evangeline's spiritual practices and experiences over the course of all five cantos of part 2. The first teaching is presented by Father Felician, and is prompted by Evangeline's rejection of her fellow exiles' suggestion that she should forget Gabriel and marry someone else:

> Then would they say, "Dear child! Why dream and wait for him longer?
> Are there not other youths as fair as Gabriel? Others
> Who have hearts as tender and true, and spirits as loyal?
> Here is Baptiste Leblanc, the notary's son, who has loved thee
> Many a tedious year; come, give him thy hand and be happy!
> Thou art too fair to braid St. Catherine's tresses."
> Then would Evangeline answer, serenely but sadly, "I cannot!
> Whither my heart has gone, there follows my hand, and not elsewhere.
> For when the heart goes on before, like a lamp, and illumines the pathway
> Many things are made clear, that else lay hidden in darkness."[45]

---

43. Longfellow, "Evangeline," ll. 619–20.
44. Longfellow, "Evangeline," ll. 659–60.
45. Longfellow, "Evangeline," ll. 708–17. Here were can see Evangeline's final rejection of the "youths" who idolized her in part 1. Baptiste Leblanc was very likely one of

As far as they go, Evangeline's words are not religious or theological, but are instead a sort of erotic doctrine, which expands upon her earlier assurance to Gabriel on the shore in 1.5: "if we love one another / Nothing, in truth, can harm us, whatever mischances may happen!"[46] In 2.1 Evangeline seems to still be operating on this principle, believing that if she follows her heart after Gabriel, the great mischance that has befallen their love will indeed prove to be temporary, and they will remain unharmed. Further, Evangeline uses a metaphor of light, hearkening back to the earlier images of both natural and celestial light in part 1. The within/without dialectic which first appeared in the ambiguity of the phrase "shone on her face" in part 1, canto 1, is more pronounced in this image, for the heart, which is within the human, "goes on before" and "illumines the pathway," acting as if it were something external to the human.

Father Felician, however, sees in Evangeline's erotic doctrine a theological truth about human perfection:

> Thereupon the priest, her friend and father-confessor,
> Said with a smile, "O daughter! thy God thus speaketh within thee.
> Talk not of wasted affection, affection never was wasted;
> If it enrich not the heart of another, its waters, returning
> Back to their springs, like the rain, shall fill them full of refreshment;
> That which the fountain sends forth returns again to the fountain.[47]
> Patience, accomplish thy labor, accomplish thy work of affection!
> Sorrow and silence are strong, and patient endurance is godlike.
> Therefore accomplish thy labor of love, till the heart is made godlike,
> Purified, strengthened, perfected, and rendered more worthy of heaven!"[48]

Felician begins with the claim that God, not merely she, is "speak[ing] within" Evangeline. This situation of the voice of God "within" Evangeline is

---

those same youths who considered Evangeline the "saint of his deepest devotion" in 1.1. In this passage Evangeline rejects that form of sainthood once and for all.

46. Longfellow, "Evangeline," ll. 559–60.

47. It is likely that Longfellow got this image from Dr. Noyes, a Unitarian minister whom he heard preach while he was writing *Evangeline*. In his journal, on November 15, a month before he finished *Evangeline* part 2, canto 1, Longfellow writes: "Dr. Noyes preached. In his sermon he had this poetic figure: 'Our duties to God ascend like the vapors, not to refresh the sky, but to fall again in the genial showers upon ourselves.'" Longfellow, *Life of Longfellow* 2:63. Though the figure is converted to be about affection, the image of waters being sent forth and returning remains.

48. Longfellow, "Evangeline," ll. 719–27.

a step beyond "God's benediction" resting "upon her" in part 1—Evangeline seems to be slowly uniting with God.

Next, Felician explains how affection works: it is like a fountain whose waters, if they do not "enrich another," return back to the source from which they sprang and "refresh" it. Like Evangeline's previous image of the lamp, Felician's description of affection as a fountain contains a sense of the procession of what is within to something that affects from without. But Felician's image goes another step further, for "that which the fountain sends forth returns again to the fountain." Affection, then, is never wasted, for it either enriches another, or enriches the heart that sent it forth. It is not clear yet, however, what this "enriching" entails, especially for the spring—the heart of Evangeline—to which it may return. In the next section of this brief sermon, Felician drops the metaphor of the fountain and speaks more plainly.

The "work of affection," Felician explains, is the "labor" that Evangeline should "accomplish." This will entail three activities of the heart and body: "sorrow and silence . . . and patient endurance." Sorrow and silence are "strong," and will result in Evangeline being "strengthened." More remarkably, "patient endurance is godlike," and if Evangeline accomplishes her work of affection, her heart will be "made godlike." In the conclusion of his short sermon, Felician describes three other qualities in addition to strength and godlikeness that Evangeline will gain through her work of affection: purification, perfection, and worthiness of heaven.

To summarize, in part 2, canto 1, Father Felician presents a theological teaching in which unrequited affection returns to and enriches the heart through a process in which the heart becomes godlike, strong, purified, perfected, and worthy of heaven through sorrow, silence, and patient endurance. Though each of the five promised qualities (godlikeness, strength, purification, perfection, and worthiness of heaven) are desirable, it is godlikeness that seems the most exalted and surprising of the promised benefits of the work of affection. In part 1, Evangeline is likened to Old Testament saints; but now godlikeness, not just saintliness, is promised her, if only she can "accomplish [her] work of affection."

There is one more theological teaching in part 2, which, while more minor than the 2.1 keynote, is worth examining. As Evangeline waits in sadness at the Jesuit Mission in the Ozark mountains, the priest tries to comfort her with a teaching about faith and passion:

> "Patience!" the priest would say; "have faith, and thy prayer will be answered!
> Look at this delicate plant that lifts its head from the meadow,

> See how its leaves all point to the north, as true as the magnet;
> This is the compass-flower, that the finger of God has suspended
> Here on its fragile stalk, to direct the traveller's journey
> Over the sea-like, pathless, limitless waste of the desert.
> Such in the soul of man is faith. The blossoms of passion,
> Gay and luxuriant flowers, are brighter and fuller of fragrance,
> But they beguile us, and lead us astray, and their odor is deadly.
> Only this humble plant can guide us here, and hereafter
> Crown us with asphodel flowers, that are wet with the dews of nepenthe."[49]

As in Felician's earlier teaching, Evangeline is again exhorted to have patience. But now there is added a teaching about the necessity to reject the allure of passion and to cling to faith, which alone "can guide us." Nature once again teaches spiritual truths, this time through the imagery of the "compass flower." And here we find a clarification of what exactly Evangeline's ascesis entails: true ascetic activity does not reject nature, does not close its eyes to flowers, trees, or prairies, for through these can come "Divine Sensations" to lead the pilgrim aright. True ascetic activity entails the rejection of "the blossoms of passion," which "beguile us, and lead us astray."

## Spiritual Practice and Experience in Part 2

Immediately after Felician's sermon in 2.1, Evangeline submits and obeys:

> Cheered by the good man's words, Evangeline labored and waited.
> Still in her heart she head the funeral dirge of the ocean,
> But with its sound there was mingled a voice that whispered, "Despair not!"
> Thus did that poor soul wander in want and cheerless discomfort
> Bleeding, barefooted, over the shards and thorns of existence.[50]

---

49. Longfellow, "Evangeline," ll. 1216–26.

50. Longfellow, "Evangeline," ll. 728–32. In line 728, there is another echo of Longfellow's *Voices of the Night*, this time from the famous poem "A Psalm of Life," which ends with these lines:

> Let us then be up and doing
> With a heart for any fate
> Still achieving, still pursuing,
> Learn to labor and to wait.

Longfellow, *Complete Poetical Works*, 4.

These lines reveal the difference between the spiritual climate of part 1 and the spiritual climate of part 2. Though Evangeline is "cheered" by the words of Father Felician, as the villagers were in part 1, canto 4, this cheer is temporary. Her future wanderings, which are chronicled in cantos 2–5 of part 2, will be filled with "cheerless discomfort." And the note of consolation offered by nature, which brought her great peace before her exile, is now mixed with "the funeral dirge of the ocean" that ended part 1. Thus Evangeline's spiritual practices in part 2 will be more uncomfortable, more cheerless, than those in part 1. Gone is the world where spiritual practices immediately work. We as readers will have to wander and labor along with Evangeline in order to see whether her practices will ever work, whether the promised godlikeness can ever be attained in the world of exile.

Evangeline's spiritual experiences in part 2 are often connected with the natural world. As we have already seen, the dirge of the ocean in canto 1 whispers, "Despair not!" In the next canto, Evangeline has a mystic vision of Jacob's ladder as she watches the hummingbirds flit through the trees and summer heat on the Mississippi:

> Swinging from its great arms, the trumpet flower and the grapevine
> Hung their ladder of ropes aloft like the ladder of Jacob,
> On whose pendulous stairs the angels ascending, descending,
> Were the swift humming-birds, that flitted from blossom to blossom.
> Such was the vision Evangeline saw as she slumbered beneath it.
> Filled was her heart with love, and the dawn of an opening heaven
> Lighted her soul in sleep with the glory of regions celestial.[51]

Once again Longfellow describes Evangeline as illumined by celestial light, this time specifying that it is "her soul," in particular, that is "lighted." Unbeknownst to her, this is when Gabriel is sailing past. When she awakes from sleep, she tells Father Felician of a premonition that Gabriel is near. He reassures her, using a language reminiscent, once again, of Origen's defense of the visions of the prophets as partaking in "Divine Sensations":

> "Daughter, thy words are not idle, nor are they to me without meaning.
> Feeling is deep and still; and the word that floats on the surface
> Is as the tossing buoy, that betrays where the anchor is hidden.
> Therefore trust to thy heart, and to what the world calls illusions."[52]

---

51. Longfellow, "Evangeline," ll. 820–26.
52. Longfellow, "Evangeline," ll. 851–54.

In the following cantos, Evangeline has many opportunities to heed Felician's advice.

In 2.3, Evangeline is alone in Basil's garden, having learned that Gabriel departed only the previous day:

> Nearer and round about her, the manifold flowers of the garden
> Poured out their souls in odours, that were their prayers and confessions
> Unto the night, as it went its way, like a silent Carthusian.
> Fuller of fragrance than they, and as heaved with shadows and night dews,
> Hung the heart of the maiden. The calm and magical moonlight
> Seemed to inundate her soul with indefinable longings,
> As, through the garden gate, and beneath the shade of the oak trees,
> Passed she along the path to the edge of the measureless prairie.
> Silent it lay, with a silvery haze upon it, and fireflies
> Gleamed and floated away in mingled and infinite numbers.
> Over her head, the stars, the thoughts of God in the heavens,
> Shone on the eyes of man, who had ceased to marvel and worship,
> Save when a blazing comet was seen on the walls of that temple
> As if a hand had appeared and written upon them, "Upharsin."[53]

In this detailed description of the garden and prairie, Evangeline experiences the whole natural setting as a host of spiritual signs: the flowers pour out odors like confessions—not unlike her own soul in part 1 when it exuded "celestial fragrance"—the night is like a confessor, the prairie is "measureless," the fireflies are "infinite," and the stars are "the thoughts of God." As in part 1, divine sensations abound. As if this were not enough, when Evangeline speaks, nature speaks back:

> And the soul of the maiden, between the stars and the fireflies,
> Wandered alone, and she cried, "O Gabriel, O my beloved!
> Art thou so near unto me, and yet I cannot behold thee?
> Art thou so near unto me, and yet thy voice does not reach me?
> Ah! How often thy feet have trod this path to the prairie!
> Ah! How often thine eyes have looked on the woodlands around me!
> Ah! How often beneath this oak, returning from labor,
> Thou hast lain down to rest, and to dream of me in thy slumbers!
> When shall these eyes behold, these arms be folded about thee?"

53. Longfellow, "Evangeline," ll. 1031–44.

> Loud and sudden and near the notes of a whippoorwill sounded
> Like a flute in the woods; and anon, through the neighboring thickets,
> Farther and farther away it floated and dropped into silence.
> "Patience!" whispered the oaks from oracular caverns of darkness:
> And from the moonlit meadow, a sigh responded, "To-morrow!"[54]

This is the most that Evangeline speaks in all of part 2, and in her words we hear her turmoil and disconsolation. Yet in the surrounding landscape there are indications that Evangeline is further along than she might realize, for her soul is described as being "between the stars and the fireflies." Stars and fireflies are the two dominant light-filled objects in this canto and, in the case of stars, in the entire poem. Evangeline's soul is midway between the earthly light of the firefly and the celestial light of the stars.[55] Further, the landscape, which in part 1 consoled her and reminded her of God's justice, here preaches "patience" to her, reinforcing Father Felician's sermon. Yet we are not told whether Evangeline is consoled; in the world of exile even the mystic utterances of nature may not be enough to bring consolation to the one accomplishing the work of affection.

In canto 4, as she listens to the tales of the Shawnee woman, Evangeline feels that "the region around her / seemed like enchanted ground and her swarthy guest the enchantress."[56] But this enchantment is not the same as consolation, and though Evangeline joins in with the familiar Catholic worship at the Jesuit Mission in the Ozarks, and listens "meek and submissive" to the priest's encouragement, her soul remains "sad and afflicted"[57] as she waits there for Gabriel, who never comes.

Finally, at the beginning of 2.5, Evangeline settles after many years in Philadelphia, and there experiences yet another vision:

> So, when the fruitless search, the disappointed endeavor,
> Ended, to recommence no more on earth, uncomplaining,
> Thither, as leaves to the light, were turned her thoughts and her footsteps.
> As from the mountain's top the rainy mists of the morning
> Roll away, and afar we behold the landscape below us,
> Sun illumined, with shining rivers and cities and hamlets,

---

54. Longfellow, "Evangeline," ll. 1145–58.

55. It is probably safest to read the stars as symbols of celestial light, not as literal celestial lights. For "celestial light" in Evangeline seems to be reserved for the light of heaven itself, or of those into whom it has been infused by grace, such as Evangeline after confession, or Moses coming down from Mount Sinai.

56. Longfellow, "Evangeline," ll. 1151–52.

57. Longfellow, "Evangeline," ll. 1202–3.

> So fell the mists from her mind, and she saw the world far below her,
> Dark no longer, but illumined with love; and the pathway
> Which she had climbed so far, lying smooth in the distance.[58]

In this first part of her vision, Evangeline finally sees that her "endeavor" is "ended," and upon seeing so, her pathway, previously dark, is now "illumined with love." This is the fulfillment of the erotic doctrine that Evangeline preached in 2.1, namely that "the heart goes before, like a lamp and illumines the pathway" and "many things are made clear that else lie hidden in darkness." Evangeline is like a leaf that turns toward the light. We have already seen, in canto 2, that God's light has never been wholly absent from her. Still, Evangeline's new clarity remains vague to us; what exactly has been made clear to her? And what must she do now? This is recounted in the second part of her vision:

> Gabriel was not forgotten. Within her heart was his image,
> Clothed in the beauty of love and youth, as last she beheld him,
> Only more beautiful made by his death-like silence and absence.
> Into her thoughts of him time entered not, for it was not.
> Over him years had no power; he was not changed, but transfigured;
> He had become to her heart as one who is dead, and not absent;
> Patience and abnegation of self, and devotion to others,
> This is the lesson a life of trial and sorrow had taught her.
> So was her love diffused, but, like to some odorous spices,
> Suffered no waste nor loss, though filling the air with aroma.
> Other hope had she none, nor wish in this life but to follow
> Meekly, with reverent steps, the sacred feet of her Savior.
> Thus many years she lived as a Sister of Mercy.[59]

Evangeline's vision has now "transfigured" Gabriel: he is loved, remembered, beautiful, and timeless in Evangeline's mind. Her affection is not gone, but it did not, after all, enrich the heart of another. If Father Felician is to be believed, the return of Evangeline's affection back to her own heart should have some pretty dramatic results, not least of which is the attainment of godlikeness. And the beginnings of these results are recounted in this passage. Evangeline has indeed endured and learned from the "patience . . . and sorrow" that Father Felician recommended. Further, Evangeline now desires to "follow . . . her Savior," and takes the practical step of becoming

---

58. Longfellow, "Evangeline," ll. 1267–75.
59. Longfellow, "Evangeline," ll. 1276–88.

a member of the Sisters of Mercy, a Roman Catholic order in Philadelphia. In wanting to follow Christ, Evangeline is showing at least a desire to be godlike. And in having learned the "patience" which Felician called godlike in 2.1, Evangeline now possesses one prominent quality of godlikeness. In addition, her love is now "diffused" in a way that recalls Felician's fountain metaphor, now translated into olfactory imagery. But there is not yet a dramatic indication that she has reached that state of godlikeness, purification, perfection, and worthiness of heaven that was promised her.

This state is reached, if it is reached at all, in the next stanza—and keynote—of 2.5, when Evangeline is ministering to the sick and dying during an epidemic:

> Thither, by night and by day, came the Sister of Mercy. The dying
> Looked up into her face, and thought indeed, to behold there
> Gleams of celestial light encircle her forehead with splendor,
> Such as the artist paints o'er the brows of saints and apostles,
> Or such as hangs by night o'er a city seen at a distance.
> Unto their eyes it seemed the lamps of the city celestial,
> Into whose shining gates erelong their spirits would enter.[60]

For the first time since 1.1, Evangeline is described as being bodily illumined by celestial light. This is a more detailed description than before, and Longfellow gives us two images to help us understand this transfiguration: the halo of the painted saint, and the glow of a far-off city. He then clarifies that the city that Evangeline resembles is not an earthly city, but heaven, the "city celestial." In 2.5, then, Longfellow provides us with a dramatic physical indication of the godlikeness that Evangeline has attained by learning patience though her work of affection: she shines with the light of heaven itself.

There is one final religious experience that Evangeline has before the final discovery of Gabriel and epilogue. In the next stanza after her transfiguration in celestial light, Evangeline, ascending the stairs of the poorhouse and listening to the bells of Christ Church, again hears a voice, this time coming from herself:

> Soft as descending wings fell the calm of the hour on her spirit:
> Something within her said, "At length thy trials are ended;"
> And, with light in her looks, she entered the chambers of sickness.[61]

In these three lines we find a spiritually restored Evangeline: she is consoled by the calm of the hour, with no lingering doubt or turmoil; she hears and

60. Longfellow, "Evangeline," ll. 1313–19.
61. Longfellow, "Evangeline," ll. 1329–31.

trusts the mystic utterance which, formerly given to her by nature, now comes from within herself; finally, she is still shining. Not only is there a voice that guides Evangeline from within, but also the light that previously "shone on" and "encircled" Evangeline is finally described as being "in" her. She is fully united to the celestial light that has flitted in and out of her body and soul throughout her life. This light re-manifests itself visibly on her body in the previous scene, and continues to emanate from her, for it is "in her looks." Thus, in these penultimate stanzas of 2.5 we find an Evangeline who has accomplished her labor and has begun to enjoy the rewards of such an accomplishment. Her spiritual labors, so easily accomplished and rewarded in part 1, in part 2 take a lifetime to complete, a lifetime to be rewarded with godlikeness.

## Religious Language in Part 2

While much of the religious language of part 2 of *Evangeline* has already been seen in the quoted passages that describe the teaching and practice of part 2, a few instances merit closer examination. Continuing in the vein of part 1, there remains throughout part 2 a sanctification of nature through similes. In 2.2, the hummingbirds flit through the tree-branches like "angels ascending and descending" on "the ladder of Jacob."[62] In a more pagan image, the sun, no longer resembling Moses, "like a magician extended his golden wand o'er the landscape."[63] Further, the mockingbirds sound like "frenzied Bacchantes,"[64] and the Druids of the introduction make another appearance, for the mistletoe of in the Louisiana trees is "mystic . . . such as the Druids cut down with golden hatchets at Yuletide."[65] The enchantment that Evangeline feels after listening to the Shawnee woman's legends is not the celestial brightness of 1.1, but instead is a "mysterious splendor" that seems to issue from the "magical words" of a "swarthy . . . enchantress."[66]

Though there are more pagan figures in part 2 than in part 1, they do not outweigh the Judeo-Christian imagery. The odor of the flowers in Basil's garden pours out like "prayers and confessions," and moves "like a Silent Carthusian."[67] Basil himself likens the wayward Gabriel to both "the Prodigal Son" and the "Foolish Virgin" of Christ's parables.[68] The sky over

62. Longfellow, "Evangeline," ll. 821–23.
63. Longfellow, "Evangeline," l. 865.
64. Longfellow, "Evangeline," l. 878.
65. Longfellow, "Evangeline," ll. 889–90.
66. Longfellow, "Evangeline," ll. 1151–54.
67. Longfellow, "Evangeline," ll. 1032–33.
68. Longfellow, "Evangeline," ll. 1063–64.

the prairies is "like the protecting hand of God inverted,"[69] and the native peoples of the plains are likened to "the scattered tribes of Ishmael's children."[70] Longfellow saves the final biblical simile of the poem for the description of the dying Gabriel:

> Hot and red on his lips still burned the flush of the fever,
> As if life, like the Hebrew, with blood had besprinkled its portals,
> That the Angel of Death might see the sign and pass over.[71]

Thus, though the spiritual climate of part 2 is one of difficult, lifelong labor and delayed consolation and reward, it is still a climate wherein the natural world and the persons who live in it are often put into symbolic relationships with religious principles, figures, and stories.

## The Spiritual World of Evangeline

Now that we have examined the theological teaching, spiritual practice and experience, and religious language of the poem, we are ready to provide an initial account of the spiritual world of *Evangeline*. What would such an account look like? It would, of course, take into account the theology taught in the poem, but it would need to go beyond this, ideally describing how the spiritual world of the poem is structured and how it operates, a sort of anatomy and physiology of *Evangeline*'s cosmos. As we have seen from our investigation of part 2, this will need to end up accounting for Evangeline's extraordinary experience in 2.5, where she shines with celestial light like a saint, like heaven itself. Finally, a complete account would explore the kinship between the poem and Longfellow's Unitarian and patristic theological sources. In the rest of this chapter, we will explore the spiritual world of *Evangeline* as a whole, and in the next chapter account for the 2.1 and 2.5 keynotes and the Unitarian and patristic influences discernible therein.

### *A Christian Cosmos*

At the most basic level, *Evangeline* presents a world where God is present and involved in the affairs of humans. This God is the creator of humans and the natural world, and the ideal state of human community is one where the lives of humans "reflect . . . an image of heaven," and all dwell "in the love of

---

69. Longfellow, "Evangeline," l. 1105.
70. Longfellow, "Evangeline," l. 1095.
71. Longfellow, "Evangeline," ll. 1354–56.

God and man." In these simple statements we can discern two basic teachings of Scripture: first, that man is made in the image of God, his heavenly Father, and his life should reflect this kinship;[72] and second, the two greatest commandments are to love God and one's fellow man, as Jesus teaches in the New Testament gospels.[73]

Further, there is a church, the Roman Catholic Church in particular, where men can worship God rightly. Right worship seems to be comprised largely of singing songs together, both in praise of God and in devotion to Mary and the saints. As Higgins has argued, however, Longfellow does not present the Catholic Church as the only church capable of right worship, for in part 2, canto 5, Longfellow presents the worship of the Quakers in Philadelphia as equally idyllic and proper as the worship of the Catholics in part 1. Thus, according to Higgins, Longfellow's is an ecumenical Christian vision, not an exclusively Catholic one.[74] Be this as it may, Grand-Pré is nowhere presented as being spiritually or culturally poorer for its lack of denominational diversity.

The priest acts as the central authority in the Catholic Church of *Evangeline*, and his duties include preaching, blessing, and acting as a father confessor in the sacrament of confession. Chevalier has argued that part 1, canto 1, is "rife with tension" between the sinlessness of a Romantic Eden and the sinfulness of the biblical Fall.[75] But read at the literal level, at least, the presence of Evangeline's participation in confession is an indication that the Christian community—post Fall and pre-glory as it is—is working as it should. Confession is the proper, sacramental response to sin in the ideal, earthly, Christian community. Further, whatever iniquity Evangeline confesses is dealt with through the sacrament, and does not seem to do lasting damage; in fact, the sacrament of confession seems to result in the illumination of some of its participants by celestial light.

The sin that does do lasting damage in the world of *Evangeline* is tyranny and oppression, which comes from outside the ideal human community. This sin effectively destroys the ideal community, and separates humans from the twofold love in which they used to dwell: the love of man and the love of God. Evangeline not only loses her father to death and her beloved to exile, but also finds herself, by the beginning of part 2, in a state of relative imperfection, impurity, weakness, and dissimilarity to God. Evangeline has not herself sinned in any major way, but sin—the sin of British tyranny— has nevertheless caused her whole community to experience a kind of fall.

72. Genesis 1:26–27 (ESV).
73. Matthew 22:37–39 (ESV).
74. Higgins, "Evangeline's Mission," 547.
75. Chevalier, *Semiotics, Romanticism, and Scriptures*, 1.

Redemption from the effects of sin—imperfection, impurity, weakness, and dissimilarity to God—is found through the "work of affection," which entails sorrow, silence, and patient endurance, all of which can be categorized under the general term *ascesis*.[76] As we have seen above, this ascesis is not a wholesale rejection of all created things. In fact, it is as much through the natural world as it is through other humans that Evangeline is encouraged and led on her long journey. This is because true ascesis, in Evangeline, is the rejection not of the created order, which teaches divine truths to those properly attuned to it—who are, as Origen says, "Partakers of these Divine Sensations"—but of "passion," which would include frivolous living, loquaciousness, despair, sloth, and all other vices that are contrary to the sorrow, silence, and patient endurance to which Evangeline is called.

Further, as Franchot and Chevalier have convincingly argued, the spiritual world of *Evangeline* is not merely one in which ascetic practice leads to redemption. For the work that Evangeline must carry out is also fundamentally erotic; it is a work of *affection*—in particular, affection for Gabriel practically realized in the physical search for him. But this work of affection is not just a persevering love for Gabriel, but also an act of submission and obedience to Felician as father confessor.[77] And though it might appear that Evangeline moves more and more toward freedom from spiritual authority over the course of part 2, she does the opposite. After obeying Father Felician for many years as a member of the Catholic laity, Evangeline submits even further to the Catholic Church by taking religious orders and becoming a Sister of Mercy. Strangely, it is only in the last canto of part 2 that we hear of Evangeline's relationship with Jesus. He is described as Evangeline's "Savior," and it is out of her desire to follow him that she becomes a nun.

According to the theological teaching of the 2.1 keynote, the final stage of redemption in the spiritual world of *Evangeline* is the attainment of godlikeness. This is beyond mere saintliness, which Evangeline experienced

---

76. True to Chevalier's observation that Longfellow sublimates explicitly theological language to natural, pastoral language, we do not find any explicit references to salvation or redemption in *Evangeline*. Calling Jesus "Savior" is the closest Longfellow comes. Instead, redemption is characterized most clearly in *Evangeline* as that same strengthening, purification, perfection, and becoming godlike to which Father Felician calls Evangeline in 2.1.

77. There is a strange tendency on the part of contemporary critics to see such obedience as oppressive and necessarily against the natural wishes of the one who is being obedient. But this is not the case in *Evangeline*; after all, it is Evangeline who first claims that she will follow her heart in pursuit of Gabriel, and this is what prompts Felician to reveal the theological and redemptive nature of such a labor. Thus there is little contention between Evangeline's natural wishes and the mission that her father confessor gives her.

both literally and analogically in Grand-Pré. After confession, Evangeline is encircled in "celestial brightness," and is likened to Moses himself, who shone with divine light on Sinai. The youths of Grand-Pré treat Evangeline as a saint in an erotic analogy, whereby their desires for her are characterized as devotion, and she, as the object of their desires, is characterized as a saint. Evangeline, however, rejects this analogical role twice over, first in her choice of Gabriel over the other youths in part 1, and second in her rejection of the youths again in part 2, when she is offered the chance to forget Gabriel and marry Baptiste Leblanc. It is immediately after this second rejection that Father Felician presents her with the opportunity to pursue godlikeness.

Whether Evangeline attains godlikeness—in effect revealing the final stage of soteriology in the created cosmos of the poem—is still unclear. We have seen that she learns patience and sorrow, but has she become purified, perfected, and godlike? If so, we have said that it must be in the keynote passage of 2.5 where Evangeline again, for the first time since before the fall of Grand-Pré, shines with celestial light. Is the witness of this scene enough to conclude that Evangeline has been rendered godlike? If the answer is yes, then this is the heart of the spiritual world of Evangeline—namely, that the end of human striving, of proper ascetic and proper erotic labor, is the attaining of a state of godlikeness wherein one's face shines with the light of heaven.

## *Evangeline's Success*

There are several reasons to think that by the end of 2.5, Evangeline indeed has accomplished her work of affection, and can thus be called strong, pure, perfect, godlike, and worthy of heaven. These reasons include both the internal evidence of the poem and the external evidence of the critical tradition. There are two passages in 2.5 that suggest Evangeline has indeed accomplished her work of affection. First, the narrator states at the beginning of part 2, canto 5, that "Patience, abnegation of self, and devotion to others" are the "lesson a life of trial and sorrow had taught her."[78] This is stated in the past tense; she is not currently learning from sorrow and trial, but has already been "taught" by them. Given that sorrow and patience were two of the key components of the "work of affection" as described by Father Felician in the 2.1 keynote, it seems reasonable to conclude that Evangeline has already accomplished at least some of her work of affection. Further, as we have mentioned before, according to the theological teaching of the 2.1 keynote, it is "patience" or "patient endurance" that is godlike, and if

78. Longfellow, "Evangeline," ll. 1282–83.

Evangeline has "been taught" patience, then she is in some way godlike, for she possesses a godlike quality. If this were not enough to convince us that Evangeline has begun to succeed at her mission, two stanzas later, as she is ministering to the sick, she hears a voice within her say, "'at length thy trials are ended.'"[79] There is no indication from this voice that the trials are ended because she has failed.

Between these two indications of Evangeline's successful accomplishing of the work of affection is her experience of light, which is compared to "the lamps of the city celestial."[80] Father Felician lists worthiness of heaven as part of the reward of the work of affection, and now Evangeline is shining with the light of heaven. She does not just shine with light that resembles that of heaven—this is literally the light of heaven, and indicates in a powerful visual way that Evangeline is now not only worthy of heaven, but is already participating in heaven by shining bodily with its celestial light. There is no longer any apparent weakness, impurity, or imperfection in her; even her love for Gabriel, as we learned in the previous stanza, is now untouchable by time or circumstance.

Further, the critical tradition of Hawthorne and Demarest attests to the interpretation of the keynote passage in 2.5 as a description of Evangeline's successful accomplishment of her mission. Hawthorne, as we have seen, says that in the "transfiguration" of Evangeline in 2.5, "the joy" which Father Felician prophesies in 2.1 is "realized within her."[81] And Demarest writes that 2.5 "leave[s] behind a calm feeling that the highest aim of Evangeline's existence has been attained."[82] Neither Hawthorne nor Demarest, however, uses the term "godlikeness" to describe the state that Evangeline attains. But we will see in the next chapter that the concepts of "transfiguration" and "the highest aim of existence" are both compatible with the concept of godlikeness, or ethical deification, and its theological counterpart, realistic deification.

Now that we have gained an overall picture of the spiritual world of *Evangeline*, we will next explore in detail the illuminating relationships between the keynote passages of *Evangeline* 2.1 and 2.5 and the doctrines of Channing and Longfellow's Fathers. We will bring to our aid the witness of Hawthorne and Demarest, and will add to and unify their interpretations of *Evangeline* through concluding that in the poem Longfellow has indeed created a world wherein the patristic doctrines of deification and divine light are described and enacted.

79. Longfellow, "Evangeline," l. 1330.
80. Longfellow, "Evangeline," l. 1318.
81. Hawthorne, "Hawthorne's Review of *Evangeline*," 234.
82. Demarest, *Evangeline*, 148.

# 6

# Deification and Divine Light in *Evangeline*

THUS FAR WE HAVE proposed that the religious elements of *Evangeline* form a Christian vision of the cosmos—God creates humans to reflect his image and love one another and him; true worship involves praise of God, Christ, and the saints in song, along with obedience to a priest and participation in the sacraments; humans sin when they hate and oppress, rather than love, other humans, as well as when they choose to follow passion rather than faith; and spiritual growth and maturity are found in patient, long-suffering love in imitation of God and Christ. Beyond these basic teachings, there are two religious elements that warrant close examination—godlikeness and the spiritual experience of transfiguration.

Though these two elements are centered in the keynote passages in 2.1 and 2.5, part 1 of *Evangeline* includes a number of images that foreshadow these passages. We will begin this chapter by examining these foreshadowings in part 1, and then move on to the keynotes of part 2, exploring their relationship to those passages in Channing and Longfellow's Fathers that the keynotes parallel in imagery and concept. We will conclude by setting our Unitarian/patristic reading of *Evangeline* into the wider critical tradition, taking issue with the views of Pearce, Lewis, Franchot, Chevalier, and Higgins, while extending and lending theological nuance to the interpretations of Hawthorne and Demarest.

## Part 1: Foreshadowings

The most important and memorable foreshadowing of the part 2 keynotes is the post-confession scene of *Evangeline* 1.1:

> But a celestial brightness—a more ethereal beauty—
> Shone on her face and encircled her form, when, after confession,
> Homeward serenely she walked with God's benediction upon her.
> When she passed, it seemed like the ceasing of exquisite music.[1]

Using the terminology of chapter 3, we can say that this is a clear instance of being *illumined by* celestial light. Soon after this passage, Evangeline will be compared to a saint; but here she appears more like Christ himself. In his *Apology*, Justin Martyr uses similar words to describe Christ's coming in glory at the end of the world: "He shall come in his own form, encircled in celestial glory."[2] Longfellow, consciously or not, borrows Justin's main terms as he found them in Reeves's English translation: "form," "encircled," and "celestial." In describing Evangeline's experience in terms of Christ's second coming, Longfellow implies two things: first, that resemblance to the glorified Christ is the destiny of the Christian; and second, that, in particular, the light that shines on and encircles the Christ-like human is the glory of heaven, not the merely physical light of earth. The implications of this parallel in terminology between Longfellow and Justin go beyond the claim of Chevalier, who sees Evangeline here as an example of the "woman clothed in the sun" described in Revelation. But the sun is not quite the right image for the type of light that encircles the serene Evangeline. She is illumined by *divine* light, not *sun*light.

The timing of Evangeline's initial experience of divine light is also important. It is "after confession," one of the seven sacraments of the Catholic Church, that she appears like the glorified Christ. Turning again to Justin's *Apology*, we find that, in Justin's theology, the sacraments both illumine the believer and unite her to Christ. "Baptism," Justin explains, "is called illumination, because the minds of the catechumens who are thus washed are illuminated."[3] It is curious, then, that Longfellow chooses neither the sacrament of baptism—which Justin says "illumines" the mind—nor the sacrament of the Eucharist—which Justin says unites one to Christ—as the sacrament that precedes Evangeline's first experience of illumination and Christ-likeness. Instead, in canto 1, Longfellow takes illumination and

---

1. Longfellow, "Evangeline," ll. 78–81.
2. Justin, "First Apology," 91.
3. Justin, "First Apology," 107.

Christ-likeness and makes them the result of the lesser-discussed sacrament of confession. Chevalier provides a possible explanation for the selection of this sacrament by arguing that the intrinsic connection between sin and confession ominously foreshadows the fall and exile from Eden soon to be experienced by the Acadians.

As we noted in the last chapter, Evangeline seems to retain this illumined state in the next canto:

> Up the staircase moved a luminous space in the darkness,
> Lighted less by the lamp than the shining face of the maiden.[4]

Though Longfellow does not here use the term "celestial light," he centers the luminous imagery on Evangeline's face, the same feature he highlights in the previous illumination passage, as well as in the 2.5 keynote.

The next two foreshadowings of deification and divine light in part 1 involve brief references to Elijah and Moses, in the context of similes. In canto 4, Longfellow describes the "souls" of the Acadian men, now trapped in the church by the English soldiers, who, nevertheless, "with devotion translated / Rose on the ardor of prayer, like Elijah ascending to heaven."[5] Moses appears in the next stanza, as Evangeline waits, lonely, for the imprisoned men to be released:

> Down sank the great, red sun, and in golden, glimmering vapors,
> Veiled the light of his face, like the Prophet descending from Sinai.
> Sweetly over the village the bell of the Angelus sounded.[6]

"The Prophet" is, of course, Moses, whose face shone after he talked with God on Sinai, as described in Exodus. Not only is this passage the second description in *Evangeline* of a godly person whose face shines, but it also parallels the previous description of Evangeline's own facial illumination in the structure of its images within the stanza. Both Evangeline's illumination and Moses's illumination are described at the end of a stanza, both include a description of light in the third-to-last lines, and both include an aural description in the last line of the stanza: Evangeline's passing seems like "exquisite music" in canto 1, and in canto 4, "sweetly . . . the Angelus" rings from the belfry. In part 1, then, Evangeline's illumination with divine light is described in such a way that she resembles both the glorified Christ and the illumined Moses.

Further, the presence of Moses and Elijah as the major Old Testament figures mentioned in part 1, coupled with several descriptions of figures

---

4. Longfellow, "Evangeline," ll. 358–61.
5. Longfellow, "Evangeline," ll. 485–86.
6. Longfellow, "Evangeline," ll. 506–8.

illumined by and shining with "celestial brightness" should put the careful reader in mind of the particular scene in the New Testament that involves Elijah, Moses, and Christ all shining with divine light—the Transfiguration. We have already seen that Longfellow was familiar with Origen's description of the Transfiguration as a central revelation of the union of human and divine natures in Christ. "On the Mount of Transfiguration," Origen explains, Christ "displayed the Glory of his Raiment, and the Heav'nly lustre of Moses, and Elias, who . . . discoursed with him."[7] And Hawthorne, we remember, interprets the Transfiguration as Longfellow's model for the 2.5 keynote. Further, part 1, in its various biblical references, serves to place the main imagery and characters involved in the Transfiguration in the imagination of the reader, providing a pre-exile image of what Evangeline will again experience when her labor is complete: the transfiguration in divine light experienced by one who has become godlike.

## 2.1: The First Keynote

Let us look, once again, at Father Felician's 2.1 speech to Evangeline:

> Thereupon the priest, her friend and father-confessor,
> Said with a smile, "O daughter! thy God thus speaketh within thee.
> Talk not of wasted affection, affection never was wasted;
> If it enrich not the heart of another, its waters, returning
> Back to their springs, like the rain, shall fill them full of refreshment;
> That which the fountain sends forth returns again to the fountain.
> Patience, accomplish thy labor, accomplish thy work of affection!
> Sorrow and silence are strong, and patient endurance is godlike.
> Therefore accomplish thy labor of love, till the heart is made godlike,
> Purified, strengthened, perfected, and rendered more worthy of heaven!"[8]

We have already interpreted this passage as the key theological teaching of part 2, in which Felician presents the clearest account of soteriology in the poem. The theology taught in this homily can be categorized as both *ascetic* and *ethical*. It is ascetic because Evangeline is called to several activities traditionally associated with Christian ascetic practice: sorrow, silence, and patient endurance. But Felician's teaching is also ethical, for the main activity that Evangeline is called to is love, the greatest of the theological

---

7. Origen, *Against Celsus*, 163.
8. Longfellow, "Evangeline," ll. 719–27.

virtues in traditional Christian thought. Of course, this love is also erotic, for the primary object of Evangeline's love is her fiancé Gabriel. But Felician in his sermon draws the erotic love of the beloved up into the greater activity of affection in and through ascesis. And the ascetic practices of sorrow, silence, and patient endurance are all in service of the work of affection, not in service of the eradication of desire, nor of academic contemplation.

There are a number of indications that godlikeness is the central quality that Felican calls Evangeline to acquire. First, "godlike" is positioned as the key, last word for two lines in a row. Second, though strength and godlikeness seem to be put on equal footing in line 725, Felician clarifies, in lines 726–727, that godlikeness is the prime quality that the labor of love is working toward. And grammatically speaking, line 727 can be seen providing a list of those qualities that godlikeness involves: purification, strength, perfection, and worthiness of heaven.

## 2.1 and Channing

Though Longfellow used Channing's "Objections to Christianity Considered" to proselytize on his college campus, it was in Channing's "Christian Worship" that he found the most robust account of the Unitarian doctrine of godlikeness. In "Christian Worship" we find union with God and spiritual perfection highlighted as the goal of Christian life and worship. Channing variously describes union with God as "recepti[on] of divinity," "likeness to God," capacity for "godlike virtues," God's uniting the human soul "more intimately with himself," and "participation of a divine nature." If we apply Russell's deification terminology, these descriptions include both ethical and realistic deification terms. But in *Evangeline* 2.1, Longfellow does not borrow Channing's language of participatory union with God, opting instead for the repeated use of the ethical term "godlike." Longfellow uses the same language of "perfection" as Channing, and in speaking of the "strength" gained by the godlike soul parallels Channing's description of the soul being "lift[ed] above its present weakness."[9]

Felician's homily also shares with Channing's sermon the idea that it is ascetic struggle that most surely leads to godlikeness. Channing writes: "Were I called upon to prove God's spiritual parental interest in us, I would point to the trials, temptations, evils of life; for to these we owe . . . the development of what is divine in human nature.[10] While Longfellow uses the terms "sorrow," "silence," "patience," and "labor" instead of Channing's

9. Channing, *Works*, 4:326–27.
10. Channing, *Works*, 4:330–31.

"suffering," "trial," and "temptation," both agree that those experiences and activities that are difficult and disconsoling are those by which the human may become godlike.

It is in 2.1 that the doctrine in *Evangeline* most resembles Channing's Unitarianism. Longfellow presents, though Feliciain, a doctrine that closely parallels Channing's teaching that God's ultimate purpose for humans is a state of godlikeness in which the human is both strengthened and perfected. And though he does not use Channing's terminology, Longfellow also incorporates into Felician's speech the Unitarian idea that ascetic struggle is a sure path to becoming divine.

## 2.1 and Longfellow's Fathers

Though Felician's homily in 2.1 closely parallels key Unitarian doctrines, these doctrines are not exclusive to Unitarianism. For we find in Longfellow's Fathers as well the doctrine that the goal of Christian living is the achievement of godlikeness, spiritual perfection, and worthiness of heaven through ascetic struggle.

In *Against Celsus* Origen argues, in language reminiscent of Evangeline 2.1, that "the sincere Desire" of the Christian's soul is the attainment of a "life which is far more excellent, and, in a word, is every way worthy of a God."[11] St Cyprian of Carthage speaks similarly in his treatise "On the Lord's Prayer." According to Cyprian, one of the central lessons of the Lord's Prayer is that the Christian should desire "to be like God" and "to be of heaven."[12] This is accomplished, in part, through the sacrament of Baptism, "being born of water and of the Spirit." In Cyprian, then, we are reminded of the role of sacraments in the ethical deification of the believer. Further, in Origen and Cyprian we find a language of worthiness and being "of heaven" that is absent in Channing, but present at the end of Felician's homily as the last quality of godlikeness—being "rendered more worthy of heaven."

Mosheim—one of Longfellow's main secondary sources on the Fathers—provides a detailed account, as we have seen, of the ascetic road to union with God. Origen and the early mystic Christians, Mosheim explains, "denied that men could, by labour or study, excite this celestial flame in their breasts; and therefore, they disapproved highly of the attempts of those who, by definitions, abstract theorem, and profound speculations, endeavored to form distinct notions of truth, and to discover its hidden nature."[13]

11. Origen, *Against Celsus*, 114.
12. Cyprian, *Treatises*, 410.
13. Mosheim, *Ecclesiastical History*, 215.

So far the mystical views described by Mosheim share with Felician's homily a rejection of academic effort as an element in becoming godlike. And Mosheim continues: "On the contrary, they maintained that silence, tranquility, repose, and solitude, accompanied with such acts of mortification as might tend to extenuate and exhaust the body, were the means by which the hidden and internal word was excited to produce its latent virtues, and to instruct men in the knowledge of divine things."[14] Both Mosheim and Felician list silence as the first of the ascetic activities that lead humans to divinity. Later on in the same passage, Mosheim uses another quality of godlikeness present in Felician's homily, namely the purification of the soul from earthly distractions. Those who successfully reject the terrestrial and the material are led to a "happy union" with God, a "communion with the Supreme Being" wherein truth is finally contemplated in purity.[15] Contemplation, for Mosheim's mystics, is an activity of the final stage of the mystical path—first comes ascetic struggle, then divine union, then contemplation.

Though Longfellow includes the ascetic activities of silence and purification in Felician's doctrine of godlikeness, he makes clear through the Jesuit priest in part 2, canto 3, that it is sinful "passion," not nature itself, which must be rejected in the journey toward God. The terrestrial and the material can become sacramental messengers of God for the Christian who has begun to be, in Origen's words, a Partaker of Divine Sensation. Also, Longfellow shies away from the language of union in Mosheim just as he does the language of union in Channing. He explicitly, however, uses the language of likeness to and worthiness of God that he found in Channing, Origen, and Cyprian. And he makes clear that the path Evangeline must take to godlikeness is an ascetic path of patience, sorrow, and silence similar to that which Channing and Mosheim describe. Returning to Russell's terminology, then, we can read the 2.1 keynote passage as presenting a clear account of ethical deification through love and ascetic activity that is in agreement with and uses the major theological terminology of both Channing and the Fathers. But it also lacks another concept shared by Channing and the Fathers: the realistic deification of the believer through participatory union with the divine nature.

## *Divine Light in Part 2*

Though part 1, canto 1, and part 2, canto 5, of the poem contain passages in which Evangeline herself is illumined by divine light, these are not the only

---

14. Mosheim, *Ecclesiastical History*, 215.
15. Mosheim, *Ecclesiastical History*, 215–16.

passages where she experiences divine light. In part 2, canto 2, and at the beginning of part 2, canto 5, divine light shines upon Evangeline, acting as a consolation and a guide:

> Filled was her heart with love, and the dawn of an opening heaven
> Lighted her soul in sleep with the glory of regions celestial.[16]

> Thither, as leaves to the light, were turned her thoughts and her footsteps.
> As from the mountain's top the rainy mists of the morning
> Roll away, and afar we behold the landscape below us,
> Sun illumined, with shining rivers and cities and hamlets,
> So fell the mists from her mind, and she saw the world far below her,
> Dark no longer, but illumined with love; and the pathway
> Which she had climbed so far, lying smooth in the distance.[17]

The first of these passages is from canto 2; Evangeline lies asleep on the boat that carries her down the Mississippi, and "the glory of regions celestial" shines on her as she sleeps. Longfellow's use of the word "celestial" should immediately make us think of the 1.1 post-confession passage. The light Evangeline was illumined by in 1.1 is still with her, even in the world of exile; however, in part 2, canto 2, it is her soul, not her face and physical form, that is illumined.

The second passage speaks not of Evangeline herself being shone upon, but of her path, which, once cloudy, is now "illumined with love." Though neither "celestial light" nor "glory" is used in this passage, the description of the illumination of one's path after long struggle bears a strong resemblance to Synesius's "Hymn 1," wherein "light divine" illumines the path of the long-suffering mystic. There are a number of parallels between Evangeline's experience and Synesius's hymn: Evangeline and Synesius's mystic have both undergone "labor" and experienced disappointment and anxiety. Both are aided by a light that shines on their path: Evangeline sees "the world far below her," and "the pathway / Which she had climbed" now "illumined with love." Synesius's mystic similarly sees "unbroken sunbeams shining / On the path laid out before" him.[18] Further, the light in Synesius's hymn is provided by a divine "other," which "strengthens [the] affections" of he who is illumined, a phrase reminiscent of the "work of affection" by which Evangeline will be "strengthened." And both Evangeline and Synesius's mys-

16. Longfellow, "Evangeline," ll. 825–26.
17. Longfellow, "Evangeline," ll. 1269–75.
18. See Synesius, "Hymn 1," ll. 113–27 for the whole passage referred to here.

tic are on the road to deification—Evangeline seeks the ethical deification of becoming godlike, and the mystic is on the road to a union with God the Father wherein, Synesius deems, the mystic may be called "god."

Longfellow, then, does not let us forget Evangeline's pre-exile state of illumination even in her long, disappointing search through the world of exile. Divine light repeatedly lights her soul and leads her, but it is not until late in her life that she regains her pre-exile state, illustrating that central patristic doctrine that the Christian seeks to return to the likeness to God lost in the Fall, to shine again physically with the heavenly raiment of divine light. In a poem filled with images of that which is within venturing without and then back again, Evangeline proceeds from a pre-exile state of physical, divine illumination into a post-exile world where God's light is not easily seen, back to a state of physical, divine illumination, which is found in a Philadelphia, a city that in its brotherly affection resembles the old, loving harmony of Grand-Pré.

## 2.5: The Second Keynote

We are now ready to return to the "transfiguration" passage Hawthorne praised as Longfellow's "triumph":

> Thither, by night and by day, came the Sister of Mercy. The dying
> Looked up into her face, and thought indeed, to behold there
> Gleams of celestial light encircle her forehead with splendor,
> Such as the artist paints o'er the brows of saints and apostles,
> Or such as hangs by night o'er a city seen at a distance.
> Unto their eyes it seemed the lamps of the city celestial,
> Into whose shining gates erelong their spirits would enter.[19]

Here again Evangeline's face is "encircle[d]" by celestial light. As mentioned in the last chapter, Longfellow presents us with a number of different images by which we might picture Evangeline's illumination: the halo of the painted saint or apostle, the glow of a city at night, and "the lamps of the city celestial." If one had any doubt that by the term "celestial" Longfellow means "heavenly" or "divine," this scene clarifies the term by placing heaven and its inhabitants as central images. Except for the second image, Longfellow's language in this passage is wholly religious.

The 2.5 keynote stands as the most intense and detailed of the spiritual experiences in *Evangeline*. Further, it is a shared experience. No longer is it

19. Longfellow, "Evangeline," ll. 1313-19.

just Evangeline who feels or sees the light of heaven, but also those to whom she is ministering—to them, as well, this light is a great consolation, leading them along in their heavenward journey. These dying poor, in fact, resemble the Evangeline of 2.2, who, in sleep, saw celestial light shining out from the gates of heaven. Now the poor see the same image mediated through Evangeline. It is her God-illumined face that is the gateway to the stars.

## *2.5 and Channing*

Given the deep doctrinal affinities between the 2.1 keynote and Channing's "Christian Worship," it is surprising how little of Channing's thought can be found in the 2.5 keynote. In those sermons that Longfellow read and praised, Channing simply does not speak of humans shining with light, let alone being encircled by halos of glory like "saints and apostles." The closest Channing comes to a language of divine light is in "Objections to Christianity Considered," where he calls virtue "the very image of God in the human soul, a ray of his brightness, the best gift which He communicates to his creatures, the highest benefit which Christ came to confer, the only important and lasting distinction between man and man."[20] Here "a ray of [God's] brightness" is one of Channing's descriptions of virtue, which is, indeed, the most important quality God can give to someone in his viewpoint, for it is "the very image of God." This notion fits into Channing's larger understanding of likeness to God as the supreme end of the Christian life. If we were to extrapolate from Channing's words a doctrine of divine light, we might propose that if virtue is a ray of God's brightness, then the more virtuous one was, the brighter with God one might be. Channing, however, does not speak in such a way.

In the passages of "Christian Worship" that tend toward a doctrine of participatory union, we find concepts that could be developed into a doctrine of divine light. As quoted above, Channing teaches that "celestial influences" can "descend into the human soul."[21] Further, "when I call God the Father," Channing writes, "I understand that he communicates Himself, his own spirit, what is most glorious in his own nature to his rational offspring ... This is the great paternal gift of God. He has greater gifts than the world. He confers more than the property of the earth and heavens. The very attributes from which the earth and heavens sprung, these he imparts to his rational offspring."[22] If God communicates "celestial influences" and "what

20. Channing, *Selected Discourses and Essays*, 76.
21. Channing, *Works*, 4:326–27.
22. Channing, *Works*, 4:325–26.

is most glorious in his own nature" to his children, could we not also say that God's glory itself is communicated to his children? Though this would make theological sense, it is not something that Channing himself concludes. It is important to see that Longfellow found in Channing a principle similar to the one he found in the Fathers—namely, that those who participate in God receive his characteristics. It was only in the Fathers, however, that Longfellow found this principle again and again illustrated through descriptions of Christ and his saints shining with divine light.

## 2.5 and Longfellow's Fathers

Beginning in Cyprian and Origen we are presented with images of godlike Christians shining with light, along with descriptions of Christ himself shining with light in those instances when his divine nature is seen "through the Glass," as it were, of his human nature.[23] Cyprian, using the words of Isaiah, encourages his readers to

> Break thy bread to the hungry, and bring the poor that are without shelter into thy house. When thou seest the naked, clothe him; and despise not those of the same family and race of thyself. Then shall thy light break forth in season, and thy raiment shall spring forth speedily; and righteousness shall go before thee, and the glory of God shall surround thee.[24]

These words could easily describe not just the appearance of the shining Evangeline, but also the context in which she shines. For Evangeline is performing exactly those loving, ascetic activities that Cyprian describes; she is ministering, "by day and by night" to the dying poor when she experiences her illumination. Just as in Cyprian's words, "the glory of the Lord ... surround[s]" the Christian, so "gleams of celestial light encircle" Evangeline's head.

That which Cyprian describes so vividly using Old Testament language, Origen describes using the language of Alexandrian metaphysics. First, he writes that Christ "left the Realms of Light and Glory ... to come down into this miserable and sinful world."[25] For Origen, the pre-incarnate Christ dwelled in heaven, the natural realm of God's glory. From time to time, Origen then explains, the incarnate Christ's divine nature is revealed in brilliant light. This takes place both at the Transfiguration, where Christ

---

23. Origen, *Against Celsus*, 162.
24. Cyprian, *Treatises*, 410.
25. Origen, *Against Celsus*, 181.

"display[ed] the Glory of his Raiment,"[26] and also "after he had honorably and happily accomplished the Work of our Redemption," when his "Divinity shone with much brighter rays, through the Glass, if I may so say, of his Humane Nature."[27] Finally, according to Origen, "other Persons" than God may "bear the Characters of Divinity."[28] Given that glory is one of the characteristics of God that Origen highlights, it is no wonder that in his description of the Transfiguration, he highlights the "Heavenly Lustre" of Moses and Elijah. For, according to Origen's metaphysics, they share "the Characters of Divinity," including the heavenly glory of God. In *Against Celsus* books 1 and 2, then, Origen lays out the principle, articulated so well by Russell, that governs the illumination of Christians with divine light—those who participate in the divine nature receive the characteristics of God, foremost among them his light.

Though in 2.5 Longfellow presents us with a vivid image of a mature Christian transfigured in divine light, he does not include a doctrinal description of the metaphysical principle at work in this transfiguration. He could have done so, of course, for he found it in Origen and Boethius, and proves himself quite capable of such description in the 2.1 keynote where Felician preaches a basic doctrine of ethical deification. But instead of presenting another doctrinal description through the mouth of a priest, in the 2.5 keynote Longfellow illustrates the doctrine of participatory union leading to illumination by divine light through dramatic enactment of the doctrine within the narrative. *Evangeline* as a poem has advanced beyond doctrinal conversations. It has become a poem of ascetic actions and mystical experiences.

By opting for dramatic presentations of transfiguration rather than a metaphysical treatise, Longfellow reveals his kinship with his favorite Father, St John Chrysostom. Let us return again to Chrysostom's panegyric on the martyrs Juventinus and Maximinus:

> Blessed Babylas, along with three children, recently drew us together here. Today it is a matched pair of soldier saints that has stationed Christ's army in battle array . . . Of such a nature is the Church's treasure, containing young and old pearls. But the beauty of all of them is one and the same. Their bloom doesn't fade, it doesn't flow away with time. By nature this brilliance doesn't succumb to age's rust. For whereas physical riches fade

---

26. Origen, *Against Celsus*, 163. In using the term "raiment" to describe the light that surrounds Christ, Origen hearkens back to both Cyprian and Isaiah.

27. Origen, *Against Celsus*, 162.

28. Origen, *Against Celsus*, 193.

and pass away with the passage of time—indeed, clothes wear out and houses collapse and jewelry rusts, and with time the entire essence of these riches we see and touch perishes and vanishes—in the case of the spiritual treasures it is not like this. Rather, the martyrs always and perpetually remain brilliant in equal vigor and youth, brightly reflecting the glory of their innate brilliance.[29]

Chrysostom revels, rather like a poet, in the brilliant appearance of the martyrs and the beauty of their example rather than taking the characteristically Alexandrian route of Origen, who uses the philosophical language of "divinity," "Humane Nature," and sharing the "Characters of Divinity." Chrysostom also calls the light with which the martyrs shine "innate." Longfellow echoes this sense of the innateness of divine light in his final description of the illumined Evangeline in part 2, canto 5, where she approaches her final meeting with Gabriel with "light in her looks." She now clearly shines with the light by which she was illumined from time to time throughout her journey toward godlikeness. This light is both truly hers and truly God's, for she has become like God, and bears the characteristics of his divinity.

In *Evangeline* 2.5, then, Longfellow presents us with a portrait of Evangeline's transfiguration in divine light that shares much in common with the writings of Cyprian and Chrysostom and is conceptually compatible with the complex metaphysics of Alexandrian doctrine. It is more important to Longfellow in *Evangeline* 2.5, however, to show than to tell, and what he shows us is a heroine transfigured like Christ, Moses, and Elijah, brilliant like Juventinus and Maximinus, whose "light shines forth" as promised by Cyprian and Isaiah. Evangeline has been led to this experience by a process of ethical deification through love and ascetic activity which rejects the lures of passion and follows instead the divine sensations communicated by the sacramental activity of nature, by the light of heaven which illumines her path, and by the active charity of caring for the sick and dying poor in Philadelphia.

Throughout his poem, Longfellow avoids the philosophical language of realistic deification found in both Channing and the Fathers; nevertheless, he paints a picture of human spiritual destiny in line with third- and fourth-century patristic doctrine, namely a godlike state of purity, perfection, strength, worthiness of heaven, and illumination with the light of God. Though Evangeline may be a French Catholic, she is, in her spiritual maturity, a picture of patristic deification.

---

29. Chrysostom, "Juventinus and Maximinus," 92.

What, however, of Channing? As we have seen, his influence upon the 2.5 keynote is as negligible as his influence over the 2.1 keynote is pronounced. *Evangeline* 2.5 shows a Longfellow who seems to have stepped out beyond the influence of Channing and embraced the deification and divine light imagery of Cyprian, Origen, and Chrysostom—writers who, according to Channing, are puerile, credulous, and unnecessary for the Christian to read. But even though Channing rejects the Fathers, Longfellow does not reject Channing. He imitates Channing in using the term "celestial" for that which descends from heaven to earth. Further, *Evangeline* 2.1 stands as a careful and largely successful articulation of the one doctrine that Channing and the Fathers really do share: that of ethical deification. In avoiding discussion of the union of human and divine natures in Christ's incarnation, Longfellow avoids the inclusion of a doctrine that would have seemed heretical to his Unitarian readers. But in 2.5 he introduces the uniquely patristic imagery of shining with divine light as the pinnacle of spiritual maturity, with which his Unitarian readers would find no parallel in Channing.[30]

## Hallonsten's Caveat

At this point an important caveat is in order—we must be careful that we are not claiming too much for the text of *Evangeline*. It is a poem, not a theological treatise, and any claims about its theological content must be tempered by a close attention to the text and to the distinctions within and boundaries of the theology which we claim to find in that text. In his helpful 2007 essay, Gösta Hallonsten worries that the recent boom in interest in deification has led to a sloppy over-eagerness to find a doctrine of deification or theosis in authors and texts that do not warrant such a claim. He warns that "the doctrine of theosis is not necessarily connected to theosis language," and that the true, comprehensive doctrine of deification

> comprises a certain view of creation, especially of human beings, a soteriology, including the meaning of the incarnation; a view of Christian life as sanctification connected to church and the sacraments; and the final goal of union with God. The whole structure of this comprehensive doctrine is determined by a teleology that implies that creation and human beings from the

---

30. One might wish to see *Evangeline* as the poem wherein Longfellow personally converts from a youthful Unitarianism vision to a more orthodox Christian vision. The external evidence of Longfellow's creedal pronouncements and his church attendance, however, does not back up this interpretation. While it is tempting to apply the soteriology in the spiritual world of *Evangeline* to Longfellow's personal theological beliefs, we must avoid doing so at this point.

very beginning are endowed with an affinity and likeness that potentially draws them to God.[31]

Central to this comprehensive doctrine, Hallonsten urges, is

> a certain anthropology, often based on the distinction between image and likeness, and always teleologically oriented in a dynamic way toward the prototype. The prototype, the real image of God, is Christ. Thus the importance of the Incarnation as the central point in the economy of salvation. This anthropology is characterised by a formal causality and implies the continual presence and activity of grace and the energies of God from the beginning to the end.[32]

The distinction between image and likeness and the anthropology that undergirds it is precisely what Hallonsten does not find in those writers who are guilty of over-eagerness to find doctrines of deification everywhere:

> As a matter of fact, what is so striking when the Western present-day authors to which I have referred are compared with Orthodox descriptions of the doctrine of deification, or with that of the Greek Fathers, is this: the lack of references to anthropology and especially to the notion of image and likeness. Many present day Orthodox theologians, on the other hand, put precisely this distinction at the basis of their description of deification. Humanity is created in the image of God—referring to the constitutional aspect of anthropology, and in the likeness of God—referring to the goal of growing into communion with the Creator.[33]

Thus, if one is to claim to find a doctrine of deification taught in or illustrated by a poem, one must be careful to show that the anthropology, soteriology, and teleology that undergird this doctrine are discernible in the text. If they are not, then we might conclude, with Hallonsten, that the mere language of theosis has tricked us into seeing a doctrine where there is none.

There are four major elements to a "comprehensive doctrine" of deification, according to Hallonsten: an anthropology based on humans being created in the image of God and intended to achieve a likeness to God; a soteriology that sees Christ as both incarnate savior and the archetype of perfect image and likeness of God; a view of the church and sacraments as central to sanctification and the Christian life; and a teleology in which

---

31. Hallonsten, "*Theosis* in Recent Research," 285.
32. Hallonsten, "*Theosis* in Recent Research," 285.
33. Hallonsten, "*Theosis* in Recent Research," 285.

the goal of human life is union with and likeness to God, and where God's energies and grace guide the human to this end.

Longfellow presents an anthropological and teleological vision that is compatible with Hallonsten's criteria. It is true that Longfellow does not use the phrase "image of God," but he does speak of the lives of the Edenic Acadians "reflect[ing] an image of heaven."[34] In addition, likeness to God is, according to Father Felician, a supremely desirable state, in which one is "purified, strengthened, perfected, and rendered more worthy of heaven." If godlikeness, according to Felician, is a state of perfection for a human, then this implies a theological anthropology and teleology where God and his attributes are normative for humanity, and the highest human end is to become like God, as much as is possible. The grace and energies of God, in the form of celestial light, are present with Evangeline throughout her whole journey, illuminating her in the Edenic Grand-Pré, lighting her soul and leading her through the world of exile, and finally shining out from her to others in the transfigured state of the 2.5 keynote.

Further, in *Evangeline* Christ acts as both savior and archetype for the one seeking godlikeness. In 1.5 Father Felician describes Christ as "the Prince of Peace" who, in his crucified state, is the example of "holy compassion" and forgiveness for all.[35] In part 2, Christ is described as Evangeline's "Savior" whose "sacred feet" Evangeline has no "other hope . . . nor wish in life, but to follow."[36] In the very next stanza, Evangeline is transfigured in divine light. Thus, there is a textual connection between Christ's role as savior, his role as sole example for the one seeking godlikeness, and the spiritual experience of deification and illumination by the one who imitates him. While avoiding the language of incarnation, Longfellow clearly depicts Christ as a crucified savior and the prime figure that the one who seeks godlikeness should imitate, and like whom she sometimes shines.

In addition to the inclusion of an anthropology, teleology, and soteriology compatible with the comprehensive doctrine of deification, Longfellow also portrays the Christian life as necessarily connected to the church and the sacraments. From first to last canto, Evangeline is an obedient member of the church who partakes in the sacraments, including, in part 1, canto 1, confession. For a large portion of her life, Evangeline is guided daily by her priest, and she ends up in a religious community wherein, as Longfellow was surely aware, she would have lived a life of submission and obedience to

---

34. Longfellow, "Evangeline," l. 11.
35. Longfellow, "Evangeline," ll. 472–75.
36. Longfellow, "Evangeline," ll. 1288–89.

her abbess, love and duty to her fellow Sisters of Mercy, and daily participation in the sacrament of the Eucharist.

*Evangeline* is imbued with an anthropology and teleology in which the ideal human life is a reflection of the image of heaven. The soteriology of the poem resides in the ideas that human perfection is a state of likeness to God, and that Christ is both the savior of humans and the prime archetype for those seeking godlikeness. Finally, Longfellow presents the church—including its authorities and sacraments—as central to the life of the maturing Christian.

With regard to Hallonsten's criteria, then, we can conclude that in *Evangeline* Longfellow both describes and dramatically illustrates most of the key elements of the comprehensive doctrine of deification as taught both by the Fathers and the Orthodox Church today. Still, it is important to note that Longfellow does leave out an explicit language of incarnation—a doctrine that is absolutely central to the anthropology, teleology, soteriology, and ecclesiology of the Fathers, and, as we have already seen, was rejected by a Unitarian Church that regarded it as unbiblical. But it is equally important to see that Longfellow includes in his poem an anthropology, teleology, soteriology, and ecclesiology wholly compatible with the doctrine of the incarnation, and does so at a time in American history when the whole drift of theology was moving away from the incarnation as a central doctrine.

## DEIFICATION AND THE CRITICAL TRADITION

The interpretation of *Evangeline* that I have set forth—namely, that *Evangeline* is a poem in which a theology of ethical deification through love and ascetic activity is taught and a deified state of transfiguration in divine light is achieved—is at odds with several trends in *Evangeline* criticism, though it finds affinity with others. Most obviously, if Evangeline's mission is, in part, one of seeking godlikeness through ascetic activity, then the critical tradition represented by Pearce and Lewis—according to which Evangeline is a conventional, domestic figure who is rewarded for her domestic piety—appears largely to be a misreading of the poem. My interpretation agrees with Pearce insofar as we both see Evangeline as rewarded for her piety. But Pearce and Lewis stress a domesticity in Evangeline that simply does not accord with the plot of the poem, let alone the readings of Chevalier, Higgins, and Franchot. It is not in her home surrounded by her family, but in the poor-house surrounded by dying strangers that Evangeline finds her highest end. And though the doctrine of ethical deification preached to Evangeline in 2.1 does include love and affection, neither wifehood nor motherhood is portrayed as central to the love or the ascesis to which Felician calls Evangeline. As we have already mentioned, Evangeline forever rejects even the possibility of wifehood and motherhood when she becomes a nun in 2.5. Finally, even if Gabriel had not died, and had finally married Evangeline in their old age, this achievement of domestic bliss would be rather incidental to the great, spiritual accomplishment of deification and transfiguration prior to the lovers' rediscovery of one another. Though domestic bliss is a desire of Evangeline's, it is simply not her primary aim in part 2—her primary aim is the attainment of godlikeness.

The interpretation of *Evangeline* as a product of the careful multiculturalism and religious pluralism of Longfellow's American Unitarianism, formulated recently by Franchot and Higgins, is somewhat tempered and called into question by my interpretation. In arguing that the theological teaching of 2.1 is in part a recapitulation of central doctrines found in Channing's sermons, I have shown that Longfellow's Unitarianism exists not just at the political and ecclesial level of the poem, but also at the theological level. But in arguing that Longfellow moves beyond Channing's doctrine to a uniquely patristic vision of deification and illumination by divine light, I have shown that Longfellow's ultimate spiritual vision in *Evangeline* reaches beyond his own Unitarian tradition and Evangeline's French Catholic tradition, back to the very roots of Christian doctrine. While Higgins may be right that Longfellow had a characteristically Unitarian "vision of America as a Christian multi-culture,"[37] the poet's fondness for the Church Fathers and their writings puts him at odds with Channing, the father of American Unitarianism, who rejected the Church Fathers in favor of the Christian writers of the Enlightenment.

In the demonstration of Longfellow's familiarity with and use of the Fathers, we have advanced beyond Chevalier's exploration of Longfellow's use of the scriptures. We see, especially in Longfellow's use of Cyprian's interpretation of Isaiah, that Longfellow read key scripture passages through the eyes of the Church Fathers, and dramatically illustrates those patristic readings in the final canto of *Evangeline*. In his use of Isaiah's descriptions of illumination through love to illustrate what it means to be "of heaven," Cyprian demonstrates a patristic synthesis of Old and New Testament doctrine and imagery, and it is this patristic vision, not merely the vision of the Old Testament, that Longfellow most clearly illustrates in *Evangeline*.

Patristic understandings of the relationship between ascetic activity and love could also help us understand more clearly Chevalier's paradox

---

37. Higgins, "Evangeline's Mission," 549.

of "feasting on fasting,"[38] of uniting human love and ascetic activity in the journey toward God. Despite Chevalier's claim that Evangeline's uniting of love and ascesis is a meeting point of two disparate philosophies—Romanticism and Christianity respectively—the Fathers, as we have seen, teach that human love and human ascesis are not only compatible, but are necessarily linked in the journey toward union with God. Further, Chevalier at one point says that Evangeline's mission goes beyond just the marrying of the ascetic and the erotic, becoming a larger mission of "closing the distance that separates . . . God from Man."[39] In reading the 2.1 and 2.5 keynotes as, respectively, theological teaching about and dramatic enactment of human deification, we have shown that Evangeline does indeed "clos[e] the distance" between divine nature and human nature within herself.

As for the twentieth-century biographers, Thompson's claim that Longfellow was a lax and theologically uninterested Unitarian bears final comment. As we have shown, Longfellow understood the central doctrines of Unitarianism and incorporates Channing's doctrine of ethical deification through trial and suffering into *Evangeline* as a major theological teaching. Whatever Longfellow's personal beliefs about Unitarian theology, he seamlessly incorporates it into the plot of his first major narrative poem, an achievement that demonstrates neither spiritual laxity nor theological disinterest.

We come, finally, to Hawthorne and Demarest, whose suggestive comments on *Evangeline* part 2, canto 5, have been so helpful throughout our study. But, as we also saw, no critic after Demarest has built upon either critic's foundation. Now that we have discerned in *Evangeline* both the theological doctrine of ethical deification and the spiritual experience of illumination by divine light, we have the tools to unite and advance their interpretations in several ways. First, in speaking of Evangeline's mission as one of deification and illumination, we have provided a theological context for the concept of transfiguration. As we see in Origen, the Transfiguration of Christ is an event in which the doctrines of the incarnation of Christ and the deification of man converge in an experience of divine light. In calling the 2.5 keynote a scene of transfiguration, Hawthorne paves the way for the very investigation of the doctrines of incarnation, deification, and divine light that we have undertaken. And in our theological explorations we have shown that Longfellow was familiar with key theological texts that

---

38. The writings of Clement in particular, especially his placing of love as the highest form of *gnosis*, could reveal a higher unity between human eros and human ascesis. Such a juxtaposition of Chevalier and Clement, however, goes beyond the purview of this book.

39. Chevalier, *Semiotics, Romanticism, and Scriptures*, 113.

teach that the Transfiguration of Christ, Moses, and Elijah is a model for all Christians to aspire to, for it is a scene in which a living person, Christ, whose human nature is perfectly united with his divine nature, is illumined by and shines with divine light, and wherein we can see that those saints who are already in and of heaven, Moses and Elijah, live perpetually in this state of divine illumination.

Though Demarest does not use the terms *deification* and *transfiguration*, he does say that we feel, after reading *Evangeline* 2.5, that Evangeline has reached the highest aim of her existence. We are now familiar with the theological anthropology and teleology that can substantiate such a claim. We feel that Evangeline has reached her highest aim because we have heard that her mission is one of ethical deification, and we have seen proof of this deification in her illumination by and shining with divine light. She has reached her highest end, which is to be truly godlike. The doctrines of deification and divine light, then, unify and give theological nuance to the religious criticism of *Evangeline* by Hawthorne and Demarest.

## Future Directions

The discovery of the doctrines of deification and divine light as theological linchpins of the spiritual world of *Evangeline* has enabled us to reject some critical readings of *Evangeline*, and to temper, clarify, and advance others. And we have shown that the exploration of Longfellow's theological—especially Unitarian and patristic—sources and the interpretation of his poems in light of them can prove fruitful.

Perhaps the biggest question still remaining pertains to Gabriel and his role at the end of the poem. As we have seen, Gabriel puzzles critics, and some, including Hawthorne, Demarest, and the present book, portray Evangeline's transfiguration, not her discovery of Gabriel, as the true climax of the poem. Future *Evangeline* critics are left with a significant task: to work out how Gabriel himself fits into Evangeline's love, ascesis, deification, and illumination. Whittier's identification of God and Gabriel as dual and perhaps warring objects of Evangeline's love and devotion is still a live and perplexing issue.

What is clear is that in the Church Fathers, Longfellow encountered the teaching that active charity and love for one's neighbor is an essential step on the journey toward godlikeness. And it is also clear from part 2, canto 5, that it is Evangeline's abiding love for Gabriel along with her selfless love for the poor that renders her godlike, receptive of divine characteristics, including divine light. But what part does Evangeline's discovery of Gabriel in 2.5 play in the spiritual world of the poem? We have hitherto held Dante's *Commedia* at arm's length on account of its magnitude. Further, Longfellow did not begin his famous, thorough study and translation of Dante's *Commedia* until well after he researched and wrote *Evangeline*. But perhaps it would not be improper to turn to the *Commedia*'s main love triangle, namely the Pilgrim, Beatrice, and God, as a way to begin to unravel the dilemma of Gabriel and God as the warring objects of Evangeline's affection.

There are several affinities between the Pilgrim–Beatrice–God relationship in the *Commedia* and the Evangeline–Gabriel–God relationship in *Evangeline*. Just as Dante's Pilgrim pursues his lost love, Beatrice, through the realms of the afterlife, so Longfellow's pilgrim Evangeline pursues her lost love, Gabriel, through America. And just as the Pilgrim's initial reason for setting out on his journey—namely, that Beatrice waits for him in paradise—changes, as the poem develops, into a quest for the beatific vision of the essence of God (which St Thomas characterizes as the highest human end) through the journey toward Beatrice, so Evangeline's initial stated reason of setting out on a journey to find Gabriel is re-interpreted by Father Felician as a quest for godlikeness through the journey to find Gabriel. Also, as we saw briefly in chapter 4, Dante's pilgrim ends up in an illumined state just like Evangeline does—though the pilgrim enters the transhumanising light of Paradise, whereas Evangeline shines with celestial light amid human death and darkness.

Given these affinities, we might begin to reconcile the God/Gabriel dilemma by interpreting Gabriel as a Beatrice figure through whom Evangeline is led toward, not distracted from, God. Thus Longfellow can be seen, in *Evangeline*, as characterizing human romance—just as he characterizes nature—as a sacramental path to God, a way of affirmation that calls for an ascetic rejection of sinful passion—the real enemy of the human soul—and a wholehearted embrace of both God's created order and the hallowing power of human *eros*.

# Conclusion

## EVANGELINE AMONG HER PEERS

OVER THE COURSE OF this book, we have attempted to show that Longfellow was better versed in the theology of his Unitarian contemporaries and of the early Christian tradition than is often claimed. In following Higgins's suggestion that we take Longfellow's Unitarianism more seriously, we have found that the theological language of Channing is indeed present and central in *Evangeline*. But, in the end, we have seen that Longfellow's ultimate vision of earthly human perfection in *Evangeline* is not Unitarian, but, instead, patristic, and accords with the theological anthropology still being discussed today by theologians who base their thought on the writings of the Fathers. It remains, then, to place *Evangeline* among its peers in American literature, and so see more clearly its shape and contribution to the history of American literature.

### EVANGELINE AND THE PURITAN DIALECTIC

The patristic vision of salvation as deification, as "an existential participation in the life of the Trinity," is at odds, Valerie Karras has recently argued, with the more Puritan "juridical notion of justification [as] being made right with God."[1] The reading of *Evangeline* as illustrating a more Eastern, non-Puritan, concept of salvation has the potential to change how we look at *Evangeline* and its place in nineteenth-century American literature. In *Evangeline*—arguably Longfellow's best long poem and one of the few long narrative poems of lasting quality in all of the American nineteenth century—the state of godlikeness, manifested as transfiguration in celestial light, is the vision of the human that is offered. The implications of this can and should be explored in more detail. For all of Longfellow's apparent con-

---

1. Karras, "Eschatology," 250.

servatism, especially compared to the Transcendentalists, *Evangeline* shares little in the realm of theological outlook with those American poets whose immediate religious context is Puritanism, whether as spokespersons of Puritan theology, as was the great eighteenth-century poet Edward Taylor, or as critics of it, as was the greater nineteenth-century poet Emily Dickinson.

Edward Taylor's poetry, though neither published nor widely read until the twentieth century, stands as a prime example of the Puritan verse of Colonial America. The Calvinist "juridical notion" of salvation, as Karras calls it, abounds in Taylor's work. Perhaps the best example of this is in his 1690 poem "Meditation 38," where the poet envisions "A Court of Justice" which God "in heaven holdst" to try the sinner's soul.[2]

> But Justice hath her Glory here well tri'de:
> Her Spotless Law all Spotted Cases tends
> Without Respect or Disrespect them ends. . . .
>
> God's Judge himself: and Christ Atturny is:
> The Holy Ghost Resgesterer is founde.
> Angells the Sergents are, all Creatures kiss
> The booke, and doe as Evidence aboundе.
> All cases pass according to pure Law
> And in the Sentence is no Fret, nor flaw.
>
> My Case is bad. Lord, be my Advocate.
> My sin is red: I'me under Gods Arrest.
> Thou has the hit of pleading; plead my State.
> Although its bad thy Plea will make it best.
> If you wilt plead my case before the King:
>
> I'le Waggon Loads of Love, and Glory bring.[3]

In Taylor's heavenly court, each member of the Trinity and all the angels are imagined in judicial roles, and the principles that govern the proceedings are Justice and Law. The sinner's only hope for pardon is Christ, his attorney. In this model, God the Father is set up as the Judge to whom God the Son must appeal in order to make the sinner right before the Law. This pitting of the Father as a stern judge against Christ as a loving advocate is central to the juridical, Puritan understanding of salvation.

---

2. Johnson, "Edward Taylor," 313.
3. Johnson, "Edward Taylor," 313–14.

While "Mediation 38" ends with the request that Christ argue the sinner's "case before the King," in Taylor's long verse drama "God's Determination touching his Elect," the poet imagines a conversation between Justice and Mercy wherein the sinner is pardoned at last:

> Justice:
> Unto the humble Humble Soule I say,
>   Cheer up, poor heart, for satisfied am I.
> For Justice nothing to thy Charge can lay,
>   Thou hast Acquittance in thy Surety.
> The Court of Justice thee acquits: therefore
> Thou to the Court of Mercy are bound o're.
>
> Mercy:
> ... Justice in Justice must adjudge thee just:
> If you in Mercies Mercy put thy trust.[4]

Whereas in "Mediation 38" Christ the attorney is the one in whom the sinner must trust, here it is Mercy itself which acquits the sinner and satisfies justice. Thomas H. Johnson sees in these lines a good example of the "orthodox Puritan Taylor stress[ing] Christ's mercy without denying God's justice."[5] Roy Harvey Pearce goes even further than Johnson, arguing that those readers and critics who ignore Taylor's confidence in the Puritan doctrine of "God's order in his world" can understand neither his poetry nor his poetics. "Reading Taylor's poetry," he concludes, "we read his Puritanism."[6]

A Puritan-influenced poetry more familiar and palatable to contemporary readers is the nineteenth-century verse that questions and criticizes Puritan theology, of which Emily Dickinson is the master. From her early lyrics like "23" where she playfully riffs on the New Testament trinitarian dictum, substituting "the Bee ... the butterfly ... And ... the breeze" for the Father, the Son, and the Holy Spirit,[7] to her late meditations on immortality and art, Dickinson is "unequalled among the other poets of her day," according to Helen Vendler, in "her defiant critique of Christianity and her uninhibited scrutiny of its concepts."[8]

---

4. Johnson, "Edward Taylor," 299.
5. Johnson, "Edward Taylor," 299.
6. Pearce, "Edward Taylor," 46.
7. Vendler, *Dickinson*, 27.
8. Vendler, *Dickinson*, 17.

Dickinson seldom opts for outright protest. Instead, she uses the language of Puritan theology to explore non-theological topics. In "279" she begins:

> Of all the Souls that stand create
> I have Elected—One—[9]

As the poem continues, it becomes clear that this is a romantic poem, not a theological one, and that the "One" who is "Elected" is Dickinson's earthly beloved. But the poet's language from the outset could be mistaken for a description of the Puritan doctrine of election from the viewpoint of God, wherein he chooses from all existing souls those that he will graciously save.[10] While there is not an explicit critique of the Puritan doctrine of election in the poem, Dickinson is clearly using the language of serious theology to describe the experience of choosing a lover, not the other way around. Vendler calls this a reversal of "the usual homiletic procedure ... Whereas the preacher uses the human to illustrate the divine, Dickinson coopts the divine to illustrate the human."[11] Such a co-opting often leads, it turns out, to the estimation of the human above—or at least on par with—the divine:

> The Brain is just the weight of God –
> For—Heft them—Pound for Pound—
> And they will differ—if they do—
> As Syllable from Sound—[12]

Such an equivalence of the human brain and God is closer to Emerson's ego-theism than to Longfellow's ethical deification. But Dickinson, likely, has neither in mind. Instead, she sees God as the "sound" that the "syllable," the brain, makes. God turns out to be a pronounced language derived from the natural, human world. If this is Dickinson's meaning, then her habit of using the language of Puritan Theology to describe non-religious human

---

9. Vendler, *Dickinson*, 98.

10. In his 2000 volume *Nimble Believing*, James McIntosh breaks down the five major tenets of Calvinism and Dickinson's attitude toward each one. See McIntosh, *Nimble Believing*, 5–6. Overall, McIntosh agrees with Vendler that Dickinson's "transcriptions of Christian ideas and reworkings of Christian texts are not dogmatic but experimental." McIntosh, *Nimble Believing*, 3. McIntosh, however, does not conclude that Dickinson was devoid of all faith. Rather he argues that one can discern in Dickinson's work a "'Nimble believing,' that is believing for intense moments in a spiritual life without permanently subscribing to any received system of belief." McIntosh, *Nimble Believing*, 1.

11. Vendler, *Dickinson*, 510.

12. Vendler, *Dickinson*, 17.

life makes sense: having played the agnostic when it comes to the literal truth of Puritan theology, she re-imagines it as a fancy, even fitting, figure by which to understand the natural world.[13]

When we compare the religious elements of Taylor and Dickinson's verse to those of *Evangeline*, we see that Taylor and Dickinson are caught up in a dialectic from which Longfellow's poem seems largely free. For Taylor, the language of Puritan theology is a serious matter to be vividly dramatized, for it concerns the fate of the human soul. For Dickinson, the language of Puritan theology is not nearly so sacrosanct; instead, it is a potent, poetic plaything. But the language of Puritan theology simply does not factor into *Evangeline*—there are no divine courtrooms, no impartial law condemning the human soul, no legal opposition between God the Father and Christ, and no doctrine of unconditional election, whereby some souls are saved and some damned according to God's whim. In *Evangeline*, Christ is "Savior," but not attorney, and God is just, but never a condemning judge. And humans freely choose to follow Christ or not, with no sense of irresistible grace or reprobation. Thus, in comparison with Taylor, a staunchly Puritan poet, and Dickinson, who stands on the other side of the dialectic as an anti-Puritan poet, Longfellow in *Evangeline* is simply non-Puritan, deriving his theological outlook from a religious tradition that predates Puritanism by over a millennium. And even in his employment of Unitarian theological language and categories, Longfellow avoids those explicitly anti-Puritan digressions that pepper the writings of Channing.

## Evangeline and the Long Poem in the American Nineteenth Century

If contributing to the poetic struggle between Puritanism and anti-Puritanism is not what Longfellow is involved in in creating the spiritual vision of *Evangeline*, then what is he up to? I would argue that *Evangeline*'s place in American poetry can best be mapped—and its theological uniqueness understood—by placing it in conversation with the other two great long poems of the American nineteenth century: Whitman's famous "Song of Myself" and Melville's under-appreciated *Clarel*.

Admittedly, Whitman's "Song of Myself," continually adapted and expanded by the poet from 1855 to 1893, shares little in structure with *Evangeline*. Whereas Longfellow's narrative is linear and follows the classical plot patterns of Greco-Roman epics like the *Odyssey* and *Aeneid*, Whitman's

---

13. Along similar lines, Vendler writes, "Re-writing the Bible was one of Dickinson's constant amusements." Vendler, *Dickinson*, 70.

poem is a rambling lyric pastiche of nineteenth-century America. But it is no less epic in tone and scope than *Evangeline*, and features a no-less-heroic protagonist: the human self. Whitman's conception of this self owes much to Emerson's doctrines of self-reliance and ego-theism, but Lawrence Buell argues that Whitman develops the idea of the identity of God with man much further than Emerson does. Whitman, according to Buell, carries "the idea of the self as God" to the point that "the 'I' is capable of the same infinite variety as nature and that every thought and act is (at least potentially) significant and holy."[14] In "Song of Myself" every human act, whether virtuous or vicious, is a divine doing of a divine being:

> Divine am I inside and out, and I make holy whatever I touch or am touch'd from;
> The scent of these arm-pits aroma finer than prayer.
> This head more than churches, bibles and all the creeds.[15]

In Whitman's vision the concept of God is subsumed into the democratic idea of a self that transcends the church, Bible, and creeds. All religious institutions like the Catholic Church, religious authorities like priests, and religious texts like scriptures or missals are left far behind.

If Longfellow and Whitman do share anything, it is a tendency toward natural theology. Just as the prairie whispers spiritual consolations to Evangeline, so the wind and river teach ultimate truths to Whitman's self. But the selves to whom nature's revelations are made in the two poems are very dissimilar, anthropologically speaking. Longfellow's understanding of the human potential for godlikeness is quite different from Whitman's, and the departure point may be rightly seen as Longfellow's rejection, alongside Channing, of Emerson's ego-theism, in contrast to Whitman's acceptance and development of it. In Longfellow's vision the exiled self seeks to follow and become like the God who is revealed in Scripture through, in part, obedience to church authority. Further, godlikeness for Longfellow is much more strictly defined than for Whitman—instead of all human acts, moral and immoral, it is found in the specific practices of sorrow, silence, patient endurance, and, most of all, love.

In his late and too-little-read epic poem *Clarel: A Poem and Pilgrimage in the Holy Land*, Melville outstripped both Whitman and Longfellow in terms of sheer length. At 150 cantos and well over 500 pages, *Clarel* still stands among the longest poems in American literature. The plot, which centers around the Holy Land adventure of an American student named

14. Buell, *Literary Transcendentalism*, 324–25.
15. Whitman, *Leaves of Grass*, 49.

Clarel, is less classically epic than that of *Evangeline*, and often reads more like a travel memoir, not dissimilar from Longfellow's own prose works *Hyperion* and *Outre-Mer*, which also feature young American protagonists wandering through scenic, Old World landscapes. But in *Clarel* Melville is not interested in the landscape of the Holy Land as much as he is in the mental landscapes of characters who converse and clash over rival theologies and philosophies. According to William Potter,

> in *Clarel* the eternal need for faith is projected against the backdrop of the inexorable evolution of humanity through history. This evolution, the poem asserts, has now led to the spiritual crisis of the nineteenth century, where Western Protestantism— rejecting mysticism and embracing reason—is left in a spiritually vapid materialism largely of its own devising . . . *Clarel* is nothing less than a hugely conceived study of the very nature of all belief.[16]

Clarel, the protagonist, is a portrait of the doubting American Protestant, who, according to Potter, is employed by Melville in his "most embittered and sustained critique of America, a critique that is, at its core, religious in nature. . . . The three main characters—Clarel, Vine, and Rolfe—suffer for their American Protestant background; each is painfully aware of the degree to which this background has contributed to his spiritual emptiness."[17]

Clarel's journey is both less transcendental than that of Whitman's self, and less successful than that of Evangeline. In the poem's conclusion Melville's protagonist, far from being transfigured, fades, forlorn, into the exotic biblical scenery. Recently Martin Kevorkian has summed up the spiritual arc of *Clarel* quite nicely: "On the circuit of his pilgrimage, Clarel fails to secure the spiritual certainty, guidance, or even friendship he seeks. The poem opens and closes in Jerusalem, with Clarel in his room, alone with his doubts."[18] Kevorkian, however, sees a hope that where Melville's plot line leaves the character in a state of general doubt, the more hopeful epilogue may reveal "a more seasoned perspective, of wisdom that speaks from the

---

16. Potter, *Melville's* Clarel, xiii.
17. Potter, *Melville's* Clarel, xv–xvi.
18. Kevorkian, *Writing beyond Prophecy*, 132. Potter is a bit more hopeful about Clarel's final fading into the Jerusalem background, calling it a Schopenhauer-esque "denial of self" which leads to an identification with all living and suffering beings, a final rejection of Emersonian self-reliance. Potter argues that the positive tone of the epilogue supports this more positive reading of the final canto. Potter, *Melville's* Clarel, 144–45.

heart, to the heart, from beyond such a moment of intellectual perplexity."[19] Melville's narrator ends the epilogue by encouraging the forlorn Clarel:

> Who in life's pilgrimage have baffled striven—
> Even death may prove unreal at the last ...
> Then keep thy heart, though yet but ill-resigned ...
> Emerge thou mayest from the last whelming sea,
> And prove that death but routs life into victory.[20]

This is a theological teaching worthy of Father Felician, but it *ends* the poem. In *Evangeline* Longfellow places this sort of theological exhortation in the middle of the poem, and then shows his heroine emerge from a "whelming sea" of her own and find, in the face of death, the victory of deification. In contrast to Melville, Longfellow does not divorce his vision of human spiritual destiny from the plot of his poem. Thus Longfellow presents a more difficult and ethical vision of human divinity than Whitman does, and incorporates the attainment of spiritual victory into his narrative in a way that Melville does not.

From these comparisons the unique shape of *Evangeline* emerges: it is a poem firmly Christian, but not Puritan, in its metaphysics, ethics, and politics; nor is it concerned with anti-Puritan polemics. It is a poem interested in showing spiritual consolation, transformation, and victory, but not at the expense of de-emphasizing spiritual disconsolation. But this disconsolation is not the *ennui* of the post-Protestant intellectual, as one finds in *Clarel*, but rather the more immediate and practical disconsolation of the exile, cut off from *polis* and beloved. The landscape of the poem—especially part 2—is neither the Holy Land of *Clarel*, vied for by Christian and non-Christian sects, nor is it the post-Revolution east coast of Whitman, but rather the western wilderness, caught between pre-colonial nature and nativism and the slow incursion of Catholic missions. It is in the westward wilds of *Evangeline*'s second part that Longfellow anticipates the whole troubled genre of the Western, and, with grace and care, cuts a path for future writers and future scholars. In Longfellow's vision the "untamed West" need not be a place of violence—let alone masculine violence—but may be a place of healing, of search, of spiritual maturation. Evangeline finds there what Clarel cannot find in the wilderness of the Holy Land: real guidance and real growth. In this, Longfellow imagines that America, especially the American wilderness, can provide for the human what the early Christian monastics sought

---

19. Kevorkian, *Writing beyond Prophecy*, 144.
20. Melville, *Clarel*, 4.35.24–25, 27, 34–35.

in the deserts of the Middle East, and what, in *Clarel*, some Americans can no longer find in those deserts: an arena of soul making.

Many pages are filled scholars' attempts to articulate what is unique about the American vision of the human being, what new perspectives on human struggle and flourishing arose in the great lines of nineteenth-century American verse. It is time we recognize that *Evangeline*, too, has something to say about what it means to be human, something that still—in this disconsolate age—holds power to shape human minds, increase human worth, and direct the very movements and practices of the human body in the journey toward God.

# Bibliography

Arnold, Matthew. *On Translating Homer*. London: Longman, Green, Longman, and Roberts, 1861.
Arvin, Newton. *Longfellow: The Man and his Work*. Boston: Little, Brown, 1963.
Athanasius. *The Letters of Athanasius Concerning the Holy Spirit*. Translated by C.R.B. Shapland. London: Epworth, 1951.
———. *On the Incarnation*. Translated and edited by a Religious of CSMV. Crestwood, NY: St Vladimir's Seminary Press, 1993.
Bailey, Elmer James. *Religious Thought in the Greater American Poets*. Boston: The Pilgrim, 1922.
Bartos, Emil. *Deification in Eastern Orthodox Theology*. Benchley: Paternoster, 1999.
Basil. *Letters and Select Works*. Nicene and Post-Nicene Fathers 8. New York: Christian Literature, 1895.
Bloom, Harold. *The Anxiety of Influence: A Theory of Poetry*. Oxford: Oxford University Press, 1997.
Boethius. *The Consolation of Philosophy*. Translated by Victor Watts. New York: Penguin, 1999.
Bregman, Jay. *Synesius of Cyrene: Philosopher-Bishop*. Los Angeles: University of California Press, 1982.
Brownson, Orestes. "Longfellow's Evangeline and Kavanaugh." *Brownson's Quarterly Review* 4 (1850) 59–87.
Buell, Lawrence. *Emerson*. London: Belknap, 2003.
———. *Literary Transcendentalism*. London: Cornell University Press, 1973.
Calhoun, Charles. *Longfellow: A Rediscovered Life*. Boston: Beacon, 2004.
Carroll, Timothy. "Being Clothed in Righteousness; Being Dressed for Salvation." Paper presented at A Celebration of Living Theology conference at Durham University, July 2012.
Channing, William Ellery. "Likeness to God." In *Transcendentalism, A Reader*, edited by Joel Myerson, 3–20. New York: Oxford University Press, 2000.
———. *Selected Discourses and Essays: From the Works of William Ellery Channing D.D.* London: Philip Green, 1895.
———. *The Works of William E. Channing, D.D.* Vol. 4. Boston: Walker, Wise, 1862.
———. *The Works of William Ellery Channing*. Boston: American Unitarian Association, 1903.
Chasles, Philarète. *Anglo-American Literature and Manners*. New York: Charles Scribner, 1852.

## BIBLIOGRAPHY

Chevalier, Jacques. *Semiotics, Romanticism and the Scriptures*. Berlin: Mouton de Gruyter, 1990.

Christensen, Michael J., and Jeffrey A. Whittung, eds. *Partakers of the Divine Nature*. Madison, NJ: Farleigh Dickinson University Press, 2007.

Clement of Alexandria. *The Writings of Clement of Alexandria*. Translated by William Wilson. Ante-Nicene Christian Library 4. Edinburgh: T and T Clark, 1867.

Crawford, W.S. *Synesius the Hellene*. London: Rivingtons, 1901.

Cyprian of Carthage. *The Treatises of Cyprian*. Vol. 1. Edinburgh: T and T Clark, 1868.

Dorrien, Gary. *The Making of American Liberal Theology: Imagining Progressive Religion, 1805-1900*. London: Westminster John Knox, 2001.

Eleanor, Mary. "The Catholic Spirit in Longfellow." In *Certitudes*, 23-31. New York: Books for Libraries, 1968.

Emerson, Ralph Waldo. "Divinity School Address." In *Transcendentalism: A Reader*, 230-45. Oxford: Oxford University Press, 2000.

———. "Holiness." In *Early Lectures of Ralph Waldo Emerson 1836-1838*, 341-47. Cambridge, MA: Belknap, 1964.

———. "The Over-soul." In *Essays and Lectures*, 383-402. New York: Library of America, 1983.

Finch, Annie. *The Ghost of Meter: Culture and Prosody in American Free Verse*. Ann Arbor: University of Michigan Press, 1993.

Finlan, Steven, and Vladimir Kharlamov, eds. *Theosis: Deification in Christian Theology*. Eugene, OR: Pickwick, 2006.

Franchot, Jenny. *Roads to Rome: The Antebellum Protestant Encounter with Catholicism*. Berkeley: University of California Press, 1994.

Gale, Robert L. *A Henry Wadsworth Longfellow Companion*. London: Greenwood, 2003.

Gartner, Matthew. "Longfellow's Place: The Poet and Poetry of Craigie House." *The New England Quarterly* 73 (2000) 32-57.

Gavrilyuk, Paul N. "The Retrieval of Deification: How a Once-Despised Archaism Became an Ecumenical Desideratum." *Modern Theology* 25 (2009) 647-59.

Gioia, Dana. "Longfellow in the Aftermath of Modernism." In *The Columbia History of American Poetry*, edited by Dana Gioia, 64-96. New York: Columbia University Press, 1993.

Gregory Nazianzus. *Nicene and Post-Nicene Fathers*. Vol. 7. New York: Christian Literature, 1894.

Gregory of Nyssa. *Selected Writings and Letters*. Translated by William Moore. New York: Charles Scribner, 1917.

Griffiths, Naomi. "Longfellow's 'Evangeline': The Birth and Acceptance of a Legend." *Acadiensis* 11 (1982) 28-41.

Gross, Jules. *The Divinization of the Christian according to the Greek Fathers*. Translated by Paul A. Oncia. Anaheim, CA: A and C, 2002.

Gosta Hallonsten, "Theosis in Recent Research: A Renewal of Interest and Need for Clarity." In *Partakers of the Divine Nature*. Grand Rapids, MI: Rosemont, 2007.

Hawthorne, Nathaniel. "Hawthorne's Review of Evangeline." Edited by Hubert H. Hoeltje. *The New England Quarterly* 23 (1950) 232-35.

Hickey, Father Richard. *Catholic Influence on Longfellow*. Kirkwood, MO: Maryhurst, 1928.

Higgins, Andrew C. "Evangeline's Mission: Anti-Catholicism, Nativism, and Unitarianism in Longfellow's *Evangeline*." *Religion and the Arts* 13 (2009) 547-68.

Hippolytus. *The Ante-Nicene Fathers*. Vol. 5. New York: Charles Scribner's Sons, 1919.
Hirsh, Edward L. *Henry Wadsworth Longfellow*. Minneapolis: University of Minnesota Press, 1964.
*The Holy Bible: English Standard Version*. Wheaton, IL: Crossway, 2003.
Irenaeus. *Against Heresies*. Translated by John Keble. Oxford: James Parker, 1872.
Irmscher, Christoph. *Longfellow Redux*. Chicago: University of Illinois Press, 2006.
———. *Public Poet, Private Man: Henry Wadsworth Longfellow at 200*. Boston: University of Massachusetts Press, 2009.
John Chrysostom. "Homily of Praise on the Holy Martyrs Juventinus and Maximinus who were Martyred under Julian the Apostate." In *The Cult of the Saints: Select Homilies and Letters*, translated by Wendy Mayer and Bronwen Neil, 89–100. Crestwood, NY: St Vladimir's Seminary Press, 2006.
Johnson, A.J.B. "The Call of the Archtype and the Challenge of Acadian History." *French Colonial History* 5 (2004) 63–92.
Johnson, Thomas H. "Edward Taylor, Puritan 'Sacred Poet.'" *New England Quarterly* 10 (1937) 290–322.
Justin Martyr. *Dialogue with Trypho*. Translated by A. Lukyn Williams. New York: MacMillan, 1930.
———. "The First Apology of St Justin." In *The Apologies of Justin Martyr, Tertullian, and Minutius Felix, in Defence of the Christian Religion, with the Commonitory of Vincentius Lirinensis Concerning the Primitive Rule of Faith Translated from the Originals*, translated by William Reeves, Vol. 1, 14–134. London: A. and J. Churchhill, 1709.
Karras, Valerie. "Eschatology." In *Cambridge Companion to Feminist Theology*, edited by Susan Frank Parsons, 243–60. Cambridge: Cambridge University Press, 2002.
Kevorkian, Martin. *Writing beyond Prophecy: Emerson, Hawthorne, and Melville after the American Renaissance*. Baton Rouge: University of Louisiana Press, 2013.
Larson, Kerry. Introduction to *The Cambridge Companion to Nineteenth Century American Poetry*. Edited by Kerry Larson. Cambridge: Cambridge University Press, 2011.
Lejay, Paul. "Louis Ellies Dupin," in *The Catholic Encyclopedia*. Vol. 5. New York: Robert Appleton. http://www.newadvent.org/cathen/05204a.htm.
Lewis, Paul. "Longfellow's Serenity and Poe's Prediction: An Antebellum Turning Point." *New England Quarterly* 85 (2012) 144–58.
Longfellow, Henry Wadsworth. "The Christian Fathers," MS Am 1340, 58–59. Houghton Library: Harvard University.
———. *Christus: A Mystery*. Boston: Houghton Mifflin, 1890.
———. *The Complete Poetical Works of Henry Wadsworth Longfellow: Household Edition*. Cambridge, MA: Belknap, 1907.
———, trans. *The Divine Comedy of Dante Alighieri*. Boston: Houghton Mifflin, 1867.
———. "Evangeline." In *The Complete Poetical Works of Henry Wadsworth Longfellow: Household Edition*. Boston: Houghton Mifflin, 1907.
———. *Evangeline: With Biographical Sketch, Explanatory Notes and Critical Opinions*. Edited by A.J. Demarest. Philadelphia: Christopher Sower, 1911.
———. *Evangeline: With Biography of Author, Critical Opinions, and Explanatory Notes*. New York: Maynard, Merrill, 1893.

———. "Handbook of the Anglo-Saxon Tongue. Selections from King Alfred's Version of Boethius with an Interlineary Translation," MS Am 1340, 14. Houghton Library: Harvard University.

———. *The Letters of Henry Wadsworth Longfellow*. 4 volumes. Edited by Andrew Hilen. Cambridge, MA: Belknap, 1966.

———. *Longfellow's Evangeline, Edited with Notes, Outline Study and Examination Questions*. Edited by Maud Elma Kingsely and Franck Herbert Palmer. Boston: Palmer, 1909.

———. *Longfellow's Evangeline, with biographical and Critical introductions and notes*. Edited by H.I. Strang and A.J. Moore. Toronto: Copp, Clark, 1890.

———. *Outre-Mer and Driftwood*. Boston: Houghton Mifflin, 1886.

———. *The Prose Works of Henry Wadsworth Longfellow*. Vol. 2. Boston: Houghton and Mifflin, 1892.

———. *The Works of Henry Wadsworth Longfellow*. Vol. 7. Boston: Houghton Mifflin, 1886.

Longfellow, Samuel. *The Life of Henry Wadsworth Longfellow with Extracts from his Journals and Correspondence*. 3 volumes. Edited by Samuel Longfellow. Boston: Houghton Mifflin, 1891.

Lossky, Vladimir. *The Mystical Theology of the Eastern Church*. Crestwood, NY: St Vladimir's Seminary Press, 1957.

Lot-Borodine, Myrrah. *La Deification De L'Homme Selon la Doctrine des Peres Grecs*. Paris: Editions Du Cerf, 1970.

Macarius. *Fifty Spiritual Homilies*. Translated by A.J. Mason. London: Society for Promotion of Christian Knowledge, 1921.

MacCrie, George. *The Religion of our Literature*. London: Hodder and Stroughton, 1875.

McIntosh, James. *Nimble Believing: Dickinson and the Unknown*. Ann Arbor: University of Michigan Press, 2000.

McLaughlin, J. Fairfax. "Father Livingston on Longfellow." *The Catholic World* 58 (1894) 528–37.

Melville, Herman. *Clarel: A Poem and Pilgrimage in the Holy Land*. Evanston, IL: Northwestern University Press, 1991.

Meyer, D. H. "The Saint as Hero: William Ellery Channing and the Nineteenth-Century Mind." *Winterthur Portfolio* 8 (1973) 171–85.

Mosheim, Johann. *An Ecclesiastical History, Ancient and Modern, from the Birth of Christ, to the Beginning of the Present Century*. Translated by Archibald MacLaine. New York: Duyckinck, Collins, 1824.

Origen. *Contra Celsum*. Translated by Henry Chadwick. Oxford: Oxford University Press, 1953.

Origen. *Against Celsus*. Translated by James Bellamy. London: B. Mills, 1660.

*The Orthodox Study Bible*. Nashville, TN: Thomas Nelson, 2008.

Palamas, Gregory. *Gregory Palamas: The Triads*. Translated by John Meyendorff. London: Society for Promoting Christian Knowledge, 1983.

Pearce, Roy Harvey. *The Continuity of American Poetry*. Princeton: Princeton University Press, 1961.

———. "Edward Taylor, The Poet as Puritan." *New England Quarterly* 23 (1950) 31–46.

Peck, George Washington. "A Review of Mr. Longfellow's *Evangeline*." *The American Review* (1848) 1–15.

Plato. *Theaetetus and Sophist*. Translated by Harold North Fowler. Cambridge, MA: Loeb Classical Library, 1961.
Potter, William. *Melville's Clarel and the Intersympathy of Creeds*. Kent, OH: Kent State University Press, 2004.
Prichard, John Paul. "The Horatian Influence upon Longfellow." *American Literature* 4 (1932) 22–38.
Russell, Norman. *The Doctrine of Deification in the Greek Patristic Tradition*. Oxford: Oxford University Press, 2004.
Seelye, John. "Attic Shape: Dusting off *Evangeline*." *Virginia Quarterly Review* 60 (1984) 21–44.
Strong, Augustus Hopkins. *American Poets and their Theology*. Philadelphia: Griffith and Rowland, 1916.
Synésios de Cyrène. *Hymnes*. Translated by Christian Lacombrade. Paris: Les Belles Lettres, 1978.
Synesius of Cyrene. *The Essays and Hymns of Synesius of Cyrene*. 2 volumes. Translated by A. Fitzgerald. London: Oxford University Press, 1930.
———. *The Ten Hymns of Synesius, Bishop of Cyrene*. Translated by Alan Stevenson. Edinburgh: T. Constable, 1865.
Tertullian. *The Ante-Nicene Fathers*. Vol. 3. New York: Charles Scribner's Sons, 1903.
———. "Apology." In *The Apologies of Justin Martyr, Tertullian, and Minutius Felix in Defence of the Christian Religion with the Commonitory of Vincentius Lirinensus, Concerning the Primitive Rule of Faith Translated from the Originals*, Vol. 1, translated by William Reeves, 153–388. London: A. and J. Churchhill, 1709.
Thompson, Lawrance. *Young Longfellow*. New York: MacMillan, 1938.
Vendler, Helen. *Dickinson: Selected Poems and Commentaries*. Cambridge, MA: Belknap, 2010.
Vincent of Lerins. "The Commonitory of Vincentius Lirinensis." In *The Apologies of Justin Martyr, Tertullian, and Minutius Felix, In Defence of the Christian Religion, with the Commonitory of Vincentius Lirinensus, Concerning the Primitive Rule of Faith Translated form the Originals*, Vol. 2, translated by William Reeves, 219–399. London: A. and J. Churchill, 1709.
Wagenknecht, Edward. *Longfellow: A Full Length Portrait*. New York: Longman's, Green, 1955.
Whitman, Walt. *Leaves of Grass: Author's Copyright Edition*. London: David Bogue, 1881.
Whittier, John Greenleaf. *The Works of John Greenleaf Whittier*. Vol. 7. Boston: Houghton Mifflin, 1892.
Williams, A.N. *The Ground of Union: Deification in Aquinas and Palamas*. Oxford: Oxford University Press, 1999.
Williams, Cecil B. *Henry Wadsworth Longfellow*. Boston: Twayne, 1964.
Willis, Lloyd. "Henry Wadsworth Longfellow, United States National Literature, and the Canonical Erasure of Material Nature." *ATQ* 20 (2006) 629–46.

www.ingramcontent.com/pod-product-compliance
Lightning Source LLC
Chambersburg PA
CBHW051737230426
43670CB00012B/2063